79.	658.802	6504	£65.00	July 14.

Obstructive Marketing

Obstructive Marketing

Restricting Distribution
of Products and Services
in the Age of Asymmetric Warfare

MAITLAND HYSLOP
Northumbria University, UK

GOWER

Gower Applied Business Research
Our programme provides leaders, practitioners, scholars and researchers with thought provoking, cutting edge books that combine conceptual insights, interdisciplinary rigour and practical relevance in key areas of business and management.

Published by
Gower Publishing Limited
Wey Court East
Union Road
Farnham
Surrey, GU9 7PT
England

Ashgate Publishing Company
110 Cherry Street
Suite 3-1
Burlington, VT 05401-3818
USA

www.gowerpublishing.com

British Library Cataloguing in Publication Data
A catalogue record for this book is available from the British Library.

Library of Congress Cataloging-in-Publication Data
Hyslop, Maitland.
  Obstructive marketing : restricting distribution of products and services in the age of asymmetric warfare / by Maitland Hyslop.
    pages cm
  Includes bibliographical references and index.
  ISBN 978-1-4724-1604-9 (hardback) – ISBN 978-1-4724-1605-6 (ebook) – ISBN 978-1-4724-1606-3 (epub) 1. Marketing–Management. 2. Strategic planning. 3. Equality. I. Title.

  HF5415.13.H97 2014
  658.8'02 – dc23

                                                                        2013026260

ISBN 9781472416049 (hbk)
ISBN 9781472416056 (ebk – ePDF)
ISBN 9781472416063 (ebk – ePUB)

Printed in the United Kingdom by Henry Ling Limited,
at the Dorset Press, Dorchester, DT1 1HD

Contents

List of Figures

List of Tables

Preface

This book has its origins in the thinking, articles and theses developed by the author in the Army Academies, Durham and Northumbria Universities in particular, and the Institute of Information Infrastructure Protection Working Group(s) in the USA. In many ways it is a blinding glimpse of the obvious; so it would be inappropriate to attribute to this work a great deal of original thought. There is of course some original thought but there is also the bringing together of a range of linked subjects under a single approach. The idea that marketing has an antithesis might seem obvious; but it has not been seriously developed. The idea that such an antithesis is linked to modern warfare might also seem obvious; but equally has not been seriously developed. The idea that both could be used to destabilise organisations and even countries may be a little less obvious; but commentators such as Donnelly and Angell have been warning about this for a decade.

First defined by the author in 1997 the subject of Obstructive Marketing is now timely and relevant. The newspapers on a daily basis carry some sort of story about it. Its military counterpart, Asymmetric Warfare, is now an accepted strategy by superpowers and 'no powers' alike. The rise of the South and East at the expense of the North and West has brought some Obstructive Marketing stratagems into sharp focus. This book aims to explain what Obstructive Marketing is, who practices it, where and when and how. The formal links to Asymmetric Warfare and terrorism are explained – as is the need for a strong government/business partnership to counter the effects.

Before their respective deaths in 2008 and 2012 both Professor Thomas W. Dunfee of the Business Ethics School at Wharton, Pennsylvania, USA and Dr Stephen R. Covey, he of the *7 Habits of Highly Effective People*, were both kind enough to endorse the general approach of this book.

Acknowledgements

The inspiration for this book came from a number of sources. Professor Thomas W. Dunfee of Wharton School, University of Pennsylvania, Pennsylvania, USA; Professor Gerald Blake, of Durham University; Professor Andrew Collins of Northumbria University; Professor David Alexander of University College London; Dr Peter Trim of Birkbeck College, University of London; Lieutenant General Sir Edmund Burton KBE; Chris Donnelly CMG; Robert Leitch MBE; Amanda Goodger, now of Cambridge University; General Gordon Sullivan, formerly US Army Chief of Staff; Eric Goetz formerly of the Institute of Information Infrastructure Protection at Dartmouth College, New Hampshire, USA; Michel Frenkiel; my occasional writing partner on business continuity, resilience and 'Hardening' James Royds, immediate past Chairman of the Business Continuity Institute; and all those who spared their time anonymously or otherwise to give me their views on this and related subjects.

I would like to thank my family, friends and colleagues at Durham Consulting Group, the NHS, Goodwin plc and Microdat Limited for their support and advice whilst writing this. Alastair Waite, my business colleague, has, as always, indulged me by giving me time to complete this book. Above all Jenny Gray of ITV News gave me space, support and assistance over many months.

Martin West and the team at Gower Publishing gave me the opportunity of writing this book. They are all thanked both for that and for their patience over various impinging events and timescales as the manuscript became due; not least the worst snow in over 25 years as I attempted, and eventually succeeded, to move house to Cumbria, UK; change my job; complete a university course; and write this in the first three months of 2013. My risk assessments may have left something to be desired; certainly my critical path was distorted and my home path required a JCB (thank you Morris Fisher) to clear it for the removal van.

So there is not a great deal of hubris in this book! Events count, and plans don't always survive their initial practical engagement; whether with the enemy or the snow! So be warned!

Introduction and Definition

1

It was the age of wisdom, it was the age of foolishness, it was the epoch of belief, it was the epoch of incredulity, it was the season of light, it was the season of darkness, it was the spring of hope, it was the winter of despair, we had nothing before us, we were all going direct to heaven, we were all going directly the other way.

Charles Dickens – A Tale of Two Cities

In the Cold War there was a clear division between the West, East and the non-aligned states. Everyone, more or less, knew where they stood in relation to the political power blocs of the time. In economic terms the capitalist West operated to a set of rules understood by all, the communist East operated to a different set of rules. The interface, though difficult, was manageable as both the then USSR and China generally stuck to contracts once they had been agreed. Socially there was more stability than today. Technology was driven by the two superpowers. The environment had yet to withstand the onslaught of four major economic blocs competing for resources. Legally there was a system of international law that looked civilised in many respects compared to today. This essentially bi-polar world was easily understood.

This book links the concepts of Obstructive Marketing, Asymmetric Warfare and Asymmetric Obstructive Marketing. The following recent examples will help position the concepts. On 11 January 2013 French air strikes began an involvement by France and others in removing an Al Qaeda break-away group from Northern Mali. Apart from removing a political, social and cultural threat this activity also protected valuable uranium resources. On 16 January 2013 the gas facility at In Amenas in Algeria was attacked by an Islamic force. The gas facility was run by BP (UK/US), Statoil (Norway) and Sonatrach (Algeria). On 31 January 2013 the BBC news carried the story of the *New York Times* being hacked by the Chinese for revealing the accumulated wealth of the outgoing Chinese premier. This followed similar events at the *Washington Post* and *Wall Street Journal*.

These attacks are notable for a number of reasons:

- one is an attack by a State on a stateless organisation to both preserve another state and access to economic resources;

- one is an attack by a stateless organisation on a business;

- one is a cyber-attack by a state on a business;

- all are related to military attacks on businesses and an attempt to stop businesses operating.

There is not a nuclear weapon or an aircraft carrier in sight and neither would have been useful in the circumstances. However, this is the face of modern warfare. These attacks linked casual, competitive, criminal, cultural, critical infrastructure and capitalist issues together in contests designed to affect businesses in a war dominated by small forces attacking, or being attacked, by larger ones in a largely asymmetric military contest and/or the use of critical infrastructures as either targets or conduits in the contest. This book is an attempt to look at how modern marketing and warfare have become intertwined in a manner that would be foreign to the original international marketers and globalisation gurus. Today the international landscape is very different. Today's landscape is multi-polar and difficult to understand.

Politically, there are some states wishing to become democracies; some seeking independence; some joining federations; some leaving federations or unions; some providing facades for religious groups that actually extend across so-called international boundaries; and some stateless groups that operate with impunity across land or marine boundaries. Militarily effects-based operations, shock and awe tactics, have given way to the much more subtle interplay of forces that is Asymmetric Warfare. The rules of war change over time and today the rules are changing apace.

Economically, the global financial crisis of 2007/2008 has seen a rebalancing of economic power. Simply, this has seen the relative decline of the North and West of the world against the South and East. The increasing dominance of China, and to a lesser extent India and Asia in general, adds two more resource hungry blocs to the traditional West and what is now Russia. The former global multi-national giants are being challenged by the likes of Gazprom in Russia, Goodbaby in China and Tata of India for a share of what the West has traditionally seen as its global market. Goldman Sachs's Jim O'Neill, for example, has described this process more than once and coined the term BRICKS for the emerging economies of Brazil, Russia, India, China, Korea and South Africa as long ago as 2001 (O'Neill, 2001).

Socially, the world has fragmented from the clear social fabrics that bound the major Western democracies and the Eastern monoliths for decades. Perhaps this clarity was an illusion or mirage; as frequently what went on underneath political systems was very different to the image officially portrayed. This is apparent from the way in which the communist system crumbled, the current social challenges in India and China, and the many facets of and catalysts for the Arab Spring. Socially the world has to deal with Facebook and the Taliban, often in the same place. This is new territory and the end result unclear. Expectations are raised by a global information stream; local reality is often disappointing, repressive, disease ridden and violent.

Technology has had a massive impact on political systems and economic growth. This has been liberating, the Internet and the Boeing 747; enterprising, Microsoft, Oracle, Apple; challenging, Google and Facebook; and uplifting, Apollo, disease control and keeping everyone fed. Electronic data works its way round the world in a similar way to the old trade routes of the sixteenth and seventeenth centuries; and suffers from similar attacks from pirates and technophobes. Not everyone is keen on technology and those that believe that technology challenges the supremacy of God will become themselves an increasing challenge to the technophiles of this world.

Environmentally the planet is under threat from pollution, population and the plunder of resources to feed the demand for products. In the coming decades these four horsemen of the environmental apocalypse will hold sway over the world in a similar but much more aggressive way than climate change has over the last two or three decades. Such is the momentum behind these that, in the short term, it is likely that less can be done to stop their effects than has been achieved for climate change.

In 1999 most American businessmen asked about threats to their business commented that most of the time business was conducted within the capitalist system in an honourable manner. The UK's *Sunday Times* came out with a similar story at about the same time. Today, life is not so simple. The legal basis for trade is continually challenged by different laws, different systems (sometimes no systems), and a trading system that has different interpretations of the word capitalism. Trade is not conducted legally in such a simple manner as it used to be.

The major writers on marketing emphasise only the positive side of the subject. A review shows that over four decades nobody has addressed the 'negative' of marketing and globalisation effectively. This negative side is a major part of what this book is about. As will be seen later this negative side acts much more like a modifier than a true opposite; and is akin in physics to the modifying action of black holes in the universe.

The starting point is the original definition of Obstructive Marketing in Hyslop (1997):

> *Any process, legal or not, which prevents or restricts the distribution of a product or service, temporarily or permanently, against the wishes of the product manufacturer, service provider.*

An improved definition followed reader comments on the original article:

> *Any process, legal or not, which prevents or restricts the distribution of a product or service, temporarily or permanently, against the wishes of the product manufacturer, service provider or customer.*

When thinking of Obstructive Marketing for the first time it was very much the case that it was Western companies and organisations that were thought to be subject to this sort of activity. A decade or so after the initial thoughts much has changed. Today there are multi-nationals and globalising companies from all parts of the world. Some of these practice their trade in a traditional capitalist manner; and some do not. Companies and organisations out of China have a heavy state input; the same can be said of Russia and, to a lesser extent, India. The link between capitalism and governments was strong in the West, but is arguably now weaker than it was 50 years ago. Today, the links between government and companies and organisations in many of the so-called emergent, some would say now fully emergent, BRICKS (Brazil, Russia, India, China, Korea, South Africa) countries is so close that the term state-sponsored capitalism is not far-fetched.

In the West and the East the companies and organisations face a multiplicity of challenges to their marketing objectives. These can be summarised as the 6Cs: casual, competitive, criminal, cultural, critical infrastructure and capitalism. The casual is the disgruntled former employee; the competitive other companies or organisations; the criminal is terrorism and organised crime; the cultural the many obstacles faced by companies and organisations in selling goods and services into different political, social and religious arenas. These four areas constituted the original thinking of challenges to marketing and globalisation. More recently it has become clear that critical infrastructure represents a threat to marketing. This can be in the shape of various threat vectors from the Internet; lack of water; or lack of energy; or lack of protection. Even more recently the addition of a sixth C, capitalism, reflects the banking crisis of 2007 onwards, some of the issues surrounding the use of 'Quants' in the financial markets, and the growth in influence of sovereign wealth funds.

This book now starts to explore some of these issues in more detail. The subsequent chapters are split into two main sections. Section 1 deals with the who, what, why, when and how of Obstructive Marketing. Chapter 2 therefore starts with the origins of the thinking behind Obstructive Marketing. It looks at philosophical parallels that suggest the idea has some basis in logical thought. It then turns to what the marketers have been saying. Few have commented on any anti or Obstructive Marketing thinking. An exception would be the scholars at Wharton who have identified a number of related issues. Writers such as Sun Tsu, Machiavelli and Clausewitz are looked at, as they all had ideas on how Obstructive Marketing may be conducted.

Chapter 3 deals with the principal Obstructive Marketing casual, competitive, criminal, cultural, critical infrastructure and capitalism challenges. In each case the issues that cause the Obstructive Marketing problem are described. These are then followed by a series of case studies that demonstrate the point. Every day in the newspapers and online there are now stories of an Obstructive Marketing nature. It is sometimes legally and ethically difficult to describe these stories accurately. They may be subject to outstanding legal discussions or court cases; and, ethically, some cases may still be a problem for individuals to deal with. Therefore many of the case studies are from the late 1990s and early 2000s. They illustrate the point and allow comparisons to be made to contemporary studies and reviews.

The case studies relate back to a traditional marketing mix so the tie to the marketing discipline can be clearly understood. Chapter 3 also deals with those periods in which Obstructive Marketing attacks are likely to happen by looking at the times when businesses or organisations are strong, weak, entering new markets, innovating or undergoing change. Each circumstance presents a different Obstructive Marketing challenge and each needs to be dealt with in a different way.

Section 2 looks at preventing Obstructive Marketing. To prevent Obstructive Marketing context is important and Chapter 4 looks at the modern context in which businesses and organisations have to operate. As the new business continuity standard, ISO 22301, is introduced, context is writ large. Context is a major addition to this standard. The thinking in this book has had an impact on that standard. Few businesses spend time really examining the context in which they operate. The theme moves on to look at Obstructive Marketing and challenges to globalisation in more depth, reviewing a number of key issues.

Chapter 5 introduces risk. Risk management is important because it prevents Obstructive Marketing attacks if managed correctly. This is looked at generally through the lenses of the 6Cs. This discussion on risk shows that many risk management issues have escaped from the true control of management; and thereby represent a risk themselves. Some ideas are presented that may make the dealing with risk a little more simple than it is at the moment. In particular, the difficulties around the description and measurement of risk are discussed and some suggestions made as to how to deal with them. The management of risk is dealt with through the mechanism of dependencies. Building a picture of dependencies within and without an organisation confirms the description and measurement of risk and allows risk management to be handled in a structured manner. How this is done is demonstrated through a model of Obstructive Marketing.

Chapter 6 introduces the concept of Asymmetric Warfare. Obstructive Marketing attacks are often undertaken by people with fewer resources than those that seek to market their products or services in the first place. This has significant parallels with Asymmetric Warfare where small forces take on larger ones. This chapter therefore examines the various military doctrines related to Asymmetric Warfare and suggests why this form of warfare may have a present and future impact on organisations.

Chapter 7 looks at the markets, finance and sovereign wealth funds. In addition to the capitalism issues discussed in Chapter 2 this chapter seeks to demonstrate the increasing influence of Sovereign Wealth Funds in the global economy. These are relevant to Obstructive Marketing because they can have significant distorting effects, as well as beneficial ones. To understand the influence of these funds is to understand how they can impact Obstructive Marketing. Chapter 8 brings all these themes together. In this chapter Obstructive Marketing and Asymmetric Warfare are discussed together. The new concepts of the Asymmetric Military Balance, or see-saw theory, and Asymmetric Obstructive Marketing are proposed and the consequences of each explained. Chapter 9 suggests specific ways in which Obstructive Marketing can be prevented, and describes how such a preventative model might look. Chapter 10 provides a summary and Chapter 11 a look forward to the future.

2

Obstructive Marketing Origins

Marketing has become a branch of economic science. It is taught at universities and institutes of professional competence, such as the UK's Chartered Institute of Marketing, now educate marketers to various levels in the subject. A century has passed since the first marketers started to practice their discipline and now there is a philosophical and doctrinal background to the profession which is well-grounded in research.

The philosophical background of marketing reaches back to the early years of the twentieth century and Bartels (1988) in *The History of Marketing Thought* categorised the development of marketing theory decade by decade from the beginning of the twentieth century thus:

- 1900s: discovery of basic concepts and their exploration;

- 1910s: conceptualisation, classification and definition of terms;

- 1920s: integration on the basis of principles;

- 1930s: development of specialisation and variation in theory;

- 1940s: reappraisal in the light of new demands and a more scientific approach;

- 1950s: reconceptualisation in the light of managerialism, social development and quantitative approaches;

- 1960s: differentiation on bases such as managerialism, holism, environmentalism, systems and internationalism;

- 1970s: socialisation; the adaptation of marketing to social change.

But nowhere in this discourse was the subject of 'anti' or Obstructive Marketing raised.

The modern day gurus include Kotler and Keller in the US and McDonald in the UK.

Kotler and Keller (2008, p6) state:

> *Marketing is one of the most important, yet misunderstood, activities in modern life. Too many people think of marketing as the advertising and selling of goods, whereas in truth marketing starts long before the goods exist and continues long after the goods are sold.*

Marketers have the responsibility of helping their organisations determine, through market research, what relevant groups of consumers and business buyers need. Then undertaking all the activities of concept development and testing, product development, market testing, distribution planning, pricing, advertising and selling to make sure that the right goods reach the right buyers and create the right satisfaction.

To accomplish all of this work efficiently marketers must be familiar with economics, management science, psychology, sociology and the mathematics of the market place. In the past, marketers were primarily found in consumer packaged goods firms and in industrial firms. Now they are evident in every organisation from Procter and Gamble to Oxfam.

This has led to specific definitions accepted by the Chartered Institute of Marketing (UK) (1976, p1 and p3):

> *Marketing is the management process responsible for identifying, anticipating, and satisfying customer requirements profitably.*

Importantly, in global companies this means worldwide. As not-for-profit organisations also have a need for marketing such a definition needs to be extended to:

> *Marketing is those activities performed by individuals or organisations, whether profit or non-profit, that enable, facilitate, and encourage exchange to take place to the satisfaction of both parties.*

This is the Chartered Institute of Marketing's UK (1976) alternate definition of Marketing. (The Institute is developing a somewhat longer definition.)

Kotler and Keller (1994, p7) put it as follows:

> *The societal marketing concept holds that the organisation's task is to determine the needs, wants and interests of target markets and to deliver the desired satisfactions more effectively and efficiently than competitors, in a way that enhances the consumer's and society's well-being.*

Emphasis on satisfying customer requirements is central to any definition of marketing. So is positive thinking. There are no negatives in these definitions. The antithesis of marketing has been described by Hyslop (1997, p2) as Obstructive Marketing and was defined as in Chapter 1. Today that definition needs to be improved to reflect the changes seen over the last decade:

> *Any process, ethical and legal or not, which prevents or restricts the distribution of a product or service, temporarily or permanently, against the wishes of society, shareholders, management, staff or procedures of the product manufacturer, service provider or customer.*

- 'any process' reflects the global nature of the issue and accepts that different mores will prevail in different parts of the world;

- 'ethical and legal or not' because what is legal and acceptable in one state is not in another; and judgement must be suspended in looking at global practices from a purely Western legal standpoint. (Otherwise, for example: it would be impossible to discuss Islam in an unbiased fashion);

- 'prevents or restricts', because the sale of goods and services can be stopped in an absolute or relative manner depending on the subtlety of the 'offender';

- 'distribution of product or service', because this is central to the marketing effort;

- 'temporarily or permanently', because time always changes the picture in international relations, and this affects business as well as politics and international relations;

- 'society', because any organisation is embedded in some society;

- 'shareholders', because these are the ultimate financiers and beneficiaries;

- 'management', because these are the people who effect the production and sale of the product and service;

- 'staff', because these are the people who earn their living from the product or service;

- 'procedures', because this is the way in which the product and service is created and delivered;

- 'product manufacturer, service provider, or customer', because these are the players in free market capitalism;

- the addition of the words 'or customer' to the original definition reflects the later thought that customers, as well as providers, can be deprived as a result of the potential techniques. This is both logical and common sense, particularly from a marketing viewpoint, and particularly where the customer is key.

Sun Tsu's work, see Krause (1995) and Chung (1995), almost a bible for some modern day executives, explores the role of spies and decoys, deception and obstruction, in winning wars. Machiavelli (1521, 1535) explores the idea of deception in winning. Newton (1664) states that, 'For every action there is an equal and opposite reaction.' In the 350 years since this statement was made it has come to be understood to apply to many walks of life, not just Newtonian Physics. More recently Angell (1995) of the London School of Economics predicted economic gloom as a result of modern corporate processes.

The essence of competition is of one or more trying to outdo others. Marketing is such a positive profession that it is difficult to conceive of any process that could be easily identifiable as 'anti-marketing' in a business sense, except, perhaps, the complete lack of marketing in the first place. However, there is a counterpoint to the marketing process and agenda. This is called Obstructive Marketing, for semantic aestheticism, and can be readily identified, categorised, and dealt with as part and parcel of the marketing mix. There are some general theories that help to demonstrate that such an idea is reasonable.

These theories also help to develop the 'in principle' idea of 'intent' behind such a process.

Angell (1995, p1) comments as follows in a paper dealing with globalisation and information systems today:

> *The alchemist treats information systems as social systems in which technology is only one element. In its required new form security must be seen in holistic terms, treating the ecology of systems as reflexive and non-linear. The difference between success and failure when dealing with uncertainty will be the management of the quality and integrity of a company's people, procedures and systems. More and more that difference will be the responsibility of security chiefs and their redesignated departments. The sheer complexity of the situation and the uncertainty necessitate corporate strategies, whose effectiveness depends on the vision of its leadership and the integrity or wholeness, the sense of identity and trust in the company, and how it deals with change. The concept of security itself will have to be redefined to encompass these ideas, which will impact on all company systems. We in the security community must see ourselves among the elite symbolic-analysts. The job of the new style security manager is to broker the identification and solution of security problems. As the old power bases collapse all around, the strategic brokers of our community must develop our own alchemy, which delivers organisational procedures and technological applications that can succeed in the midst of social, political and economic upheaval.*

To Angell (1995), even if not defined as such, the concept of Obstructive Marketing is not foreign. He was and is of his time. In terms of a response to Obstructive Marketing he is clearly aligned with the overall thrust of this book; and with Alexander's (*q.v.*) view on Jung being influential in terms of symbolic-analysts.

Competition is an element that is often seen as core to the success of any business. There is too much, too little, it is skewed in some way or missing completely; such scenarios build a range of business models that have been studied in many different ways. Companies 'beat' the competition or, sometimes, there is 'co-opetition': where, in Porter's (1995) description of the business world, there is a need for clusters of competitive businesses to co-operate for the benefit of all businesses. Understanding the competition is also critical to success. Moss Kanter (1995), and Handy (1997), amongst others, help us to understand this in a wide and 'world class' sense, but from, generally, a traditional perspective. Huntington (1996) deals with competition in a different way, he looks at the competitive pressures as between cultures. This is something the global company has to be increasingly aware of. As Huntington (1996, p68) states:

> *In an increasingly globalised world, characterised by historically exceptional degrees of civilisation, societal and other modes of interdependence and widespread consciousness thereof – there is an exacerbation of civilisation, societal and ethnic self-consciousness.*

Huntington (1996) infers that a concept such as Obstructive Marketing should exist, at least in the competition between cultures.

The anti-marketing element of Obstructive Marketing was a starting point. This was qualified by examples of particular activities in marketing that were not strictly the reverse of marketing, just not very pleasant: for example, the hoarding of agencies and vendetta sanctions. Hence the reason for describing the process looked at here as Obstructive Marketing rather than anti-marketing; or developing existing themes of counter marketing and demarketing which are more aligned with specific product targeting. A good parallel to this exists in the development of Newtonian, relative physics and quantum mechanics. All of these theories, acting in their own fields and within general boundaries are correct and give 'right' and 'wrong' answers. At the extremities, however, things are not so simple.

Hawking (1988), in a discussion on black holes, best describes this subtlety. Black holes would appear, in general, to be the counterpoint of stars, planetary, solar and various other systems. They are not strictly anti-matter, although some do behave as such, but are much more 'modifiers' of the system. Clearly, a system which operates with some efficiency, as modern day free market capitalism has done, cannot function if there is 'anti-capitalist' matter all around. When this has occurred historically there has been a polarisation, into capitalism and communism for example: as one would expect from physics. More likely there is a combination of 'anti-matter' where modern day marketing efforts will be destroyed. For example, some aspects of some Muslim societies can act as modifiers where the marketing efforts will be slowed or distorted. This is also true of some Indian practices where agencies are often undertaken just to prevent market penetration; see

Lalvani (2006). Therefore just as black holes obstruct parts of the universe by being either anti-matter or modifiers so Obstructive Marketing can do the same to a capitalist system by either stopping it or modifying it. Once again, the reason for not calling the process anti-marketing is a consequence of this subtlety.

It is possible to draw similar parallels from almost any philosophical position. Sun Tsu, noted by Krause (1995); Machiavelli (1535); Competition Theory after Porter (1980); Hawking (1988); and Angell (1995), can all be, and often have been, used to illustrate business life directly or allegorically. They give a clear indication that there is nothing unreasonable in a description of Obstructive Marketing. To confirm the issue it is necessary to look no further than the philosophy of the main defeated alternative to capitalism, Marxism, or the current main rivals to globalisation, the current incarnation of Marxist–Leninist–Maoist thought practised by the Chinese, and Islam, to understand the points clearly.

Both Marxism and Marxist–Leninist–Maoist thought encourage challenges to marketing in a philosophical sense.

Marx and Engels (1888, p104) comment as follows:

> *Of course, in the beginning, this cannot be effected except by means of despotic inroads on the rights of property, and on the conditions of bourgeois production … (and will) necessitate further inroads upon the old social order, and are unavoidable as a means of entirely revolutionising the mode of production. These measures will be different in different countries. Nevertheless, in the most advanced countries, the following will be pretty generally applicable:*

- *abolition of property;*
- *heavy and progressive income tax;*
- *abolition of inheritance;*
- *confiscation of property of all emigrants and rebels;*
- *centralisation of credit in the hands of the state;*
- *centralisation of communication in the hands of the state;*
- *extension of the means of production by the state;*
- *equal liability of all to labour;*
- *vertical integration of agriculture and manufacturing;*
- *free education, abolition of child labour.*

The Chinese, particularly TseTung (1964, p79), opined:

> *If the US monopolist capitalist groups persist in pushing their policies of aggression and war, the day will come when they will be hanged by the people of the whole world. The same fate awaits the accomplices of the United States.*

This latter developed Marxism into a philosophy much more based on the will of people to determine a future, and importantly on the concept of dialectic materialism. Lately this has softened to a more traditional Marxist view overladen with capitalist overtones; but as Rosen (1998) shows this is still highly anti-competitive. It must, therefore, be remembered that China has not totally eschewed a Marxist view. Marx himself commented that it may be necessary to make compromises along the way. Therefore China is a country which could be seen as counter to marketing in the sense discussed here. Certainly few have actually made any money out of China except the Chinese, despite the hype and investment; at least until very recently.

In Islam the position is relatively simple: the key unifying forces are the family, the tribe and religion. Religion, in particular, puts many obstructions in the path of modern companies. It is, almost by definition, counter to marketing efforts. The Holy Koran preaches the oneness of God and emphasises divine mercy and forgiveness (Dawood, 1982, p10).

> *God is almighty and all-knowing and though compassionate towards His creatures. He is stern in his retribution … The most important duties of the Muslim are faith in Allah and His apostle, prayer, almsgiving, fasting and pilgrimage to the sacred House at Mecca.*

This is not reflective of a capitalist existence. The bold demonstrates how easy it becomes for Islamic clerics, representatives of Allah and interpreters of the Holy Koran to demand Holy Wars, fatwahs and boycotts on issues which they, by right, can define as contrary to Islamic thought (Dawood, 1982).

The Koran, Dawood (1982, p311), also states:

> *Do not barter away the covenant of Allah for a trifling price. His reward is better than all your gain, if you but knew it. Your worldly riches are transitory, but Allah's reward everlasting … Allah will not guide those who disbelieve His revelations … None invents falsehoods save those who disbelieve the revelations of Allah: they alone are liars.*

These are not encouraging words, taken with clerical interpretation, for non-Muslims seeking to sell into an Islamic world.

There is every reason why the idea of Obstructive Marketing should exist. Indeed, most work would suggest that it is not only reasonable, but almost obvious, that it should. Literature has, in a philosophical context, already helped this study, through Sun Tsu, Krause (1995), Machiavelli (1535), Newton (1664) and Marx and Engels (1888) and others, to provide an introduction on how Obstructive Marketing could be deduced at a theoretical level.

To this list could be added Confucius (Chung, 1994 and Clausewitz, 1962), as further support for the idea: that there is a resistance to marketing.

> *The superior man, when resting in safety, does not forget that danger may come. When in a state of security he does not forget the possibility of ruin. When all is orderly, he does not forget that disorder may come. Thus his person is not endangered, and his States and all their clans are preserved. (Confucius)*

Confucius (551–479 BC) thoughts are preserved in the *The Analects*, or *Lunyu*, also known as the *Analects of Confucius*. These are the collection of sayings and ideas attributed to the Chinese philosopher Confucius and his contemporaries, traditionally believed to have been written by Confucius' followers. These recognise the need to have both strong and moral leadership; but acknowledge the darker side of events and the need to guard against these.

Clausewitz's writing was dialectic on war, the balance between offence and defence. He recognised that winning did not depend entirely on the superiority of forces. He recognised that other attributes were important. This is why he was fashionable in US doctrinal circles post the Vietnam War, slipped away before 2001, and has now become fashionable once again as the US comes to terms with the fact that military might alone is not enough. His famous 'war is an extension of politics (more correctly policy) by other means' is often misunderstood. It is one side of the dialectic. He recognised that political objectives could be achieved by commercial, psychological means as well as armed force. In an age of asymmetry, of Obstructive Marketing, his dialectic approach to war is important and helps us to understand how the thinking behind warfare is not one dimensional.

These thinkers also confirm 'intent'. It is with intent that spies are deployed, it is with intent that Machiavelli's 'companies' are not always virtuous, it is with intent that Islam decries earthly riches, and it is with intent that Marx seeks to outlaw free market capitalism. The list of contributing and intentional thinkers could continue. There is a clear change in context, risks, dependencies, how people operate and crises from an Obstructive Marketing perspective.

Philosophical literature throws up a particular conundrum in the area of political thought. Political thought has always dealt with the state: as machine, organism, class or revolution (Wayper, 1973). This has recently changed. The power vacuum created by the end of the Cold War has not been filled by any state. Arguably, a business philosophy and process has filled it: free market capitalism. Except for its origins in the US, in particular, this does not have allegiance to any particular state. Indeed, some states are having a problem existing under the free market capitalist umbrella. Countries from Britain to Malaysia have complained about the impact of currency trading on stability, from 1992 to 2011, most recently evidenced by the 'market' influence on the Euro-zone crisis of 2011. This begs a question of the future of political thought, as it has been understood since the Greeks. The opposition and alternatives to the current state of play may stem from Obstructive Marketing type events rather than states. Fukuyama (1992) (1996) may be right in describing the end of history, certainly in terms of many of the rules that have governed society for millennia.

Obstructive Marketing is not just a barrier to positive marketing. There are practices that act as a resistance, drag, opposite or modifier of marketing. In the final analysis, if the argument on the political thought conundrum is accepted and developed, Obstructive Marketing can be seen as a *de facto* opposition to not only globalisation but perhaps to the political as well as the business philosophy of free market capitalism. This is not only an idea that requires more study but clearly points to the need for organisations to be proactive in protecting themselves from such events.

Pretty (2000) and Hyslop (1999) demonstrate how casual sabotage, normally by employees and not usually pre-meditated, can damage a company's reputation. Table 2.1 summarises the position.

Table 2.1   Casual sabotage

Company	Catastrophe	Type of Loss
Johnson & Johnson	Tylenol	Product tamper
P&O	Zeebrugge	Liability
Exxon	Valdez	Pollution
Perrier	Benzene	Product recall
Heineken	Glass	Product recall

Source: After Hyslop, 1999 and Knight and Pretty, 2000.

Other examples include Rewick (1999, p1):

> *Analysts are punishing the Chicago-based company, whose stock hit a 52 week low last week, for one of the deadliest bacterial outbreaks and largest meat recalls in the US.*

This indicated product contamination caused by employees at Hudson Foods.

The 2010 BP oil well leak in the Gulf of Mexico promises to bring a decade of difficulty to the oil giant.

The archetypal Obstructive Marketing campaign by activists was against McDonald's. Initially McDonald's was accused of lying about the quality of ingredients and other aspects of food in the chain. McDonald's brought a libel suit in response in London. The case went on for years (McSpotlight, 1999). The suit cost McDonald's millions of pounds and exposed every part of their commercial operation to scrutiny. The company survived, but it was not the same organisation afterwards. The McSpotlight website spawned many other attacks on multi-national companies and is a key reference point for the study of Obstructive Marketing. It is a further example of different context and risks to organisations.

Huntington (1996) expressed a view that, with the Cold War over, the bi-polar nature of the world has given way to a multi-civilisation community likely to be perpetually at odds. He finds it difficult to sustain any idea of complete free market capitalist hegemony in a world re-characterised by a rise in nationalism and religious fervour. This view implicitly, and almost explicitly, supports the Obstructive Marketing idea.

Fukuyama (1992) (1996) is more positive about the future for free market capitalism. In the first of these works he describes the end of history in a Marxist–Hegelian sense and sees the world, essentially, as one organised on free market capitalist lines. In the second, he responds to some of the criticisms levelled at the earlier work by reviewing the economic basis of many different cultures. His book suggests how these differences can become a single interlocking network working in a single direction. This approach supports the idea of Obstructive Marketing by demonstrating, at a practical level, how cultures are different, and how each culture approaches perhaps the same end by different means.

Kennedy (1989) predicts the demise of the 'American Empire'. Later writers, especially Friedman (1999), suggest this is premature. From an historical perspective Kennedy's (1989) logic cannot be faulted. As free market capitalism is essentially an American philosophy, there is, again, support for a marketing modifier or opposite.

Porter (1990, p129) in describing his 'diamond' of determinants of national effectiveness:

> Cultural factors are important as they shape the environment facing firms … such influences are important to competitive advantage because they change slowly and are difficult for outsiders to tap or emulate. Social and political history and values create persistent differences among nations that play a role in competitive advantage in many industries.

Again, by implication, Porter (1990) supports much of the thinking behind Obstructive Marketing.

Moss Kanter (1995, p73) lists many positive attributes that world class organisations must adopt but also comments:

> Local distribution channels require specific, differentiated relationships … large international companies are not immune to local and national politics … the Renault–Volvo alliance fell apart on political grounds … Predictable cultural tensions arose … country differences … country rivalries … local interests.

She specifically acknowledges the paradoxes of the global economy and the existence of reactions to globalisation procedures.

Sullivan (1996) has given an insight into the battlegrounds of the future. They are information battlegrounds. These battles are more likely to be fought between organisations than armies as known today. This gives some credibility, from one of the USA's leading soldiers, of the existence of planned campaigns against organisations.

Productive sources of cases of Obstructive Marketing activity include: Fialka (1997) who covers industrial and marketing espionage; Tolchin (1992) who looks at the dangers of selling important manufacturing assets (in this case the USA's) and includes examples of Obstructive Marketing behaviour; Partnoy (1997) on Wall Street is specific regarding the ways investment houses plan to relieve clients of their money; and Naylor (1994) who finds many Obstructive Marketing issues in his review of the 'soft underbelly of capitalism'.

Critically relevant is much of the ethics and marketing research at Wharton School, University of Pennsylvania when under Professor Thomas Dunfee. Personal communications have verified Obstructive Marketing as something understood in general by this eminent ethics and marketing establishment. This is important to this book for a number of reasons, but mainly the personal support Dunfee gave to the overall approach.

French (1988), whilst at Wharton, developed the idea of corporate adulterers in work on corporate punishment. This specifically alluded to companies punishing each other for presumed or actual misdemeanours. This was often where there was no, and occasionally where there was, legal redress. This idea was derived from Hawthorne (1850) and his use of the letter 'A' on clothing to identify Hester Prynne the adulterer. The same methodology, it is suggested, can be used to identify corporate deviants beyond the reach of law.

Corlett (1989) developed the theme with his modified vendetta sanction that extends French's idea to extremely rare and infrequently identified forms of retribution against organisations.

Finally, Dunfee (1999, 2008) confirmed that Obstructive Marketing as an idea was perfectly in tune with the ideas of French and Corlett; and was certain that governments, organisations and individuals act in this sort of manner on a regular and planned basis.

Marketing is a positive profession. Little is written about the 'downside'.

Bursk and Chapman (1964), in the 1960s/1970s gave no space at all to the downside of marketing. In the same decade Drucker (1968) does not even mention marketing specifically, but does point out some dangers in the marketplace. Davidson (1975) in the 1970s/1980s steps up the marketing process but again does not mention anything of a contrary nature. McCarthy (1975) approached the subject tangentially by mentioning some behavioural idiosyncrasies.

Lace (1983) and McDonald (1999), in the 1980s/1990s only hint at difficulties in marketing internationally. Primers dedicated to international marketing such as Czinkota and Ronkainen (1995), allude to difficulties and mention, in detail, one or two instances, for example Disney's purchase plan for counterfeiters, but do not address Obstructive Marketing in any structured manner. They concentrate on how to take the US model abroad. They do warn that all countries are not the same, and give some help on identifying local differences. It is left to practitioners such as Phillips (1989), to explain the disasters awaiting the marketer.

The Internet is now an accepted source of information, and an important element in any literature search. It is almost a true market. It is a rich source of information on Obstructive Marketing, and many of the cases identified in this book have been found there (Rough Guide, 2009). Four aspects are of interest to the subject of Obstructive Marketing.

The first is that it is an anarchic medium. This means that many of the methods used by society over the last hundred years or so to suppress information damaging to business confidence and marketing are absent. This includes laws of censorship, libel, slander, intellectual property protection, contract, and privacy, amongst others, and the use of public relations (PR) 'spin'. This allows the exposure of events and processes that may previously have gone unnoticed or unrecorded. It may be that without the Internet the subject of Obstructive Marketing could not be raised at all; it is an Internet-dependent subject in many ways.

The second is the way in which Obstructive Marketing techniques, as the resistance, drag, opposite or modifier of marketing, are beginning to be applied to the medium by the very bodies and states most threatened by it. This is interesting because it not only reinforces the idea of Obstructive Marketing but confirms its use and effectiveness, even by those who normally suffer from it. Thus the various attempts to police the Internet are indicative of a process that threatens, as well as enhances, the status quo.

The third is of course the use of the Internet as a medium to perpetrate Obstructive Marketing behaviour such as 'virus attacks', confidence tricks, disinformation and misinformation.

The fourth is the influence of the medium on conflict and war: state vs state (France vs US, Russia vs US) as explained by Fialka (1997) and Vistica (1999), company vs company (British Airways vs Virgin) as reported by Tucker (1997) (amongst many others), state vs company (US vs Microsoft) by Fialka (1997) again, state vs individual (US vs Clinton) as revealed by the Drudge Report (1999).

These ideas are alluded to in much of the literature above, particularly by Sullivan (1996); Haylock and Muscarella (1999) help to make sense of the Internet itself from a commercial point of view. However, little of a specific nature has been written on the subject in the intervening years and this is an area for further study.

The key free market thinkers, and associated works, of the twentieth century are Hayek (1944) (1960) (1988), Hazlitt (1946) (1959), von Mises (1936) (1949) (1956) (1962), Rand (1943) (1957) (1966), and Snyder (1940). These writers brook no Obstructive Marketing interference in their pursuit of the free market capitalist ideal. They anticipate an ideological, but not practical, resistance. They believe that the process can be legislated for. The evidence in their support is strong, particularly in those societies where the individual and individual rights are also strong. However, as Rout (1999) points out there are challenges of an Obstructive Marketing nature not only in those parts of the world where free market capitalism has yet to take root, but also in those societies who wish to determine for themselves what sort of capitalism they want.

This discussion suggests that the pragmatic obstacles to organisations are more varied than many philosophers may understand.

In a key essay Williams (2002) comments that organised crime is primarily about the pursuit of profit and can be understood, in Clausewitzian terms (Clausewitz, 1962), as a continuation of business by criminal means. He notes that organised crime groups typically have a home base in weak states that provide safe havens from which they conduct their transnational operations; and that they, led by Colombian drug traffickers, have developed their operations along standard business practices. This provides an added degree of protection against law enforcements, minimises risk and maximises profit.

The Internet fits perfectly with such a model. Williams identifies seven major trends in organised crime and cyber crime:

- the use of the Internet: fraud, theft;

- white collar crime: stock manipulation in particular;

- cyber-extortion: and extension to the physical use of force and intimidation;

- use of nuisance tools, for example: viruses, to obtain account and password information;

- jurisdictional arbitrage: use of countries with jurisdictional voids;

- Internet used for money-laundering: use of over and under invoicing, auctions, gambling;

- the link between 'hackers', 'networks' and organised crime grows as different skills are required.

The steps taken to deal with these issues need to be international, multilateral and strategic. The G7's Financial Action Task Force (2004) has made some inroads in this respect with regard to money-laundering; and has produced nine special recommendations and 40 other recommendations of practice. The Council of Europe Convention on Cybercrime (2004) is another step. However, as the European eJustice Project (2006) demonstrated aligning the administrative processes across jurisdictions remains difficult to achieve; and thereby allows organised crime to operate more easily across boundaries. This highlights the need for mutual legal assistance treaties (MLATs).

Rider (1991) and Bosworth Davis (1988) have run various economic crime events over time and their work, with associates, in the field of economic crime, is relevant. They point out the increasing backdrop of organised crime to all events in society.

A more general review of the literature on organised crime sees a bias towards the physical and US. The following texts give a reasonable overview.

Albanese (2004) shows that the world of organised crime has changed dramatically in recent times. He reports the changes that have occurred, including Internet crime, human smuggling, transnational links, and other modern manifestations of organised criminal activity. In an earlier work, Albanese (2004) offers a different country perspective on organised crime for each of its 20 chapters.

Galeotti (2001) suggests that if the twentieth century was dominated by Cold War then the twenty-first century will be defined by the struggle against organised and transnational crime. He noted the blurring of terrorism and organised crime.

Kelly et al. (2005) address various forms of international crime: drug trafficking, money-laundering, weapon smuggling, trafficking in humans, the illicit trade in precious stones, art, and cultural objects, and the commercialisation of human body parts.

Kvashny (2003) travelled to Asia to research piracy which, after virtually disappearing for more than a century, has reappeared and is increasing at an alarming rate. The goal of his book was to determine who all the players in piracy are, how they are involved, and how piracy is being perpetrated with such force and volume today. The day-to-day monitoring of such activities is undertaken by the likes of the International Maritime Bureau (2009).

Leong (2004) discusses the overlapping relationship between organised crime and terrorism. She asserts the difficulty of defining, and therefore understanding, both terrorism and organised crime and how it affects law enforcement's ability to fight either. She further contends that a thorough understanding of the two concepts is essential in order to generate appropriate and effective policy decisions for law enforcement agencies.

Shelley (2005) undertook a peer-reviewed 18-month study that includes empirical evidence drawn from numerous case studies. The resultant report analyses the relationship between transnational organised crime and terrorism, with attention to the factors most likely to foster a link between these two networks.

Trim and Lee (2006, p126) state:

> *It is sometimes hard to quantify how much leading companies lose with respect to the illegal activities of criminals and fraudsters ... senior managers need to think in terms of putting in place an effective corporate security system ... if one accepts that counterfeiting is now a major problem then it is reasonable to put in place ... contingencies to counteract damage and plans ... to counter the activities of organised criminal activities.*

In other work Trim (2004) (2005) pushes the need for a better intelligence understanding of the threats faced by organisations. Trim and Lee (2007) introduce the Global Intelligence and Security Environmental Sustainability (GISES) model for counteracting organised crime and international terrorism. This model operates at a supra-organisation level but helps individual organisations understand how to operate in such a context. The framework for organised crime–international terrorist network risk and consequences assessment is useful. Trim et al. (2009) suggest that resilience in organisations should be developed through a built-in security management approach.

Viano et al. (2003) demonstrate through a series of essays the significant developments in crime made possible by technological advances, high-speed communications, ease of international travel, softening of borders and Internet-based transactions.

Donnelly (2001) comments that a new type of security force is required. This would combine elements of the current military and police, but would also involve Non-Governmental Organisations and business, in an effort to combat a new world in which the threats are much more from organised crime than they are from the old Cold War protagonists.

In these writings there is an explicit threat to organisations which, implicitly, needs to be met by a stronger and toughened organisation. All these writings therefore support the need for an organisation to be able to withstand a number of Obstructive Marketing and related threats.

A key point is that continuity and security as a process is reactive whereas the environment in which it operates is, from this analysis, dynamic. Organisational continuity and security should therefore be proactive.

The American preoccupation with promoting democracy around the world is, according to some, the product of a dangerous idealistic impulse.

In his book, *Diplomacy*, Kissinger (1995), cautions against this impulse, under which American foreign policy is shaped more by values than by interests. He joins a long line of American writers, from Lippmann (1955) through Kennan (1947) to Krauthammer (2001), who call on the US to check its idealism and accept the necessity of a more sober pursuit of American national interests abroad. In their view, the American democratic impulse is a distraction, an inconvenience that forces the nation's leaders to dress up needed measures in democratic rhetoric. At worst, it unleashes a dangerous and overweening moralistic zeal, oblivious to or ignorant of how international politics really operates. It fuels periodic American 'crusades' to remake the world, which, as President Woodrow Wilson discovered after the First World War, can land the country in serious trouble.

Ikenberry (1999) suggests this 'hard-headed' view, however, is a misreading of both past and present. The American promotion of democracy abroad, particularly as it has been pursued since the end of the Second World War, reflects a pragmatic, evolving and sophisticated understanding of how to create a stable and relatively peaceful world order. Liberals emphasise the role of human rights, multilateral institutions and the progressive political effects of economic interdependence. Although 'realist' critics and others complain about drift and confusion in US foreign policy, it actually has a great deal of coherence looked at in this manner.

Huntington (1996) famously warned of a coming 'clash of civilisations' that will pit 'the West against the rest'. His notion of democratic community focussed on the Atlantic world. Others suggest more generous interpretations, seeing democracy as something that runs along a gradient and is not confined to the West. Durable democratic institutions do require a congenial democratic culture and civil society, but these are not confined to only a few national, religious and ethnic settings.

Cesari (2004) has written of the dangers of the clashes between Islam and Democracy. Jenkins (2010, p1) brings this up to date with the following comments:

> The west's proudest export to the Islamic world this past decade has been democracy. That is, not real democracy, which is too complicated, but elections ... How strange to choose this moment to export it, least of all to countries that have never experienced it in their history. The west not only exports the stuff, it does so with massive, thuggish violence,

the antibook of how self-government should mature in any polity. The tortured justification in Iraq and Afghanistan is that elections will somehow sanctify a 'war against terrorism' waged on someone else's soil. The resulting death and destruction have been appalling. Never can an end, however noble, have so failed to justify the means of achieving it ... Democracy has been greatly oversold.

There is a developing agenda of confusion post-Cold War which sees context, risks, dependencies, people and crises changed. This is summarised by the change from the Cold War era to an era of terrorism.

The concept of Obstructive Marketing appears understandable in this new environment.

In Christianity, the term 'fundamentalism' is normally used to refer to the conservative part of evangelical Christianity, which is itself the most conservative wing of Protestant Christianity. Fundamentalist Christians typically believe that the Bible is inspired by God and is never wrong. The term 'fundamentalist' derives from Torrey (1909), who proposed the required Christian beliefs for those opposed to the Modernist movement.

The term 'fundamentalist' has been extensively misused by the media to refer to terrorists who are Muslim. This is not accurate as most Muslims are fundamentalists in terms of their religion. Fundamentalist Islam is described by the West as the conservative wing of Islam, just as fundamentalist Christianity is the conservative wing of Christianity. The vast majority of Muslim fundamentalists, in this sense, are pious individuals who strictly follow the teachings of Mohammed, promote regular attendance at mosques and promote the reading of the Holy Koran. Many promote the concept of theocratic government, in which Sharia (Islamic law) becomes the law of the state.

Addi (1992) addresses democratic construction in Islamic societies through the Algerian experience. Its main conclusions can be summarised as follows. First, in all Muslim societies, there exists an Islamicist Utopia that stands as an obstacle not only to democracy but also to political modernity. Until now, this Utopia has been contained only by repression that finally impedes democratisation. Second, Islam presents itself as a public religion that participates in the legitimisation of political power. The democratic ideology, however, is compatible with religion to the extent that it is lived as a private concern. Finally, the Islamicist Utopia and the public aspect of Islam aim at maintaining society's communal structures. They refuse to make the singularity of the political arena independent and reject differentiation through politics within a society that claims to be fraternal.

Omar (2011) summarised the Islam society succinctly in his BBC broadcasts wherein he emphasised the true nature of Islam as a caring religion far removed from the fanatics and terrorists that characterise the general media view of the religion today. This view is confirmed by Khan (2012) and Pervez (2012) when asked about terrorist cells in Stoke-on-Trent, UK. Their view was that few attended the Mosque from the local Muslim community, but most would see themselves as caring. Most were trying hard to make some sort of living; not radical at all. In fact getting anyone really interested in politics was very difficult. However, this is not to say that both could have been unaware of radical elements in their own community; as they certainly exist. The expansion of Islam was a religious–military campaign according to Marr (2012).

All this said fundamentalism on both sides of the Christian/Islam divide has created different contexts, risks, dependencies, people issues and crises than were evident a generation ago.

Once again the idea of Obstructive Marketing is understandable here, as part of the ideas of fundamentalism on both sides of a current global religious divide. The export of democracy and the fundamentalism of both East and West is another dynamic process.

The way in which the military interpret their role is extremely important for a complete understanding of Obstructive Marketing. This subject will be covered in more detail in Chapter 6. Suffice to say that at this point that somewhat like the ebb and flow of regulation in the banking industry, depending on how the industry is performing or perceived at the time, political interference in the military and the doctrine of the military also ebbs and flows, at least in the North and West, on how the political and military balance is seen at the time.

Staten (1997), Donnelly (2003) and others, comment that mercenaries, ideological or religious zealots would attack corporations and business networks. Some terrorists have discovered that the path to the fear and chaos that they crave most may be more easily achieved by a wide-scale attack on infrastructure/economic targets, thus causing a general breakdown in society and facilitating civil unrest and rioting. Evidence of insurgent attacks on economic targets have been clearly demonstrated in places like Corsica (banks, court houses), Greece (bank, car dealership and businesses), Colombia (multiple oil pipeline bombings), India (attack on multiple commercial buildings in Bombay), and Sri Lanka (bank and commercial building attacks).

An excellent example of this emerging situation might involve further study of a United Nations report that the gross national product of the drug and crime-driven 'underground economy' in Pakistan is probably greater than that of the official government (Staten, 1999). Although sufficient studies are currently unavailable, this is also probably true in Colombia, and it is becoming increasingly likely that the same trend is developing in parts of the former Soviet Union, where organised crime 'mafia organisations' have infiltrated or subverted legitimate business for their purposes. Needless to say, these patterns do not bode well for the future of the legitimate governments in these and other areas of the world.

Donnelly (2003, p2) made a number of seminal statements regarding security in the twenty-first century. Some of these were in regard to Asymmetric Warfare. His comments on the corporate sector are reproduced here because they are central to the argument for 'Hardening' against Obstructive Marketing:

> It is at this point that the issue becomes more than an academic one for the corporate sector. The corporate sector has always had an interest in national security, of course, but that interest was general and invested in the social and political basis of the country. Business did not usually involve itself directly except inasmuch as there was business to be done in the field of supplying the defence sector. 'Security' for the business world was mostly protection against competition, theft or fraud, and the occasional green ecological protestor. Very large conglomerates have always played a major role, especially in smaller countries, but the main focus was usually on economic and political issues, not security issues.

> The change in the nature of security, however, has created a new imperative: the need to break down the barriers not only between government agencies but between those agencies and the corporate world. As societies, under the influence of commercial competition, become ever more efficient, ever more information dependent, and ever more 'globalised', they also become more vulnerable to disruption, even catastrophic disruption. Business is the first and most immediate institutional victim of terror. Long before terrorism is a threat to governments or to social cohesion it will have put companies – especially small- or medium-sized companies – out of

business. Other threats to security, such as organised crime, corruption, and smuggling are equally threats to society because they are first and foremost threats to the health of the business sector. Genuine business needs secure conditions to flourish. The whole concept of security as developed by NATO and the EU was based on economics. But the threat that inspired Schumann to found the basis for the EEC and ultimately the EU was the threat of hot war. Today, security needs to be applied against a much wider range of threats in which business features directly, and not at a second remove as it did in the past.

More immediately, business is itself a generator of stability and prosperity and a hedge against the new threats. Therefore it is of greater interest to governments as an element of security. Business needs governmental help in order to know in which countries and in which ways the new threats to security will arise. Security becomes a major determining factor in foreign direct investment (which, for example, doubled in Poland in the year after that country joined NATO). Today, business can provide governments with intelligence that they cannot easily get from other sources. Big business may be the actual prime target of cyber-crime or terrorism pursued with a political, rather than an economic, motive. All these considerations demand a new relationship between the corporate world and the security sector.

Equally, the answers to new security problems will likely lie in the hands of corporations. We need to explore new responses to security in collaboration with business. If we seek security merely by ratcheting up old procedures we risk creating such obstacles to trade and commerce that we destroy the market freedoms which form the basis of our society and ensure our prosperity.

Governments and international institutions, in other words, can no longer solve their security problems without building a new partnership with business. Business can no longer ensure conditions for its secure operation without having a greater input into government policy. The need for partnership works both ways.

The challenge we face in the immediate future – for this is a problem which is already with us – is to develop that partnership, to make it work, and to keep it flexible so that we can keep ahead of the threats in what will, from now on, be a rapidly evolving security environment.

How this approach works in a country like the UK where up to 80 per cent of GDP is now foreign-owned is a dimension not specifically covered by this book, and a subject of further study. It is, however, a significant barrier to establishing a national approach (Heseltine, 2012). In terms of Obstructive Marketing it could possibly be said that, at a national level, the ownership of the majority of big businesses by foreigners, and thereby control of nearly 80 per cent of GDP, is an attack on the state in any event. Certainly when the current coalition Government in the UK looked to increase growth in the economy, post 2007, they faced a number of barriers. One barrier was the lack of manufacturing capacity and therefore the inability to properly launch a growth strategy led by manufacturing exports; the other was the realisation that, unlike the 1950s, 1960s, 1970s and 1980s, there was a lack of large-scale businesses that could be dictated to in order to drive growth. The economy was much more open to the whim of the market, and therefore Obstructive Marketing too, than the Government realised. Attending Secretaries of State board meetings was an eye opener if only because this was clearly not properly understood.

Jonsson (2007) spoke of sovereign wealth funds being a weapon of Asymmetric Warfare. The size of these funds, the collapse of the banking industry and the realignment of economic power over the last three to five years suggest that these will continue to be potentially so (confirmed in August 2011 as the world's currencies started to realign).

This again positions organisations as both targets and activists in a new world security scenario. Appropriate defence therefore requires global businesses and organisations to take steps against Obstructive Marketing.

The threats to the UK are as described by the Cabinet Office (2008).

The links between terrorism, organised crime, and failed states are well made. There remains a lack of understanding, at least in the explicit description in this document, of the further links with globalisation, infrastructures and, in particular, information infrastructure. These are all mentioned but not drawn together into a cohesive threat picture. This view is repeated by MI5 (2010). The City of London (2012), for example, states that London is responsible for 20 per cent of the UK's economy but this does not feature as a risk in either the Cabinet Office nor MI5's assessments, and this at a time when banking was about to collapse. The City of London is totally dependent on critical information infrastructure.

The Centre for Advanced Management and Interdisciplinary Studies (CAMIS) Workshops on Critical Information Infrastructure, under the Chatham House Rule, noted that there was no joined up thinking in Government on many aspects of the new infrastructure threats (Trim, 2010). In a parallel conversation Goodger (2010) noted that the key issue was to ensure that the business and organisational threat from virtual and logical risks was properly understood by chief executive officers (CEOs).

This suggests that the UK threat scenario has not yet fully grasped that organisations may suffer from Obstructive Marketing threats in the way that a review of the military and economic threats so far suggest.

Dorfer (2004) uses Cooper's (2003) classification of societies into pre-Modern, Modern and post-Modern to state that the threats to Europe come from all three and quotes the European Security Strategy's (2003) list:

- terrorism;

- proliferation of weapons of mass destruction;

- regional conflicts;

- state failure;

- organised crime.

Again, as with the UK, but unlike the US, the economy is not writ large as a threat; although this is the second largest economic bloc in the world. This again suggests a lack of attention to a need to 'Harden' organisations, particularly economic organisations.

The threats identified by the US since 1996 have been consistently moving away from a Cold War scenario towards one where the two top threats at the time of writing are the economy, in contrast to the UK and European position, and, according to national Intelligence Chief, Blair, UK Islamic Citizens (Blair, 2010). Generally, the threats are as stated for the UK and Europe. There is a wider perspective to the threats than in either the UK or Europe. This may just be a reflection of the sheer size of the economy, infrastructure and global position. It implicitly and, occasionally, explicitly supports the concept of Obstructive Marketing and the need for more than resilient organisations in a variety of contexts.

As a generalisation much of the rest of the world sees either the US or regional, religious and ethnic conflict as the key threats. However, this is changing as globalisation gathers pace outside the Western and Northern powers. As this happens the need for a counter to Obstructive Marketing spreads beyond the West and business.

Organisational continuity and security is reactive; globalisation and its antithesis is dynamic; the export of democracy and fundamentalism is a further dynamic process; and now the military context and threat scenarios have changed to the extent that any conflict is presumed to require civilian participation and assumes organisational and civilian involvement and casualties.

Critical infrastructures are defined as follows:

- energy;

- finance;

- health;

- food;

- government services;

- law and order;

- national icons;

- transport;

- water;

- waste water.

Historically, critical infrastructure has had a very physical feel to both the term and artefacts. Critical infrastructure could be seen. It was pipes, stockpiles or electricity pylons. However, half the critical infrastructures listed above cannot be 'seen' at all. It follows that protecting critical infrastructure has moved from defending 'things' to defending what might be generically termed as 'processes'. The defence of 'things' requires other familiar tools like walls, fences, alarms, decoys, police forces, armies, navies and air forces. In order to defend 'processes' we need the same words but used in different ways.

In the 1950s, a critical infrastructure was sometimes called a strategic national asset. In those days, most of these assets were nationalised and often had a complete government department named after them, or a 'golden share' was held by the Government in relevant organisations. In the UK these included the GPO, Shell, BP, ICI, The Gas Board, The Electricity Board, the Water Boards, the Prison Service, the British Railways Board, British Overseas Airways Corporation, British European Airways and so on. Many of them have been privatised and their survival in any 'battle' depends upon a public–private partnership. This partnership, in most countries except perhaps the US, is so far incompletely understood and certainly not formal. Critical infrastructures are no longer truly 'national', no matter what governments might want to think. But, critical infrastructures remain key to sustaining our way of life. The fact that they are not only under attack, but have also escaped from a society's control, gives great cause for concern. The necessary partnership between the public and private sectors must work in order to protect our collective futures.

All critical infrastructures are bound together today by the most important one of all: telecommunications and information. Most of the time this is hidden from view too – and from most people's consciousness – but it is always there. It is the most vulnerable point and the most fantastic achievement. It is also the major battleground in an Asymmetric War or Obstructive Marketing campaign.

Some ways in which today's critical infrastructure is protected will be familiar: such as the use of geography and physical security. Others will not, such as governance and business effectiveness. The processes of today are not in the sole hands of any government, they are in the hands of a number of different partners. Hence, there is a need for a partnership of interests. The private sector has had long experience of managing threats to processes. Most businesses depend on processes for their livelihood. They manage protection in very different ways to governments.

It is necessary to look not only at how to protect modern critical infrastructures but also why and how that protection will differ from any traditional understanding of defence. In 2003, the author, Hyslop (2003), argued that Asymmetric War fighting methods are not new. They were practised during previous World Wars, and almost all other wars. They have characteristics of total war – where balance, timing, effort and resources are deployed in different measures to deny a strong military power the full use of that power. These techniques are well suited to attacks on critical infrastructures. This is, simplistically, where the world is today concerning the attacks on the US, and their allies, and the responses in Afghanistan and Iraq.

However, this is likely to be just the start of a long campaign and it is important to understand how it might develop in regard to infrastructures and what the North and West powers need to understand in order to fight this asymmetric war well. Asymmetric Warfare is generally conducted in a covert planned military/technical, criminal or cultural manner and less frequently in a spontaneous manner. Critical infrastructure is both a target and a conduit for Asymmetric Warfare. It is a target in that it represents an infrastructure dominated largely by the major economic powers and is therefore seen as a legitimate target by those who seek to destabilise these powers. It is a conduit because the infrastructure and the applications that sit on it, the Internet/World Wide Web in particular, give an opportunity to those asymmetric combatants to plan, communicate and sometimes even execute asymmetric events. In particular, steganographic techniques are used for communication.

An understanding of the relationships between critical infrastructures and the public and private sectors is required. In order to be well protected critical infrastructures need to be resilient. The concept of resilience is relatively poorly understood. Resilience is a term that is frequently used incorrectly – and most often incorrectly in the context of recovery from disasters. Resilience in traditional critical infrastructures needs to be described in terms that will be familiar. These terms include redundancy in power distribution, stockpiles of fuel and food. However, these traditional and familiar terms are not a regular feature of these infrastructures any longer.

The privatisation of the utilities, in the UK and elsewhere, and the adoption of 'just in time' delivery techniques for food and fuel means there is very little 'give' in the system to cater for unexpected events. There is a very immature approach to both resilience and recovery in the newer and less well-defined critical infrastructures, particularly those surrounding those that now control our lives, such as telecommunications and information. In this area an exploration of the strategic importance of the relationship between telecommunications and systems resilience, recovery and security and both Asymmetric Warfare and Obstructive Marketing can demonstrate some of the issues to be tackled and suggests a number of approaches. The processes of dealing with Obstructive Marketing not only set a corporate security approach but represent the private sector's contribution to the public–private partnership.

To protect the critical infrastructures of the future will require a new approach to defining threats. Such an approach has to both acknowledge and manage context and risk. Terrorist risk has led to anti-terror legislation. Anti-terrorism legislation victimises, in general, those it seeks to protect. One has only to walk through an US or UK airport these days to understand the veracity of this statement. Anti-terrorism legislation is a victory for the terrorist and usually represents a loss for democratic freedoms. What alternative is there to anti-terrorism legislation? There are a surprising number based on intelligence, space planning, border controls, economic measures against terrorists, amendment of terrorist tools by international treaty, technological 'sniffers' on planes, trains and rails, and a belief in a way of life. All of which would not necessarily result in a definitive change for the worse in our way of life.

The efficacy of these measures can be predicted by using sophisticated risk analysis tools. A risk-based approach to Critical Infrastructure Protection (CIP) is therefore something that needs to be implemented within a public–private partnership. It needs many of the same institutional controls as exist now to be effective. Most of all, however, it requires a change in attitude. Changes in attitude are notoriously difficult to implement in any society. It is necessary to look at how a context and risk-based approach to CIP could change; by reducing the way in which our lives are affected by terrorism and our organisations and businesses by Obstructive Marketing.

The key issue behind the financial crisis of 2007 onwards was the repeal of the US Banking Act (1933) in 1990; and banking deregulation in the UK by the then UK Chancellor of the Exchequer over the period 1997–1999. The context of this repeal is important. The issues surrounding the financial markets and financial crisis are explored in more detail in Chapter 7.

3

Obstructive Marketing Challenges

This chapter is an attempt to categorise and comment through case studies on the different types of challenge posed by Obstructive Marketing. The comments in this chapter are the result of primary research by the author over the period 1999–2012. The key piece of research was a Linked-In survey conducted in 2010 of 750 representatives of the top 30 per cent of organisations, the second a set of interviews with the top 1 per cent of organisations, and third is related to the case studies later in this chapter and in the Appendix. Some additional and specific research on the financial sector was undertaken for this book.

The first category to look at is that termed 'casual'. This is potentially a misnomer because it more properly refers to timing rather than approach. Into this category come activities such as those of disgruntled employees, anarchists, some activity of the Animal Liberation Front, anti-abortionists and fundamentalists. In primary research almost a third of organisations surveyed had suffered from this type of problem or attack.

The second category is 'competitive'. Here there are issues of defensive marketing, market share issues, agency agreements and licence agreements, legal issues such as EU competition and US anti-trust laws, and non-tariff barriers. In primary research half the study was affected by these sorts of issues.

The third category is 'criminal'. In this category industrial espionage, intellectual property/copyright/patent infringement, distribution chain irregularities, extortion, long firm and financial instrument fraud and money-laundering are major problems. In primary research up to a fifth of organisations suffered from this sort of behaviour.

The fourth category is 'cultural'. This category includes a range of difficult areas such as alcohol to Arab states, Coca-Cola in a number of countries, banking in Nigeria, Oprah Winfrey in Iran, Mid-West Hogs in Israel, fertility drugs in China; to name but a few. Institutions or special interest groups (see the 'squawk' in Chapter 5) are most prone to cultural risk. According to primary research one in ten organisations suffer from cultural risk problems.

Twenty years ago critical infrastructure, the fifth category, would not have appeared on a list of Obstructive Marketing challenges. Today, this challenge is writ large particularly because of the universal dependence on information technology (IT) and the Internet. In primary research all the representatives of the top 1 per cent of organisations interviewed had suffered from problems of critical infrastructure.

Twenty years ago the sixth category 'capitalism', and finance, would also not have made up a category of Obstructive Marketing challenges. Again in primary research for this book all organisations found this to be a potential problem. This is a relatively new area. In some ways the result was expected, because of the current financial climate. However, there were a number of additional issues, more specifically explained in Chapter 7 in regard to the performance of the markets themselves.

Primary research has demonstrated that Obstructive Marketing attacks occurred during periods of weakness, strength and complacency, whilst entering new markets, at periods of innovation or change. Twenty per cent of organisations said they were attacked during periods of weakness.

Strength and complacency was characterised by an arrogant board, time served CEO or management, mature product lines, an undermined leadership position and stagnant growth. Thirty-three per cent of attacks occurred during these periods.

Entry to new markets was often accompanied by cultural misunderstanding, poor marketing skills, inappropriate products or poor leadership. Fifteen per cent of attacks occurred during these periods.

Innovative periods covered those times when new products were being launched, different distribution methods were being tried, business process re-engineering was being undertaken or new people were being brought in. Sixteen per cent of attacks occurred during these periods.

A further 20 per cent of attacks occurred during a change of management, branding, recipes, design or function.

Obstructive Marketing is clearly a critical challenge to companies and organisations. The following paragraphs look as these issues in a little more depth and demonstrate from research and case studies what the challenges look like.

Recent research by the author of the top 30 per cent of organisations in the UK, the Linked-In survey, demonstrated that:

- organisations are not proactive in continuity and security plans. This is because they have reactive plans where they have plans at all;

- organisations do not appreciate the changed global context. They do not appreciate or understand the relevant contexts;

- organisations do not appreciate the changed risk environment as they do not have proper risk management;

- organisations do not fully appreciate the dependency environment. This is because they do not review risks appropriately;

- organisations do not fully appreciate the staff environment in which they operate. They, generally, have no succession plans and have an ambivalent attitude to staff;

- organisations do not appreciate the crisis environment. This is because they have not properly planned for any continuity, risk, dependency or staff issue that could lead to a crisis eventuality;

- organisations do not appreciate the general environment. This is because of the foregoing;

There are some possible interpretations of this result:

- it is simply true;

- it is a reflection of market conditions;

- it is a reflection of ignorance;

- the questions were wrong, or not asked in the right way.

By way of further clarification all those who had agreed to be interviewed from the questionnaire were spoken to. There was unanimity in regard to pressure from the 5Cs (research for the sixth C, capitalism, was specifically undertaken later for this book); lack of continuity and security planning; in regard to a lack of risk management, staff development, in regard to crisis management and in regard to the general environment. They agreed that they all thought they were acting appropriately but also agreed that in relation to the questionnaire results, they clearly were not. They all raised the lack of time, effort and money arguments for not doing more. This tells us that for the top 30 per cent of UK organisations:

- most are unaware of the true global context in which they operate;

- most do not pay heed to risk management and Obstructive Marketing (probably because they feel they don't need them);

- most will not pay the competitive cost of doing so (this is the 'it won't happen to me' or the 'why should I pay more than my competitor scenario?');

- even when offered the opportunity of more closed questions the answers were the same.

There is a clear disconnect between how organisations believe they are operating and how they actually are operating.

The lack of focus on the 'softer' areas of continuity and security planning, the disconnect from context, the lack of risk management and dependency review, the ambivalent attitude to staff, and consequent inappropriate approach to crisis management, would suggest that general management is being looked at incorrectly.

In the alternative, it may be that the top 30 per cent is still too large a sample. In the next piece of research the sample was narrowed to the top 1 per cent of organisations.

These interview responses refer to: Alamo Group Europe (2012), Alstom (2011), British Airways (2012), Bet 365 (2012), BP (2007), British Army (2010), Buckingham Foods (2011), CNE (2011), Caterpillar (2012), Civil Service (2012), UK CPNI (2010), Control Risks (2010), Cooperation Ireland (2012), Clydesdale Bank (2010), Dana Petroleum (2012), De Beers (2011), Deloittes (2011), East of England Ambulance Service (2010), Fleetwood (2010), GCHQ (2011), Goodwin (2012), Goodbaby (2011), Grant Electricals (2012), Hadley Group (2012), JCB (2012), JLR (2012), Johnson Matthey (2012), Johnson Tiles (2012), Linklaters (2010), McLaren F1 (2010), Marsh (2010b), Metropolitan Police (2010), Maudesley (2009), Maitland Hyslop (2012), NHS South East Coast (2010), NHS Surrey (2011), OilServ (2009), RBS (2009), Rivers Capital (2012), Shell (2012), Staffordshire Police (2012), Staffordshire Fire Service (2012), Steelhenge (2012), Steelite (2012), Tata (2012), Tetra Pak (2009), UBS (2012), UK Mail (2012), US Army (2009), Dunfee (2008).

Thirty-six of these are from the UK, 4 US, 2 Irish, 2 Swiss, 1 Australian, 1 Chinese, 1 French, 1 Indian, 1 Middle East and 1 South African.

A summary of their views is also presented in Table 3.1.

Summary of Interviews

Table 3.1   Summary of primary research interviews

	Percentage	Count	Comments
Interviewee	All		All
Date	2009–2012		
Casual	100%	50	All agreed they had been subject to casual disruption.
Competitive	100%	50	All agreed they had been subject to competitive disruption.
Criminal	100%	50	All agreed they had been subject to criminal disruption.
Critical infrastructure	100%	50	All agreed they had been the subject of critical infrastructure disruption.
Cultural	100%	50	All agreed they had been subject to cultural disruption, after explanation.
Military context	58%	29	Just over half understood the military context has changed.
Risk management good	2%	4	Very few thought that their risk management was good.
Staff resilience	28%	14	Most thought that staff resilience was poor.
Crisis management	0%	0	None had a positive crisis management process.

Table 3.2   **Primary research interviews compared to primary research Linked-In survey**

	Obstructive Marketing	Military Context	Risk Management	Staff Organisation	Staff Resilience
Observed	50	29	4	47	14
Expected (Linked-In)	16	7	8	40	10
Deviation (o-e)	34	22	-4	7	4
Deviation^2 (D^2)	1156	484	16	49	16
D2/e	72.25	69.14	2	1.22	1.6
Σ^2	146.21 (5) 4.82 (3)				
Degrees of freedom	4 (5) 2 (3)				
P<0.05 = 9.49 (5) P<0.05 = 5.99 (3)	Overall there is no similarity between the samples for all five factors. However, if the chi-squared test is applied to the last three (rather than the five) there is a close similarity. This means the interview group is much more aware of Obstructive Marketing and the military context than the Linked-In survey; and aligned to Linked-In survey on risk and staff.				

The results indicated in Table 3.1 can be compared to a Linked-In survey conducted in 2011, as indicated in Table 3.2.

Also relevant are A (2012) a leading private investigator, B (2012) a former intelligence operative for the Italian secret service, C (2007) a similar individual for the French Secret Service, and D (2011) a former US Secret Service and FBI investigator and now a Director for PwC. All of these would confirm the opinions of the above interviewees.

These interviewees represent a sample of the top 1 per cent of organisations. What they tell us is that they are much more aware of the Obstructive Marketing aspects of organisational operations and activity than the Linked-In survey group. They are, however, aligned with the Linked-In survey group in respect to their attitudes to risk and staff. It is suggested that these individuals, along with the intelligence operatives questioned, are much more likely, because of their very senior positions and intelligence knowledge, to be aware of Obstructive Marketing threats than some of their Linked-In colleagues.

There is still a dichotomy between their awareness and what they do. In the Linked-In survey the sample was mostly unaware of Obstructive Marketing.

In the interview group referred to in this section they are clearly aware and have suffered from Obstructive Marketing. Risk and staff have become the main issues. None have a positive crisis management approach.

The above findings are further supported by the Chartered Management Institute (Woodman and Hutchings, 2010).

The Chartered Management Institute Business Continuity Survey 2010

The summary of the 2010 Chartered Management Institute Business Continuity Survey is as follows:

In regard to the adoption of business continuity management (BCM) the Institute found the number of organisations with specific business continuity plans covering their operations has fallen slightly to 49 per cent, compared to 52 per cent in 2009.

> *Clear challenges remain in encouraging the uptake of BCM in certain sectors. (Woodman and Hutchings, 2010, p7)*

The impact of extreme weather was the most common disruption, according to the Institute, to hit organisations over 2010. This was identified as a disruption to 58 per cent of organisations, up from 25 per cent in 2009. It replaced IT disruption as the top disruption for the first time in this research series' history. In particular, the snowfall in December 2009 and January 2010 affected 93 per cent of organisations.

The potential impact of swine flu, a concern in previous Institute studies, was not, in the event, borne out in the year. While 56 per cent of organisations reported disruption as a result of swine flu, only 3 per cent described the disruption as 'significant'.

The Institute recorded that 79 per cent of managers who had activated their business continuity plans in the past year agreed that it effectively reduced the impact of disruption. This once again emphasises the importance of using BCM to minimise disruption during crises.

Approximately half of respondents (54 per cent) reported to the Institute that they could continue to work to a great extent by working remotely in the event of a disruption. Smaller organisations continue to remain in a weaker position to support remote working.

Organisations reported that corporate governance remains the biggest driver for organisations implementing BCM, although it has dropped from the 2009 level (47 per cent in 2009 to 38 per cent in 2010). Commercial drivers of BCM remain prominent with demands from existing customers (31 per cent) and potential customers (21 per cent) acting as drivers. Central government (21 per cent) and public sector procurement contracts (16 per cent) continue to play an important role.

The Business Continuity Standard BS 25999 is known to 41 per cent of respondents who have business continuity plans. Of the organisations with a specific business continuity plan only 14 per cent use the standard to evaluate it.

Twenty-eight per cent of respondents reported they were aware of the guidance on BCM provided by their local authority or local resilience forum. The most commonly used sources of information on BCM were professional bodies (33 per cent) and internal sources (28 per cent).

Only around a quarter of managers said they had a dedicated budget (27 per cent) while around half (48 per cent) reported that they do not. Twenty-five per cent did not know. It does not appear that the recession since 2007 has resulted in extensive budget cuts.

Human Resource departments are now the most commonly involved internal stakeholder in BCM alongside IT teams having jumped from 63 per cent in 2009 to 72 per cent in 2010. This suggests an increasing recognition that people matter in business continuity planning; a perspective the Institute and the Cabinet Office strongly support.

In terms of risks the 'softer' side of continuity planning and security was not well covered. Nevertheless there was a dramatic increase from 11 per cent to 22 per cent in the concentration on corporate image/brand and reputation over 2009. Other 'softer' areas were not well-covered. The dependence of organisations on critical infrastructure was highlighted for the first time. No link was made to either cyber-warfare or the fact that the UK is at war.

There is ongoing comment on terrorism, but only marginally. The overall advice of both the survey and the National Risk Register (2012) is to adopt BS25999. As previously noted (Chapter 2) this is not sufficient and is reactive. There was no comment on Obstructive Marketing.

This report was produced in co-operation with the Cabinet Office. Looking back at the national threat landscape in Chapter 2 there was no direct link to the UK threat scenario; compared to the US threat scenario where the economy was writ large.

In regard to:

- proactive continuity and security plans, these were not in evidence. Reactive business continuity and security plans were in place in less than 50 per cent of organisations surveyed;

- changed global context, there was no mention of changed global context and the National Risk Register (2012) misses most of it;

- changed risk context, just over 30 per cent of organisations reported governance as being a driver;

- changed dependency context, commercial drivers for continuity management applied to less than 30 per cent of organisations;

- changed staff context. Human resource involvement was up on previous surveys to a record 72 per cent. This suggests that staff issues are now viewed as more important than IT. This acknowledges a changed staff context but is the only one so addressed.

Organisations do not appreciate the Obstructive Marketing risks they are running.

Marsh 2010 Business Continuity Benchmark Report

Research published by Marsh Inc. (2010a) shows that many firms appear to be over-confident in their ability to manage the business continuity and supply chain risks facing their organisations, leaving them highly vulnerable to physical disruption and economic conditions.

The research, for Marsh's 2010 Business Continuity Benchmark Report, examined the perceptions of BCM of over 220 business continuity and risk managers from 11 industry sectors, including financial services and manufacturing, across Europe, the Middle East and Africa (EMEA).

Although 83 per cent of respondents believed that BCM was integral to their risk management and that it was understood and supported by senior management, only 41 per cent said that it had given them a better understanding of their business. Moreover, just 29 per cent felt that it had led to improved risk-intelligent decision-making.

The findings also highlighted that firms concentrate business continuity plans on physical supply chain risks over non-damage related risks, such as those caused by the Icelandic volcano and air traffic disruption and the 'softer' areas of business continuity. In the manufacturing industry, 81 per cent of respondents agreed that their business continuity plan covered all their supply chain risks, whereas in financial services only 43 per cent of respondents agreed.

Hugh Morris, Managing Consultant at Marsh Risk Consulting, Marsh Inc. (2010a), explained this as follows:

> These results show that firms value BCM much more highly than when we last conducted this survey two years ago. However, our experience is that many organisations overrate their BCM capabilities and their perceptions often do not match reality ... The more obvious nature of physical supply chain risks is apparent to manufacturing firms, while only the most advanced financial services firms realise how important and vulnerable their supply chain can be ... Service firms can be equally, if not more, at risk from supply chain disruption than manufacturers due to the complex network of inter-dependencies with other financial institutions. As the recession reminded us all, the domino effect when these firms cannot supply each other with capital can have far-reaching and extremely damaging consequences.

Marsh's conclusions are:

- proactive continuity and security plans, these were not in evidence. Reactive business continuity and security plans were in place in all organisations, as the survey was directed at businesses with business continuity plans;

- changed global context, there was no mention of a general change although supply chain risks were acknowledged;

- changed risk context, just over 30 per cent of organisations reported governance as being a driver and BCM becoming integrated into an enterprise risk management strategy. Most of these were over 1,000 staff strong;

- changed dependency context, commercial drivers for continuity management applied to less than 30 per cent of organisations;

- changed staff context. Less than 30 per cent of respondents commented on staff resilience;

- crisis context. Where crises occurred planning enabled better recovery;

- general environment. The general environment was seen as less threatening than the previous year in a number of areas;

- of note is that those who have developed BCM and beyond are often the ones leading their respective industries.

The dichotomy between what people think they are doing and what they are doing is highlighted by this Marsh Inc. study. To repeat Mr Morris's comment:

> However, our experience is that many organisations overrate their BCM capabilities and their perceptions often do not match reality.

Once again it would appear that organisations do not appreciate the Obstructive Marketing risks they are running.

The Case Studies (1)

This part of the research is concerned with identifying behaviour against organisations in the empirical sense. This secondary research reflects case studies from the 1990s which identified a range of attacks against organisations. The choice of the 1990s is predicated on five points:

- the information is available;

- it is less contentious than more recent cases;

- it avoids potential legal issues;

- it shows that these issues are not new;

- it aligns with the timing of other studies relevant to this book, particularly the Knight and Pretty (2000) study on the threats to shareholder value.

The full list of cases is in the Appendix. Note that the numbers in the results tables refer to the full list of the case studies in the Appendix, not the numbers used in the examples below.

People

People are key to any Obstructive Marketing attack issue. In a practical context they are important because of the specific actions they carry out. They can be thought of as parasites or viruses, acting as individual organisms or as colonies. Such is the case with many industrial espionage cases. Here information is stolen to benefit a competitor. In many cases spies, people, are introduced to gather the information. The following examples will suffice to demonstrate how people can affect business in an intentional Obstructive Marketing attack manner.

CASE STUDIES 1 AND 2: TRW INC. AND AVERY DENNISON, 1997

The Wall Street Journal (1997) carried the report of a research scientist's guilty plea, in a Federal Court, to passing classified nuclear weapons information to China more than a decade previously. This not only deprived TRW Inc. and the US Government of important product information, it enabled competitor Chinese companies, and the Chinese Government to catch up with the US in some important areas of technical expertise. This was an archetypal example of a spy being deliberately introduced into a company to access information: competitive espionage designed to gain product and market advantage for a competitor using a person.

At Avery Dennison exactly the same thing happened. An Avery Dennison employee confessed in 1998 to being a spy for a competitor organisation (Starkman, 1997).

In both the above cases the people were working for Chinese organisations. It is not politically incorrect to identify the Chinese as a major problem area for Western firms in this respect, just a reflection of reality. Two decades ago the examples would have been Japanese; a decade ago Korean; 100 or more years ago American, with Francis Cabot Lowell stealing plans to the Cartwright Loom from the UK in 1811. China's prime intelligence agency, the 'Guojia Anquan Bu', has flooded the US with spies. About half the illegal technology transfer cases being investigated on the West Coast of the US involve the Chinese (Fialka, 1997).

Individuals generally become a problem in an Obstructive Marketing sense when they start working in one organisation at the behest of another. Groups become a difficulty when they organise as special interest groups. anarchists, trades unions, civil liberties and rights groups, and political pressure groups all have a potential interest in adversely affecting a company's marketing activities. Take the example of a company falling foul of an organisation such as the USA's AFL: CIO, or the UK's TUC, for refusing to allow unionisation. Boycotts of the company are then arranged by organised labour. This happens fairly regularly in the US, and less frequently in the UK. Companies who were regularly boycotted in this manner in the US, in the 1990s, included Wal-Mart, K-Mart, and Bristol Farms. The News International Limited 1986 move to Wapping in 1986 is a good example from the UK (*The Guardian*, 2011a). The objective of these union moves was explicitly to modify the behaviour of the company concerned. The company wanted to run a non-union organisation, the union did not want this. In order to effect a change the union tried to inhibit the sale of the company's products until it did change.

In the US people have occasionally become even more of a concern to employers. Shooting the CEO in the 1980s and 1990s was something of a habit, particularly in California (Business Insider, 2012).

As a virus people are introduced to a company to deliberately make it sick. This is an ill-researched area. Yet it appears to be widespread practice; executives move from company to company with the specific task of making their new employers sick; often with the host Chairman's blessing. During the 1990s one or two FTSE 100, later ex-FTSE, companies fitted into this scenario.

There is little room to explore this idea in this book, but it deserves further research. It is relevant to the subject of Obstructive Marketing attack because the virus is introduced to kill off the company from within. This seems, from a cursory view and as an opinion, to be concerned with asset stripping, the enrichment of key boardroom players, and the creation of near-monopolies.

An organisation protecting itself against Obstructive Marketing would anticipate and prevent any incursion or Obstructive Marketing attack in such a manner by way of an improved understanding of context, risks, dependency, crisis management and staff. 'People' are central to any business continuity issue. The introduction and use of people in this way is both competitive and illegal. Chinese illegal activity in the US is planned, paid for and recognised as illegal by the perpetrators; it is also a planned and paid for activity against companies. The intent is clearly to modify the behaviour of US companies in favour of Chinese companies and the Chinese state.

Product

PRODUCT DEPRECATION

Product deprecation and product contamination are two main areas with which an Obstructive Marketing attack may be concerned. Product deprecation is concerned with doing a product down in some way; whereas product contamination is where a product becomes damaged in some way. Both these areas are ones where there is an increase in cases; many more of them are appearing in the media. A problem here is intent. Product deprecation and contamination could happen by accident. In the examples given there is sufficient evidence that the events were planned.

Two famous cases of product defamation concern Nestlé's baby milk preparation and the Body Shop's cosmetics.

CASE STUDY 3: NESTLÉ, 1980S

In the first case Nestlé is presumed to have been causing 'baby milk powder syndrome', from the early 1980s until recently. This argument presumes that via product advertising and the largesse of the international community African mothers in particular have been encouraged to use Nestlé's baby milk preparation thereby causing extreme distress to African babies from illness brought on by the preparation. Two points stand out: the first is that in most cases the mothers themselves are sufficiently undernourished to be unable to deliver natural milk, and second, that the cause of any distress to the child is normally the use of bad water, which causes diarrhoea, not the milk preparation. The KGB (1999) admitted in a US interview that they were behind this campaign; and encouraged it once it had taken on a life of its own, as it did. The purpose was both ideological (encouraging the view that multi-nationals were raping Africa from the then Soviet viewpoint) and practical because Africa was sought as a puppet of the Soviet Union at the time.

CASE STUDY 4: THE BODY SHOP, 1980S

The Body Shop built a multi-national business on the promotion of 'natural' and 'green' cosmetics. Advertising used the founding CEO Anita Roddick as she toured the world finding natural replacements for artificially created cosmetics in the 1970s and 1980s. The Body Shop foundered, and continued to founder, after allegations were made that these products were not 'natural' or 'green' at all. The CEO and CFO were accused of lying. Even though it was impossible to prove, and Gordon Roddick (Anita Roddick's husband and the company's CFO) was persistent in denying any wrongdoing, the allegations stuck and The Body Shop suffered. A journalist was presumed to be behind the campaign, but who was behind him has never been clear. The established cosmetic companies kept largely silent on the issue, but were the prime beneficiaries (*The Guardian,* 2011b).

Product contamination is an issue that can randomly occur. Many companies suffer a consequence similar to those who suffer a major computer problem; within five years most are out of business. Two classic cases are those of Perrier (1990) and Hudson Foods (1998).

CASE STUDY 5: PERRIER, 1990

The cause was initially put down to a disgruntled employee losing a hydrocarbon soaked rag into the source; sabotage. Perrier survived after a fashion, but not without having to withdraw millions of bottles of water from the supermarket shelves and launching a major PR campaign to back the name and the product. Over time it has become, as one would expect, somewhat more difficult to determine the cause: indeed it is now difficult to find any information on the case at all. It was an extremely problematic time for Perrier, and one of the reasons it is now in different ownership.

CASE STUDY 6: HUDSON FOODS, 1998

Hudson Foods (1998) was a major supplier of minced beef to the US grocery trade. In late 1998 some products became contaminated with *E.Coli 0157*, killing several and making many more ill. The company recalled millions of pounds (weight and value) of product, but was slow in dealing with the PR aspects of the issue. The Board eventually decided the whole thing was a lost cause, closed down the business and sold on the food-processing factory. A highly efficient and profitable business was no more within a fortnight of the outbreak. This demonstrates two points: firstly how product contamination is often fatal to a company and, secondly, how quick US companies, in particular, are at forgetting the past and re-forging a future. The source of the contamination was unproven, some insiders and the PR company believe it was deliberate, but the result was the demise of the company. In the same industry the UK Bovine Spongiform Encephalitis (BSE) epidemic in beef cattle is one which may turn out to be an 'Obstructive Marketing' attack event (Booker and North, 2009).

Product Counterfeiting

Counterfeiting is a specific example of product contamination that causes damage to computer hardware and software manufacturers, aircraft spare parts and branded clothing amongst others. During the late 1980s and 1990s there was continuous coverage in the press regarding counterfeiting of computer software products, particularly in the Far East. Counterfeiters simply copy the most successful name brand products, investing nothing in research and development, marketing or advertising and next to nothing in quality control. American businesses lose over $16 billion to counterfeiters per annum. The intangible loss is more difficult to measure when the manufacturer's reputation and value of its brand is damaged by poor quality fakes (March, 1995). Crichton (1997) obviates the difficulty of identifying airline carriers who have suffered from bad spare parts by describing the issues in a fictional context.

CASE STUDY 7: LEVI STRAUSS, 1999

Levi Strauss employs various methods of keeping their jean products as 'pure' as possible. This includes hidden markers; both physical and within the denim to ensure that it is difficult for the counterfeiters to get the right cloth. It also helps Levi's brand protection personnel identify counterfeit products when they see them (Juster and Russ, 1999).

Counterfeiting costs companies billions of dollars. Good security of product development and raw materials is one way to deter it. Disney often tries to buy the offending company according to Czinkota and Ronakainen (1995) Counterfeiting is deliberate and illegal and not only restricts companies' marketing efforts and branding but is tantamount to theft.

CASE STUDY 8: TYLENOL, 1982

Some apparent product contamination issues are not. An example is the Tylenol murders of 1982. Johnson & Johnson had to withdraw Tylenol (an analgesic akin to aspirin) from stores after seven people died of cyanide poisoning between 29 September and 1 October 1982. This was a case of an individual targeting another, a spouse, and covering up by killing more than the target, and making it look like a product contamination issue (Snopes, 1997). The only difficulty was that several copy-cat murders followed, all having the same drastic impact on the manufacturer, who had to recall product.

In general product deprecation and contamination problems are 'intentional'. These issues are so common; particularly amongst leading brands and large companies that a 'Hardening' approach to the subject; looking more closely at context, risk, dependency, crisis management and staff is again appropriate.

Place

The difficulties of place and the hazards of international business are exemplified by Shell and Assi Doman.

CASE STUDY 9: SHELL, 1997

Shell had been a partner of the Nigerian Government for many years; and had overseen, as the major partner in a variety of consortia, the development of the oilfields of East Nigeria. Home of the Ibos, and what was once called Biafra, this part of Nigeria has the richest mineral wealth but the poorest human population of a country dominated, politically, by the North and West. In 1997 international attention focussed on the alleged pollution of local villages and the political campaign for redress launched by Ken Saro-Wiwa. Saro-Wiwa was eventually hanged by the repressive Abacha regime. Shell was pilloried and suffered a boycott of products around the world (Jackson, 1997).

This compounded the earlier Brent Spar oilrig disposal fiasco which had also resulted in a boycott of Shell products (but attributable largely to Greenpeace in this latter case). The result was reduced results and bad press for Shell over the period of a year or so. It also damaged Shell's 'green' image over the medium term, to the benefit of its rivals. In the years following BP, the traditional rival of Shell, was in the ascendant. Shell then looked the rather poor relation with wholesale reorganisation and cost cutting. (By the aftermath of the Gulf of Mexico oil spill in 2010 roles were reversed again.) Part of this is the result of the Nigerian problem. The risk/reward ratio of operating in Nigeria is well known. This translates into a cash figure sooner or later. It is accepted that being in Nigeria will eventually, over the long term, be worth more than these events cost. Nevertheless being in Nigeria invites these events. This is a direct consequence of place.

CASE STUDY 10: ASSI DOMAN, 1990S

Assi Doman epitomised the good and bad. In the mid-1990s Assi took advantage of 'glasnost' and pursued investment in two Russian paper operations, one in St Petersburg and one in Karelia. The St Petersburg venture went well; the Karelian was a disaster with Mafia threats, an anti-Assi campaign and threats to employees. This latter was perhaps a classic Russian response to perceived interference in local matters; but the company still lost much money. Assi later reassessed its Russian operations, particularly in Karelia (McIvor, 1998). The risk/reward ratio mentioned in regard to Nigeria applies again in this case.

Intentional actions by a group have caused both Shell and Assi to modify behaviour. It is not clear how well the risks were identified. A 'Hardened' approach to context, risk, dependency, crisis management and staff would again have been appropriate.

Price

Drug companies and car companies have a difficult time in Europe convincing everyone that differential pricing is necessary within an Economic Union where price harmonisation is a lauded keystone of the entire venture. It is difficult to cover the car companies properly, as the cases are still under review by the Commission, but the drug companies epitomise some of the problems faced by companies operating in an international environment.

CASE STUDIES 11 AND 12: GLAXO AND WYETH, 1999

Drug prices in Europe are regulated by nations, not the European Union (EU). There are high-price drug countries, for example, UK, Netherlands and Germany; and low-price drug countries, for example, Greece, Spain and Portugal. There is wide-ranging trade in buying drugs in a low-price country and selling them in a high-price country. This damages a drug company's ability to recoup the money spent on R&D in countries which have good patent protection (the high-price countries) because of actions associated with countries which have low patent protection (the low-price countries). The 1999 examples were Glaxo's anti-viral Zovirax that was $3 in Spain and $5 in the UK; and Wyeth's anti-bacterial Amoxil that was $2 in Greece and $7 in the UK (size for size). Test cases have not been helpful to the industry. EU law works against the big company that has expended the research and development (R&D) effort. This could kill drug companies as they already need to spend more on R&D to get the same result they have historically. There is more and more pressure to come to the lowest denominator on price, and this will destroy R&D in many companies. Part of the current consolidation in drug companies is as a result of this sort of practice (Taylor Johnson Garrett, 1999). This is an area, known to lawyers, but relatively poorly researched.

CASE STUDY 13: LAKER AIRWAYS, 1982

The case of Laker Airways is one of a price war causing the death of a company. The airline was a no-frills service out of the UK's Gatwick Airport into cost-effective airports in the US. This had a significant impact on the regular transatlantic services, British Airways in particular. British Airways dealt with the problem by effectively pricing Laker out of the market, and Laker's main business eventually folded. This action effectively protected the high-profit transatlantic routes of the major US and UK carriers for about a decade; broadly until the emergence of Virgin Atlantic (see below) (Bower, 1993).

The Glaxo and Wyeth example is an Obstructive Marketing attack because the drug companies are prevented, in this case by law, from marketing products across a range of countries, within a presumed single market, in the same manner. There is intent here in terms of the specific manner in which countries are approaching this issue. The Laker Airways case is a classic Obstructive Marketing attack example where one company set out to destroy another. This was done with clear intent. A 'Hardened' approach would have potentially helped both.

Promotion

Promotion is often a double-edged sword. Virgin Atlantic learnt from the Laker experience in dealing with British Airways. Virgin did not compete as a value airline as such – it went head to head on key transatlantic routes by differentiating on service.

CASE STUDY 14: VIRGIN, 1990S

Virgin Airways followed their Chairman's strategy of identifying very high-profit and margin markets; and concentrating solely on those without the difficulties of running less-effective markets/feeders. When British Airways responded with the same tricks used on Laker, Virgin responded in kind and added the results, in a subtle way, to its now famous advertising campaign (often still seen on the bottom of the back page of the *Financial Times*). Thus Virgin managed to beat British Airways at its own game by using 'knocking copy', which is not something usually recommended to clients by advertising agencies, built from British Airways's own activities. This was, in effect, a 'double whammy' with British Airways's attempts to 'attack' Virgin backfiring in the form of 'using bad press' created from its own activities. The saga continues to this day (Tucker, 1997). This is an example of Virgin using a 'Hardened' approach to context, risk and dependency. They also had a good crisis management approach and well-trained staff. They could take the 'knocks'.

CASE STUDY 15: INDIAN AGENCY PRACTICE, 1997

Some Indian practices tackle promotion in a negative way. An example would be two families, one running an instrumentation business, the other running a pipe business. To consolidate their businesses each takes on agencies for the other: the instrumentation business taking on pipe agencies, the other taking on instrumentation. The businesses then run with the agency of choice to the exclusion, in the other family's hands, of the other competitors (Hyslop, 1997). This allows a monopolistic position to be created to the clear disadvantage of those other companies hoping to enter the market.

Both these examples are clearly motivated by intent to modify or stop the behaviour of another company. This requires 'Hardening' in terms of a better understanding of context.

CASE STUDY 16: JOHNSON & JOHNSON, JAPAN, 1970S

Johnson & Johnson's experience with talcum powder in Japan is an example of many instances of poor research. Johnson & Johnson could not understand why their talcum powder was not selling in Japan. But talcum powder is white, and white is the colour of death in Japan. Sales took off when the colour was changed to pink or blue.

GM's Nova car was fine in English, but Nova means 'no go' in Spanish so did not sell as well as expected in Mexico. There are many other examples of getting it wrong internally. This is not really Obstructive Marketing attack but becomes so if done with deliberation and malice (Morgan, 1998).

Understanding context, the risks of doing business abroad, the dependencies in marketing terms, how to prevent market crises and a proper staff understanding could all have helped in these examples and therefore a 'Hardened' approach is appropriate.

Information

Institutions, particularly in non-Anglo-Saxon countries, have a completely different view of their role in accessing commercial information than is understood by companies in the US, and to a lesser extent in the UK. These institutions do not see the difference between state and the country's companies' commercial interest, they are as one. The US was, for part of the 1990s, effectively at war with France over the amount of technical espionage carried out in the US (Fialka, 1997; Tolchin, 1992). Similar activity was reported for the Chinese, Japanese and Russians. The Chinese Government, as already noted, acquires information through its own Foreign Service. The Japanese Information Centre of Science and Technology acquires information on behalf of Japanese companies, as did/does the Soviet Academy of Sciences. Similar organisations exist in Korea, India and across the Middle East and Africa. Within the US itself information gathering is conducted by a host of organisations. This gathering ranges from AC Nielsen and JD Power at the top end of a lucrative market research business to the Centre for Research Planning and the Institute of Scientific Information, whose activities are just as profitable but far more individually tailored to specific clients and targets (Fialka, 1997).

This demonstrates some of the differences between free market countries and interventionists. Government-backed organisations in interventionist countries frequently mix state and commercial interest to gain advantage from free market capitalist companies. Free market companies often do not understand this and fall foul of the plays made against them. This requires a better understanding of international context.

CASE STUDY 17: NESTLÉ AND OTHERS, 1991

During the early 1990s one particular travel agency in the UK looked after the interests of Nestlé, Company 2 and Company 3. All were going through very interesting periods in their corporate histories and the same travel agency was providing a service for their executives. The service led to tracking the executives and plays on the commodities markets to the advantage of those behind the travel agency. The travel agency had replaced in-house travel agents. There was a revision in the travel activities at all three companies once it was understood what was going on (Nestlé, 1991). This demonstrates how careful companies need to be in outsourcing their activities when sensitive commercial information can be interpreted from tasks handled by outside agencies.

All these examples demonstrate intent and require a proactive, holistic, approach to management, as described by a 'Hardening' approach.

Finance

Finance is included in this analysis because it has a major influence on all organisations. This theme is developed further in Chapter 7.

CASE STUDY 18: GOODYEAR, 1986

Goodyear was a thriving vertically integrated tyre company, not performing particularly well, when Goldsmith launched a corporate raid in 1986. The raid netted Goldsmith close to $100 million. It left a formerly strong, community employer and producer of tyres in virtual ruins, with 4,000 people unemployed, R&D farmed out, many of its key operations 'hollowed out' and the sale of its aerospace division. In a capitalist society it is a moot point whether such activities constitute unhelpful activity. Some would argue that Goodyear needed the battle and became better for it, particularly some shareholders.

Nevertheless the company was prevented from carrying out forward plans by this activity, and this clearly constituted an Obstructive Marketing attack (Tolchin, 1992).

CASE STUDY 19: JARDINE MATHESON, 1980S

In another very particular type of financial operation great efforts were made to derail Jardine Matheson, the 'Noble House' of Hong Kong, whose 1980s headquarters move from Hong Kong to Bermuda was preceded by events which can be described as a vendetta sanction. In this case Chinese financiers created a deficit in Jardine's earnings and balance sheet as retribution for the move. Retributive action is often taken against companies when the law is unable to take any action, or where a company is effectively beyond the law. This sort of activity raises interesting, and unresolved, questions of policing companies in a global economy, indeed, of policing the global economy itself (Naylor, 1994).

Politics

Politics gets in the way of international companies much more often than they think it should. It also gets in the way of domestic companies trying to grow. Douglas Hanson (1998) said:

> It's aggravating – we have nothing to do with Russia or Asia. We're just a little domestic business trying to grow, but we're being prevented because of the way those governments run their countries.

But these countries have some serious alternative agendas in running their economies. For example, Bosworth Davies (1995) explained developments in the former USSR as follows:

> The nomenklatura's principal attributes – a paramilitary hierarchy, hostility towards outsiders and a propensity for illegal behaviour – established its similarity with the criminal societies of the old Russian underworld. The similarity was no coincidence. The organisational model which the Bolsheviks found so attractive in the Russian criminal bands seventy years earlier was internalised in the modern communist party structure.

When the wall came down, therefore, neither camp was as uniform or as consistent as the stereotypes of the previous 45 years had led us to believe. In this respect, of course, within a European setting the irony was that as one end of Europe reacted strongly against belonging to a supranational organisation, the other end of Europe was moving closer to a Federal European State. It was in this environment, in 1994, that central bank funds were identified and allocated, in a manner that reflects the recipient's bargaining and political power, not on economic or financial considerations.

Such settlement was clearly not to the advantage of a company wishing to deal in Russia on normal trade terms. Effectively this approach meant there was no western style capitalist prudence within the former Eastern Bloc. Taepke, Vice President Bank One, argued that there was increasingly little in the West too, with too much money floating around (at the time) (Taepke, 1998), but this is a different issue effectively concerned with start-ups and growth and property, not settlement. The result is that payment for goods and services has often been difficult to effect legally in Russia. As the whole idea is to make a legal profit out of selling goods and services this fits the Obstructive Marketing picture well.

These organisations did not understand the Obstructive Marketing context.

CASE STUDY 20: ROCKWELL INC., 1993

The beginning of the end of the Rockwell aerospace industry in Columbus, Ohio came in August 1993 when a Chinese business group arrived at Plant 85. The Chinese Government was offering a $1 billion aircraft order in return for the missile building capacity of Plant 85 to be moved in total to China. The order did not materialise but the plant still moved east. This had severe implications for the aircraft industry, the Chinese nuclear deterrent and the US missile industry, which only became apparent much later (Fialka, 1997).

The focus here was purely on a financial deal.

Competition

An Obstructive Marketing attack is not just about stopping an organisation doing something, it can also be about manipulating a company to do something it doesn't want to do, and sometimes doesn't know it is doing.

CASE STUDY 21: DE BEERS, 1980

In a different context the battles between British Airways and its competitors have already been noted (Tucker, 1997) and this is a trend of activity which can be found in a number of different industries and structures. Cartels, for example, are notorious for keeping their markets strongly to themselves, and there was no better known cartel than De Beers (by 2012 it had undergone reform). In 1980 Zaire dropped out of the De Beers cartel. While Zaire had a small market share, there was a fear that such a move would spread throughout the cartel. The cartel responded by dumping. Prices collapsed and Zaire rejoined the cartel (Naylor, 1994).

CASE STUDY 22: WHESSOE PLC, 1992

A detailed look at the structure of the instrumentation industry would reveal the dominance of a number of key players. If the moves made by these players over the 1990s are looked at in some detail a strategy emerges. Taking the narrow example of the oil instrumentation area it could be said that the sale by US Company D of the US Company E to UK Company F in 1992 allowed Company D to develop a completely new range of oilfield instrumentation. This then effectively displaced the Company E equipment in the field (Whessoe plc, 1992). A case of making sure the competition pay for product development – especially as Company D eventually bought it and the new products back. This is a key reason why accountants alone should never be involved in take-over decisions.

Co-operation

It is said that in every joint venture one partner has to be stronger than the other, and even where this is not the case initially it becomes the case eventually. Stories of co-operation going wrong are the nightmare of sales and marketing vice presidents trying to set up international joint ventures. They deserve to be cautious; a free market does not operate across the world and potential joint ventures fall foul, relatively easily, of different cultures and ideas. Two examples demonstrate the point.

CASE STUDY 23: STOL, 1985

The US tried to enlist the support of the Japanese in a joint venture to develop and sell a new type of Short Take-off and Landing Aircraft (STOL). Instead of co-operation it got stonewalling and a classic data mining operation, in the guise of assistance, against it. The aerospace business in the US goes on, but it goes on very slowly with Japan, at least as far as the TW-68 aircraft technology is concerned. LHTEC, the US consortium, hired a major 'sogoshosha' (a Japanese trading house), C Itoh and Co Ltd to try and sell Japan on the merits of the T-800 engine. But the effort was stymied in the mid-1980s by news that a Japanese consortium of Japanese aerospace companies were developing a very similar engine of their own, and the money earmarked for co-operation seems to have disappeared from Japan's future budget plans (Fialka, 1997). This sort of tactic is relatively common in the Far East.

CASE STUDY 24: SPERO INC., 1995

Another example helps to illustrate what can happen when 'David' meets 'Goliath'. This refers to an initially trivial dispute between the giant Mitsubishi Corporation and Spero Inc. of the US, over the rights to a microwave lamp. Both companies produced such lamps, both had a form of co-operation with the other. Spero thought they had made a better lamp and tried to market it in Japan, especially to Mitsubishi, where they made little headway against that country's non-tariff trade barriers and patent laws. Spero's CEO took the fight to Washington but the company's shareholders eventually buckled under the pressure of a strong settlement from Mitsubishi, who thereby retained control of all microwave lamp technology (Fialka, 1997).

These are Japanese examples but similar examples could be given from Russia, the Middle East, Africa, South America and Europe – and all demonstrate the need to understand context, risk and dependencies.

Obstructive Marketing and Obstructive Marketing Attack

These then are practical examples of Obstructive Marketing and Obstructive Marketing attack that can be found from a study of the media, particularly the Internet and the daily newspapers in the 1990s. They have been replicated many times since. They can be grouped as:

- cultural;

- competitive;

- criminal;

- casual.

These groupings will already be familiar in this book, with critical infrastructure being added later to form the 5Cs, and capital(ism) in this book to form the 6Cs. These can be perpetrated by a range of different active or passive groups:

- institutions;

- special interest groups;

- companies;

- individuals.

A matrix could be produced as in Table 3.3.

Taking already known examples we can place them in the context of the matrix. Thus for the cases in the Appendix, by case number, the matrix would look as in Table 3.4.

Table 3.3   Obstructive Marketing prototype matrix

	Institutions	Special Interest Groups	Companies	Individuals
Cultural				
Competitive				
Criminal				
Casual				

Table 3.4   Obstructive Marketing empirical case matrix 1

	Institutions	Special Interest Groups	Companies	Individuals
Cultural	9, 45, 46, 47, 50, 52, 53, 54, 68	14, 70, 78		
Competitive	2, 15, 49, 51, 73, 74, 75, 89, 101, 102, 103, 104, 105, 106, 118, 119, 122, 126	71, 72, 84, 86, 88, 90, 134	3, 4, 5, 6, 34, 36, 55, 65, 66, 79, 80, 91, 92, 117, 121, 123, 127, 128, 129, 133, 135	7, 11, 67, 69, 108, 109, 110, 111, 112, 113, 114, 115, 124, 125
Criminal	16, 32, 136	8, 10, 82, 120	1, 12, 13, 17, 33, 60, 61, 63, 83	30, 59, 62, 64
Casual	56	18, 19, 20, 21, 22, 23, 24, 25, 26, 27, 28, 29, 31, 35, 57, 58, 76, 77, 81, 85, 87, 93, 94, 95, 96, 97, 98, 100, 101	130, 131	37, 38, 39, 40, 41, 42, 43

Note: Cases refer to the list in the Appendix.

Table 3.5   Obstructive Marketing empirical case matrix 2

	Institutions	Special Interest Groups	Companies	Individuals	Total
Cultural	9 (7%)	3 (2%)	0 (0%)	0 (0%)	12 (9%)
Competitive	18 (14%)	7 (6%)	21 (16%)	15 (12%)	61 (48%)
Criminal	3 (2%)	4 (3%)	9 (7%)	4 (2%)	20 (14%)
Casual	1 (0%)	29 (21%)	2 (2%)	7 (6%)	39 (29%)
Number of case studies	31 (23%)	43 (32%)	32 (25%)	26 (20%)	132 (100%)

Types of Obstructive Marketing by Perpetrator for 132 Case Studies

The results in Tables 3.4 and 3.5 for the cases in the Appendix reflect what common sense might suggest:

- institutions: Governments, and quasi government organisations, are interested in maintaining cultural and competitive interests;

- special interest groups: These have a range of agenda. In this example there is probably strong skew towards the casual (anarchic); largely because they are well reported;

- companies: Companies, as might be expected, are interested in pursuing their own competitive agenda, legally or otherwise;

- individuals: Get involved on a casual or competitive basis.

The overriding interest is competitive, followed by the casual (the anarchic tendency), the criminal and the cultural. This makes sense too. Most companies develop locally or within similar 'rich' pockets on a global basis. Therefore when looking at a business group highly skewed towards American literature and sources it might be expected to find less of a problem with the cultural than with the casual (anarchic anti-capitalist), criminal and competitive elements. There are no recorded interests from companies or individuals on a cultural basis. Cases can also be characterised by when, how and where events occur.

Events occur during periods of weakness, strength/complacency/entry to new markets, innovation and change. This is summarised in Table 3.6. The table suggests companies are most vulnerable during periods of strength and complacency, or weakness, the time others want to 'knock them down to size'.

Although it is not entirely clear from the sample used most Obstructive Marketing events seem to be perpetrated by third parties at the periphery of a business's market. This is an area where more work needs to be done. From these cases Obstructive Marketing appears to be, in general, perpetrated by third parties or by internal/external agents hired by third parties.

It is important to note that it is not claimed that this is necessarily how Obstructive Marketing should be ordered, more work probably needs to be done on this. The important point, as Glaser (1993) states, is whether it can be ordered at all, and if it can, can it be replicated, and if this order was unforced and emerged. This is certainly the case.

Table 3.6   Obstructive Marketing events – timing

Event	Number (%)
Weakness	25 (19%)
Strength/complacency	45 (33%)
New markets	21 (15%)
Innovation	16 (12%)
Change	29 (21%)
Total	136 (100%)

In relation to the Linked-In survey there is a strong correlation between the casual and competitive events noted in both studies. It is clear that attacks happen and that these attacks can be ordered.

Taking the practical examples a stage further, if examples can be found from a general search of the media it should be the case that the study of a specific group of businesses would determine a similar sort of result. To do this the Executive Club of Chicago was enrolled as a study group. The next section looks at Obstructive Marketing and Obstructive Marketing attack through the information available from this particular sample of organisations.

Chapter 2 identified Obstructive Marketing as a potential process for attacking organisations. These case studies have ordered events and experiences into an Obstructive Marketing model consisting of casual, competitive, criminal, cultural and critical infrastructure actions against institutes, special interest groups, companies and individuals in regard to people, product, place, price, promotion, information, finance, competition and co-operation. This effectively gives the beginnings of an Obstructive Marketing model against which organisations must guard. The ordering of these events and experiences into an Obstructive Marketing model is one of the features of this book. The case studies detailed in this chapter demonstrate a general lack of understanding of context, risk, dependency, staff, crisis and general management and thus a vulnerability to Obstructive Marketing.

The purpose of this second section on case studies is to try and confirm the results of the above case studies in a discrete population, the membership of the Executive Club of Chicago. If it is the case that Obstructive Marketing practice exists then it should be capable of testing in a defined population. Such a population should suffer the same types of events as those found in the above section.

The Case Studies (2)

The Executive Club of Chicago is one of the top three most influential business organisations in the US. In 1999 most of the major business players of the US were among the 2,000 or so members.

The aim of this study was to confirm that a group of responsible business people could understand the ideas and case studies discussed here in terms of their own business life. It was not necessary for them to define Obstructive Marketing in the manner of this study, but they had to show some understanding of the challenges. It is remarkable that a number could do neither, but this was also found in the 2010 Linked-In survey and commented upon by the Management Institute. There were a number of problems with this survey. The club was not keen on its members being polled (the Club represented itself and the US at the World Economic Forum in Davos and there was no telling what might come out of such a survey). A number of large corporations were distinctly uneasy about the questions to be asked (Koskenalusta, 1998). Unfortunately, because of the sensitivity, a less rigorous study was undertaken than originally planned. However, much of value was learned.

The key to this study was whether or not the members understood the concept of Obstructive Marketing without naming it as such, and if they did could they relate to it sufficiently well to say if they had suffered from it or not. A positive response would help remove the Obstructive Marketing issue from an individual's mind and help place it in a more general, and well recognised, business context. Too much of a positive response would question a number of issues: the approach, the questionnaire, the system, the concept. A negative response would basically stifle the idea of Obstructive Marketing. A summary of the results is as follows in Table 3.7:

Table 3.7   Summary of Executive Club of Chicago study of Obstructive Marketing

	Total	Aware of Obstructive Marketing	Suffered from Obstructive Marketing	Not Aware of Obstructive Marketing	No Reply
Individuals	1,625 (100%)	975(60%)	504 (31%)	327 (20%)	323 (19%)
Companies (SMEs)	946 (100%)	514 (54%)	143 (15%)	276 (29%)	156 (16%)
Corporate	170 (100%)	112 (65%)	57 (33.5%)	56 (35%)	N/A – All Spoken To

A key point made by the executives at the time was not to underestimate the general reliability of the free market capitalist system. Therefore, if there had been a majority who had suffered from such a problem as Obstructive Marketing – or, in the culture of the US, Berlitz (1998), accepted such a concept, then this basic reliability would have been at risk. This was a very American-centric comment as it is important to note that by 2012 many of the BRICKS countries do not fully subscribe to a free market capitalist system. China is still not a free market, India is not a true free market and does not, for example, subscribe to the Basel Financial Accords, Russia is not a free market and there are doubts about Brazil and South Africa in terms of the political leadership. The point therefore being that the free market no longer exists in quite the way anticipated by this sample at the time.

Overall somewhere over 50 per cent of the individuals within this Chicago business community understood both the term 'marketing' and had an intuitive understanding of Obstructive Marketing. It can be assumed that approximately 30 per cent of these individuals had suffered from some sort of activity that can be described as Obstructive Marketing, because they are linked to those companies who say they have. More than 50 per cent of the, predominantly, small and medium-sized enterprise (SME) group of the Executive Club understood the idea, but less than 20 per cent have suffered from it. At the major corporation level these figures jump to approximately 66 per cent understanding the term and more than 33 per cent having suffered from it. (Note: Not all respondents answered all questions. Thus only those answers that can be correctly interpreted and have been verified by personal contact are included here.)

Reviewing the narrative so far it is reasonable to expect that those companies who have had greater international exposure would be those most likely to understand and have suffered from the term (and this is confirmed by the primary research interviews earlier in this chapter). The caveat that needs to be introduced to these results is the large number of non-respondents and the minimal questionnaire eventually accepted by the Club. However, given that Chicago lies at the heart of the North American manufacturing area, with 80 per cent of North American manufacturing capacity being within a day and half's drive of the city, these results in general confirm that. In summary the idea is well understood, it has been experienced by a number of companies, particularly by larger international and global companies, and although not a major issue has been of sufficient significance to require attention (Hoffman, 1998).

This being the case it should be possible to replicate the cases by reference to the Executive Club community. These cases are from the Executive Club membership, but drawn from public sources.

CASE STUDY 25: BAKER AND MCKENZIE, 1999

Baker and McKenzie was a major target of the Melissa virus in the spring of 1999. The largest law firm in the US was effectively closed for three days after the Melissa computer virus (named apparently for Bill Gates's wife but whose wife is actually called Melinda) attacked email directories. The virus worked by taking the first 50 names on an individual email directory and emailing the virus to them, and then to their 50 and so on, and so on. In a large law firm it is frightening to speculate who would have got the virus and not surprising that it caused so much difficulty. The virus was eventually tracked to an individual who was subsequently imprisoned (Wilson, 1999). All 'Big Six', at the time (now 'Big Four') accounting and consulting firms were similarly afflicted. (This virus surfaced at the same time as the North Atlantic Treaty Organization (NATO) bombings took place on Belgrade and other targets in Serbia.) Research for this study has already identified key hackers and anti-virus champions from Belgrade. There is a known correlation between military activity and virus and other information attacks on the military, corporate and individual assets of the perpetrating country (*The Sunday Times*, 1999*)*. Although it is not suggested that it was the individual caught for the Melissa offence that was responsible for it, it is the case that sometimes countries target other countries and companies through data. (Since the 1990s this has become much more prevalent.) In a work looking at Obstructive Marketing attacks it is likely that much of the future of this subject will be found in IT.

CASE STUDY 26: BP AND AMOCO, 1999

In another people-related event the received wisdom of the middle management of the Amoco Corporation was that their own senior management sold them to BP in 1999 in return for large personal fortunes. (This would seem to be broadly correct.) It was also thought that this was followed by the wholesale termination of Amoco executives in preference for BP employees. (This is not necessarily the case but an interesting perception.) In whatever way it was done the end result was the end of the line for Amoco's marketing plans. The takeover of Amoco by BP has been acknowledged as a personal coup for Sir John Browne, then Chairman of BP (Broz, 1999).

CASE STUDY 27: ANDERSEN CONSULTING, 1999

Andersen Consulting's attempt to divorce itself from Andersen is another case in point, where people got in the way of the business's success (Winne, 1999; *The Economist*, 1997).

Product

CASE STUDY 28: MCDONALD'S, 1996 ONWARDS

McDonald's is probably the archetypal example of product targeting. Initially, in 1996, McDonald's was accused of lying about the quality of ingredients and other aspects of food sold by the chain. McDonald's brought a libel suit in response in London. The case went on for years. The suit cost McDonald's millions of pounds and exposed every part of their commercial operation to scrutiny. The company survived but it was not the same organisation afterwards in many respects. The infamous McSpotlight website is now the centre point for attacks on a whole range of multi-national corporations (Envirolink, 1999).

Place

CASE STUDY 29: NIGERIAN BOTTLING CORPORATION

The Nigerian Bottling Corporation had links with the Abacha regime in Nigeria. This company was also the local Coca-Cola franchisee. As noted with Shell in the last section, Nigeria was not the right place to be in 1997. Local political activists tried and almost succeeded (if Abacha's death had not intervened) in closing the company. An anti-Coca-Cola website was also put up and persons around the world urged to boycott the product. In areas of high political risk place takes on an unusual importance – it is often difficult to establish a company or do business without being associated with a particular political regime (Coca-Cola, 1999).

CASE STUDY 30: EDS, 1978

A combined place/politics event was EDS's position in Iran at the time of the 1978 overthrow of the Shah. Seen as the epitome of the 'Great Satan', EDS employees found themselves in the wrong place, on the wrong side of the political divide. Ross Perot mounted a personal rescue attempt and the rest is corporate folklore (Follett, 1983).

Price

CASE STUDY 31: NESTLÉ, 1992

As a big cocoa buyer, for its chocolate confectionery, Nestlé is dependent on the supply of cocoa, and consequently on cocoa commodity prices. Cocoa sellers are interested in identifying when Nestlé is going to buy and how much it is going to buy. Nestlé is such a big buyer that it can have immediate and long-lasting effects on the market. In the early 1990s Nestlé employed an outsourcing firm to act for them in a particular function. This company understood when certain executives were travelling and for what purpose. This allowed the firm to interpolate Nestlé's cocoa buying behaviour. This helped the cocoa sellers get a good price. The function was eventually brought in house. This was broadly a repeat of the Nestlé case study in the first set of case studies and demonstrates the international dimension of some attacks (Nestlé, 1992).

Promotion

CASE STUDY 32: AMERITECH, 1999

Ameritech was the telephone provider for the Chicago City and Illinois State areas. It had other interests within the US and abroad. In 1999 it had become the target of a take-over bid from SBC Inc. in Texas. The Board of Ameritech agreed this bid as being in the best interests of the company. Not all the shareholders and customers agreed. This resulted in a television advertising campaign during 1999 in which SBC was depicted as a company that would raise bills, decrease services and hassle customers in any number of ways. This threw the take-over battle into some confusion. This is a case of promotion being used directly to counter a company's plans (Channel 7, 1999).

The law regarding advertising in the US is different to the UK. It is frequently the case that advertising for one product will name the competing product as in: 'Brand X is recognised by most doctors as being more effective than Brand Y in controlling pain S.' These direct attacks are a key base to Obstructive Marketing, at least in the US, and may account for the understanding behind some of the questionnaire responses. Some aspects of Obstructive Marketing are legal in the US whereas they are not in Europe.

Information

CASE STUDY 33: IBM, 1997

IBM suffered an almost devastating theft at the hands of Hitachi in the 1980s. The theft concerned 27 'Adirondack Workbooks', known internally as the 'crown jewels', that contained secret designs IBM planned would take them into the personal computer era. Hitachi agreed with US authorities that this was a deliberate, planned operation against IBM to gain new product information for their benefit and to IBM's cost. A classic case of Obstructive Marketing. The Futures Group further developed this theme in 1997 (Aker, 1997).

> According to a recent survey of US businesses conducted by the National Counterintelligence Centre and the US Department of State, 74 US corporations reported more than 400 incidents of suspected foreign targeting against their businesses in 1996, only slightly more than half of these businesses were involved in producing technologies included on the national critical technologies list. If the full marketing ramifications of intellectual property theft and unrestricted technology transfer are factored in, estimates rise to some $240 billion a year as the cost to US commerce with a growth in the problem of 260 % since 1985. (Perry, 1995)

CASE STUDY 34: KPMG, 1998

In 1998, KPMG's aborted merger with Ernst & Young meant that each was left holding much of the other's proprietary information (MacDonnell and Lublin, 1998). Traditionally, as a 'Bull Run' closes, there is an outbreak of merger mania. In 1999, the merger mania was there, but not at the end of the Bull Run. Instead the need to be of a certain size to compete on a global basis has driven competitors to merge in order to gain the advantages of becoming a global player. When this fails much competitive and valuable information is left in each other's hands. In this case both players changed part of their operating strategy in response to what they had learnt from the other. Airlines, drug companies, chemical companies, oil companies, industrials, accountants and consultants are all examples of where this has recently occurred.

Finance

CASE STUDY 35: SARA LEE INC., 1998

A product contamination issue hit Sara Lee Inc. at the turn of the year 1998/1999. This was almost a replica of the Hudson Food issue (see previous section) but the financial consequences were different. Sara Lee Inc. had been underperforming the market whilst at the same time trying to turn itself from a manufacturing into a pure marketing company. Analysts, however, punished the company for this bacterial outbreak in one part of the company. Share prices hit a 52-week low and poor forecasts were given on the basis of an isolated incident. This damaged the company's hopes of succeeding with its immediate plans that included divestment and more moves towards becoming a marketing company (Rewick, 1999).

Politics

CASE STUDY 36: CATERPILLAR INC., 1999

Over a number of years the most difficult barrier for Caterpillar to overcome has frequently been the unilateral imposition of sanctions by the US Government. A case in point is the notification that the Sudan was a 'major threat to the State'. As Donald V. Fites, then Chairman of Caterpillar, said in 1999, Sudan cannot pose a real military, political or economic threat to the US. All that happened was that Caterpillar lost a market where it had been active and building market share for 20 years to Komatsu of Japan. At the same time the Italian subsidiary of GE made some inroads to the market because they were not affected by the political embargo. The only persons to lose out were the American workers at Caterpillar (Fites, 1999). There are a number of similar cases to this and although such political policies tend to be found most frequently against non-Western countries they can be found in Europe too. Banana wars, beef trade disagreements, homologation requirements for cars, are all relevant. The implementation of such policies is looked upon askance by most other political systems in the world.

Competition

CASE STUDY 37: NETSCAPE INC., 1998

Netscape developed a web browser. Allegedly Microsoft copied it, incorporated it into their Windows software and sold it for nothing. This, together with the Sun Microsystems Java issue, led to the US Government's anti-trust case against Microsoft in 1998. This case partially concluded with a bi-partisan deal in July 1999. Netscape was sold in the interim to America OnLine, so a de facto defeat in any event for Netscape in some respects – it was unable to hold up on its own. It remained to be seen if it was also a defeat for Microsoft in any serious and future sense. Quarterly results following the end of the case were massively up, so it was unlikely (*Financial Times*, 1999; *The Wall Street Journal*, 1999).

This case is a prototype for many future battles concerning information. Information attacks have already been noted. This case adds the difficulties of keeping proprietary software developments over the long term. Other issues arose indirectly from the case. How is the Internet to be policed? How is privacy protected on the Internet? Where are deals actually done on the Internet? Which law is applicable? How do contracts become resolved? These issues are beyond the immediate scope of this document. They are key to any future developments of the subject of Obstructive Marketing particularly as more and more business is carried out over the Internet and similar media (*The Economist*, 1999).

Co-operation

CASE STUDY 38: MOTOROLA INC., 1999

Motorola had invested heavily in the 'Iridium' global telephone network from 1996 to 1999 in a joint venture with others. Bad staff work, unreliable equipment and satellites and an ineffective product launch (which included large telephones from a company that was proud of delivering ever smaller ones) meant that Motorola's investment was unsuccessful. An engineering feat, putting 66 satellites into orbit and giving everyone on earth the potential to talk to each other, compromised by marketing failures, incorrectly identified markets, with huge cost overruns compounded by unclear joint venture management. This case is important because it shows how a big company can suffer from some complacency, both internally and externally. It is the black hole argument, which like the RB 211 engine at Rolls Royce can become an all-consuming engineering passion to the detriment of the overall health of the company (*Financial Times*, 1999).

Comparisons between the Case Studies and the Linked-In Survey

This section set out to replicate a general view in a discrete population. This has been broadly achieved but the same issues pertain. It is clear that Obstructive Marketing and Obstructive Marketing attacks are a process that is understood by many Executive Club of Chicago businessmen and women and that it is a process many have suffered from. As anticipated this understanding is skewed towards the international business community.

Examples of Obstructive Marketing practice can be found in the public domain from within this community. The same sorts of activity as seen in the primary research have been replicated here. Similar matrices can be produced to help comparison. In general these matrices show a strong correlation. This is apparent from the comparative figures from Tables 3.8 and 3.9 (below). This helps to confirm that the order placed on the subject is accurate. This is, in turn, confidence building. Further, these case studies confirm the need for some sort of response to Obstructive Marketing in terms of understanding context, risk, dependency, crisis management and staff.

Table 3.8   Obstructive Marketing Executive Club of Chicago case matrix and (in italics) the corresponding results from the general case studies

	Institutions	Special Interest Groups	Companies	Individuals	Total	Case Studies
Cultural	158	157	159		18%	*9%*
Competitive	156, 163, 164	166	152, 153, 154, 161, 165, 166, 167		58%	*48%*
Criminal			160	155	12%	*14%*
Casual		162	168		12%	*29%*
Total	24%	18%	52%	6%	100%	
Case studies	*23%*	*32%*	*25%*	*20%*		*100%*

Table 3.9   **Obstructive Marketing timing of events – executive against the general case studies (in italics)**

Weakness	4 (22%)	*25 (19%)*
Strength/complacency	6 (33%)	*45 (33%)*
New markets	1 (5%)	*21 (15%)*
Innovation	3 (16%)	*16 (12%)*
Change	4 (22%)	*29 (21%)*
Total	18 (100%)	*136 (100%)*

Correlation is calculated using the formula:

$$r = \sum (a.b)/n - \bar{a}.\bar{b}/\sigma_a.\sigma_b.$$

where:

r is the Product Moment Correlation Coefficient

a = variable 1

b = variable 2

$\bar{a}$ = mean a

$\bar{b}$ = mean b

σ = standard deviation

A positive correlation tends towards 1.0, with a random relationship being 0 and a negative correlation at -1.

In this case the product moment correlation is 0.975. This is a very strong positive correlation. The interesting point is that these organisations are attacked more frequently when they are strong and complacent.

If the findings from the 2010 Linked-In questionnaire are then added into the matrix it looks as in Table 3.10.

Table 3.10   Obstructive Marketing Executive Club of Chicago study, case studies and 2010 Linked-In study

	Institutions	Special Interest Groups	Companies	Individuals	ECC Total	Case Studies	2010 Study
Casual		162	168		12%	29%	31.4%
Competitive	156, 163, 164	166	152, 153, 154, 161, 165, 166, 167		58%	48%	33.1%
Criminal			160	155	12%	14%	6.8%
Cultural	158	157	159		18%	9%	6.2%
Total	24%	18%	52%	6%	100%		
Case studies	*23%*	*32%*	*25%*	*20%*	*100%*	*100%*	

Correlation

These three studies plotted against one another give a high degree of correlation. Using the product moment correlation coefficient r the relationship between the case studies and the Executive Club of Chicago study gives us a coefficient of 0.43. This is a positive correlation, but not particularly strong. However, this rises significantly in regard to competitive, criminal and cultural issues, suggesting, in this case, that casual is something of an outlier (this may be related to the number of case studies). For the relationship between the case studies and the Linked-In survey of 2010 the product moment correlation r rises to 0.94. This is a very positive correlation. This suggests that the case studies, the Executive Club of Chicago study and the Linked-In survey are all strongly correlated. This gives confidence that each data set is telling the same story in each example.

In general:

- the data represents the top third of UK organisations (top third of USA organisations for the 1999 Case Studies and for the 1999 Executive Club of Chicago Study);

- these organisations operate internationally;

- the UK organisations are completely separated from the political/ military position of the UK and do not understand the global context well. The US organisations are better aligned in this respect;

- most of the organisations have a business continuity plan but few test them;

- the business continuity plans do not cover the 'softer' areas of continuity to do with brands, products, capitalisation etc.;

- risk is not properly monitored or understood in most of the sample organisations;

- succession planning is deficient in these organisations;

- staff members are not always looked upon as assets to be developed;

- organisations do not feel the need to be 'Hardened';

- protecting supply chains is important;

- organisations do suffer from Obstructive Marketing/organisational attacks and these can be ordered.

Obstructive Marketing is therefore identified as a challenge to organisations.

4

Context

In physics it is axiomatic that for every action there is an equal and opposite reaction. This generally holds true in the political, economic, social, technology, environmental and legal worlds as well. While time is more of a factor in the non-physical world, Newton's third law of motion holds true for most actions. Common sense therefore, let alone game and chaos theory, suggests that globalisation (an economic action), the export of democracy (a political action), effects-based operations (a military action) and extra-territorial reach (a legal action) would inevitably provoke some sort of reaction. They have.

The rise of Obstructive Marketing, Fundamentalism, and Asymmetric War fighting techniques are all identifiable reactions to many of the actions taking place in the globalisation, export of democracy and effects-based operations fields; and these reactions are seen in all political, military, economic, social, technology, environmental and legal sectors (PMESTEL). Nature abhors a vacuum and, as a sweeping generalisation, these contemporary constructs have largely developed as a result of the vacuum left by the end of the Cold War.

The review of context suggests that the dialectic requires further and refined action to moderate current reactions. It suggests that these areas can be summarised in the following terms:

- politically: The support of 'Christian values' – shorthand for the values of the North and West as defined by the Protestant and Catholic countries in that geography. More generally a better term is morals and ethics – because these terms cover a worldwide approach;

- militarily: 'Asymmetric Military Balance' (or the 'see-saw theory') (both new terms) – a shorthand for the process that sees a large power come to terms with a much smaller force and the balance of actions between both that arrive at some sort of equilibrium;

- economic: The sustainable economy – shorthand for an economic environment sustainable from a variety of perspectives over the long term in a capitalist system;

- social: Social cohesion – shorthand for a society that clearly operates together;

- technology: Physical and virtual balance – shorthand for a technical space in which physical and virtual technologies work together in a complementary manner as they largely do in the North and West;

- environmental: Balanced earth – shorthand for ensuring an approach to the use of resources that is sustainable over the long term;

- legal: Internet and international law guidelines – shorthand for a legal environment acceptable to all.

Organised crime takes advantage of gaps, disconnects and disruptions. Associated with attempts to stop organisations doing what they wish to do, globalisation in particular, is Obstructive Marketing. This is also associated with the 'Asymmetric Military Balance'. Underpinning all actions and reactions is information and information technology. Information and the means by which it is transmitted are fundamental to sustaining 'the Western way of life' in all PMESTEL fields of endeavour and also fundamental to the antitheses of these. This thinking introduces the 'Christian Military Information Complex', a new term.

Thus the overall context model is concerned with the themes of:

- political: Democracy and Fundamentalism;

- military: Effects-based operations and asymmetric reactions;

- economic: Globalisation and Obstructive Marketing;

- social: Dissonance and resilience;

- technical: Virtual and Non-virtual (technophobes);

- environmental: The green agenda and commodity greed.

- legal: International law and the stateless.

These are the suggested main theses and antitheses that apply to global context.

These can also represent different ends of spectra. In each it is proposed that there is an optimal point along the spectrum that businesses and organisations should seek that would put them in the best position to operate. A context position for an organisation suffering from Obstructive Marketing that needs to operate becomes apparent. These positions are therefore important to the organisation that suffers from Obstructive Marketing and are crucial themes in today's world. This approach is summarised by the 'Godfearing' model. As individual contexts can be interpreted as spectra, they suggest that rather than a hierarchical model to business continuity, the traditional approach, the real approach to business continuity should also be a spectrum.

Understanding context is often the key to understanding risk. Context places the organisation correctly in its environment. From this position the description of risk, the measurement of risk and the management of risk and continuity through the control of dependencies is more successful. This model has been successfully used to place organisations in context over the last couple of years. Context, with the introduction of ISO 22301 (and its companion ISO 22313), now leaps onto the agenda – centre stage – for all within the continuity community. This model should help us to visualise our understanding of context and its importance in reducing the perceived complexity of risk and continuity management. Visually the model looks like Figure 4.1 (page 84).

This model shows a cloud that is representative of the web, the 'cloud', and the way in which information is managed (that is, a little bit woolly). It is also representative of a world in which, economically and perceptively, the North and West of the world are in relative decline and the South and East of the world are in relative ascendancy. Organised crime has an influence on everything – institutional and corporate fraud, drugs, illegal weapons and human trades – they are all part of the context of the modern world.

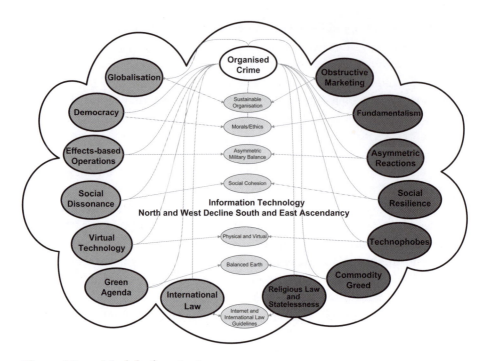

Figure 4.1   Model of context

Source: Maitland Hyslop, 2012, © Northumbria University.

In the diagram the mid-grey represents the thesis for the North and West of the world – globalisation, democracy, effects-based operations, social dissonance, virtual technology, the impact of the green agenda and the rule of international law. The dark grey shows the antitheses of these and the lightest grey a potentially useful end position.

Globalisation is no longer just a model for the North and West. The North and West and, now, the South and East will increasingly suffer from those who do not wish to be dominated by the big global firms. The antithesis of this, as should now be clear, is Obstructive Marketing where modifiers, much like a black hole in the universe, prevent the globalisers, but do not absolutely stop them, from doing just as they please. Certainly for companies in the North and West this has been a trend for a generation. The export of democracy has also been important to a broadly Western foreign policy for a generation or more. This has its benefits and challenges. In a global marketplace it is important to understand the impact of this process.

Effects-based operations is a term that has been discouraged in the Western militaries since August 2008 – but is still seen in reviews. This 'shock and awe' approach has been replaced by a more thoughtful military strategy. This has been termed by the author as the Asymmetric Military Balance. This is not such an oxymoron as it might seem, since it recognises that 'effects-based operations' alone will not succeed without some counterpart to the asymmetric reactions seen in Iraq, Afghanistan, Gaza and elsewhere. Effects-based operations, globalisation and the export of democracy have to be more subtle than they were. This requires the North and West to recognise its moral and ethical (as well as financial) purpose in an information-rich and perceptions-skewed environment and act accordingly. Organisations and businesses in response and context, therefore, must increasingly be prepared to demonstrate leadership in this asymmetric stand-off as they have now become its proponent's primary targets.

The social dissonance seen in much of the North and West is matched by social resilience in much of the rest of the world. How this resilience is achieved is not necessarily important but it is there. This is not the same as social cohesion. Social cohesion is important for all mankind and should be something to be sought by all in context.

In the virtual technology arena, how an organisation deals with the virtual world and technology generally is important for context. It may or may not be vulnerable to things such as 'hacking' and the general technophobic reactions of some communities.

The Green Agenda is becoming more important, whether it be in regard to climate change or resources. The race for resources continues and to understand the importance of this in the supply chain is key to context.

The rule of law is not universal so it is essential to understand the legal context. Many states remain lawless, or the law managed corruptly, or may be a reflection of religious beliefs rather than commercial in any way.

This means, simply put, that such an environment is subject to dynamic change on an increasingly daily basis and it is absolutely vital that we understand 'context' in setting our organisational priorities for risk, resilience, continuity, security, crisis management and so on. The launch of ISO 22301 in 2012 and its companion ISO 22313 in December 2012 place context at the heart of what it means to do business continuity effectively and represents a significant step change from guidance offered in BS 25999 parts 1 and 2. We are now compelled to step outside the confines, structures and frameworks of our organisations and understand the relationship any organisation has with its wider environment or its context. For example, in ISO 22313:2012 the guidance offered is unequivocal:

> *Organisations should evaluate and understand the internal and external factors that are relevant to its purpose and operations.*

This means that we need to understand our organisations in relation to the prevailing 'political, legal and regulatory environment whether international, national, regional or local'.

ISO 22313 also suggests we should consider and understand:

- 'the social, cultural, financial, technological, economic, natural and competitive environment whether international, national, regional or local;

- supply chain commitments and relationships;

- key drivers and trends having impact on the objectives and operation of the organisation;

- relationships with, and perceptions and values of, interested parties *outside* the organization.'

Familiarity with our supply chains has been a theme for some years now, likewise drivers and trends, but the inclusion of 'all interested parties outside the organisation' is significant and will ensure we think much more about and engage with whoever is within, or on the edges of, our spheres of organisational influence. For the continuity community this is long overdue and a most welcome development. It is also a huge opportunity!

Simply having a plan, so the argument goes, is no longer good enough (nor has this ever been the case). To do justice to our ISO obligations and demonstrate effectiveness with credible evidence means we have to be able to demonstrate a business continuity 'capability' – one in which context is key and where capability will manifest itself much more in wider management issues, management systems and the cross-over points between them. So much more then than simply having a plan. Plans are obviously implied but planning, to paraphrase Eisenhower, becomes 'everything'. It defines what makes compliance with ISO 22301 so much more interesting, challenging and strategic in nature than was ever intended with BS 25999-2.

ISO 22301 specifies that 'in establishing the context, the organisation shall:

- articulate its objectives, including those concerned with business continuity;

- define the external and internal factors that create the uncertainty that gives rise to risk;

- set risk criteria taking into account the risk appetite;

- define the purpose of the BCMS.

Many organisations are alive to this but for those new to continuity for which alignment or compliance with ISO 22301 is an aspiration, it represents a much bolder game and locks the risk and continuity communities in the same warm embrace. That alone should make us all sit up and take note.

Although the visual representation of the context model above is helpful in picturing the environment it does not give direct assistance to any organisation seeking to position itself in context. To do this we need to add a score-card that will help organisations position themselves in context. A simple score-card is required because the people who actually do this work in organisations need simple and quick models to represent context. This is not because complex models are not appropriate, it is because these tasks need to be put over in a simple manner and improved on a regular basis.

Consider for a moment a hypothetical example, of how this might work in practice. Company A has a mine in Africa. It is a joint venture with a global Western company, Company B. The Company A view is that although the joint venture has had a difficult iteration, the venture is worthwhile because of the potential profits involved. There are few of these mines in the world so obtaining access to one gives players a dominant market position. No contextual assessment has been made. Putting this through the context model leads to some potential issues. A high score give rise to a high context position. An example context score-card is in the first six columns of Table 4.1, a worked example regarding the mine example is in the last two columns.

Table 4.1   Scorecard example

Alignment Position A	Score	'Balanced' Position	Score	Alignment Position B	Score	Example	Score
Globalisation	5	Sustainable Organisation	1	Obstructive Marketing	10	The company is in a joint venture with an Australian company, Company B. Company B can be more or less co-operative depending on the state of the market. The international market can be volatile. A Chinese company is trying to acquire the mine. Transport to the docks is difficult and shipping from the docks more so; and controlled by the same Chinese company.	10
Democracy	5	Morals/Ethics	1	Fundamentalism	10	Although the mine is located in a country that has had the same Government for 25 years it is an effective dictatorship, is fighting a ten year rebel war, and has difficulty with terrorist organisations and Fundamentalists in the north of the country.	10
Effects-based Operations	5	Asymmetric Military Balance	1	Asymmetric Reactions	10	Local military activity is Asymmetric in nature and targets/kidnaps businesses/ businessmen from time to time.	10
Social Dissonance	5	Social Cohesion	1	Social Resilience	10	Local society is tribal and crosses international boundaries. There is no social resilience, and little tolerance of other cultures.	10
Virtual Technology	5	Physical and Virtual	1	Technophobes	10	The local airport regularly has its ILS stolen. There is no mobile telephony. Satellite 'phones can work.	10
Green Agenda	5	Balanced Earth	1	Commodity Greed	10	The mine is extractive. It is a potential prize for the Chinese company; who are seeking to take it over. It is not a renewable resource.	10
International Law in Some Circumstances	5	Internet and International Law Guidelines in Place	1	Religious Law and Statelessness	10	The area is lawless.	10
Some Exposure to International Crime	5	Little Exposure to International Crime	1	Heavy Exposure to International crime	10	There is heavy exposure to organised crime.	10
Public Cloud Based	5	Information Assured	1	Globally Technology Dependent	10	There is no information assurance at all.	10
				Total Contextual Score			100

Clearly, the mine operates in a very difficult context. It has a contextual score of 100/100. Profits have to be very big to think about describing, measuring and managing risk in this context. Using this context model has made an international company look again at a product approach.

So the business of risk, resilience, continuity, security, crisis management and so on often means coping with complexity. In response we strive for – even crave – simplicity in the representative frameworks or templates we use, in order to make sense of the world around us. The inclusion of 'context' and placing it centre stage challenges an easy notion of simplicity but it is a vital and necessary prerequisite for effective Governance, Risk Management and Compliance (GRC) management and management systems development – not just for business-as-usual operations but increasingly for continuity of operations following disruption. It also moves our message even further from the confines of the IT department by putting it firmly on the strategic agenda. There is no escape from this essential truth and so continuity must embrace 'context' in the same way that it must embrace risk. Any model (and there are many) which attempts to simplify the world around us will have inherent flaws (not to mention limitations) – a model cannot replace reality and perfection is not claimed for this one. But this model does help to move closer to an understanding of context.

Context is an area that has been very sketchily covered in other works. Yet it is key to our understanding of Obstructive Marketing. It is worth reprising some of the background to the approach to context described above. The idea for this 'Godfearing' model first arose during a keynote speech made by the author and James Royds (2008), the immediate past Chairman of the Business Continuity Institute. They discussed the military parallel of the author's political and economic themes: and the result was a view of globalisation, Obstructive Marketing, democracy, Fundamentalism, effects-based operations and Asymmetric Warfare or 'Godfear' for short. Other themes have since been added by the author and will be described here, which, with the addition of international law, creates 'Godfearing'.

Neither the author or James Royds would be classed as a 'practising Christian' but both share a deeply held belief in the guiding principles of Western life enshrined in such democratic instruments as the US Constitution, the Bill of Rights, The Chicago Scottish Rite Cathedral and the Roman Catholic and Anglican Communions: these are summarised as 'Christian values'. Both also uphold the basic principles of life in the US and UK Armed Services (in which both have served) and are strong advocates of UK military ethics and education as laid down in *Serve to Lead*, the book that was given to each cadet on joining the Royal Military Academy Sandhurst in the UK. Although neither of them are necessarily the best examples of such creeds, they nevertheless understand them! So the term 'Godfearing' is a happy accident, rather than a pre-planned defining acronym or mnemonic, and will hopefully focus the mind on some of the most important issues. It may also make some readers feel a little uncomfortable. This is an important and hoped-for reaction.

Of course these comments on actions and reactions are both a snapshot and an evolving picture. The time periods involved are roughly five to ten years. For example, five to ten years after the recent rise of globalisation following the end of the first Cold War, significant Obstructive Marketing events have become common place. As a result it is now necessary for global organisations in particular to protect themselves against such events. The export of democracy also followed, and Fundamentalism is one reaction, again a five to ten-year timeframe. Organisations are placed in a different context because of this change. As a result it is important to redefine the 'Christian' values of the North and West of the world.

This means organisations have to be very clear about the values they espouse, internationally, nationally and locally. Effects-based operations followed and met with Asymmetric reactions, again against a five to ten-year timeframe. As a result it is important to redefine war fighting in terms, it is suggested, of an Asymmetric Military Balance. Organisations become targets of Asymmetric Warfare under the new rules of warfare. In law there is the reaction of religious law. There may need to be, perhaps, some agreed rules of engagement on neutral territory, for example the Internet. In both these areas organisations face new challenges against which they must protect themselves further.

So in terms of political, economic, military and legal influences the timescales and reactions are significant. Where will this lead? It is conceivable that a crisis of such proportions arises that another world war breaks out, rather than the dialectic continuing to dialogue, but in the meantime we can expect the fragile status quo to oscillate thereby refining the relationship between action and reaction until a new equilibrium is reached. Note, again, that these events, actions and reactions are primarily a result of the demise of the old equilibrium, the first Cold War. In terms of how organisations must adapt then it is clear they have a range of new reactive threats to face. In the meantime business models have not changed with the same dynamism. This suggests that organisations need to further adapt and protect themselves.

Critical infrastructures are also important. Organisations that use them become targets politically (for example, so-called global companies of any origin are always associated with their country of origin – the best recent example being BP and Gulf Spill in 2010 despite it being half American owned these days), economically (because the infrastructure is used to disrupt), militarily (because in Asymmetric Warfare in particular the infrastructure is both a military conduit and means of military delivery) and legally (because of the lack of agreed rules and law). So there is a 'double-edged' sword of threats to organisations and infrastructures because of the dependencies of each on the other.

Generally any dialectic should lead to the protection of organisation against Obstructive Marketing, a redefining of 'Christian' values, or morals and ethics elsewhere, an 'Asymmetric Military Balance', and international guidelines for neutral territory. These should be reflected in a defined approach to protecting an organisation. This will be looked at in Chapter 9.

The export of democracy, Fundamentalism and Christian values may not, at first sight, have much to do with business continuity. However, with both globalisation and effects-based operations, it is part of a trio of actions that have an impact on how, for example, US businesses perform internationally.

Since the end of the Cold War the export of democracy has been a central pillar of US foreign policy. It has origins in the Christian Right of the US, and the Neo-conservatism movement. It has met with opposition around the world from Fundamentalism in many forms. Because of this reaction it is important that the underlying tenets of the export of this type of democracy, in other words Christian values, are refined since organisational values – and upholding them – have never been so important. It is possible for individuals to be atheistic or agnostic in this respect but in the context of business values it is important to understand that basic Christian values prevail.

Although society does not regularly look at the reasons for its own existence it is important to understand why resilience is important in such a context. Cynically or otherwise societies are based on certain principles. In hedonistic times these get blurred or confused. However, at the root of society is a certain set of beliefs. It is worth reprising these because they help to define society as a whole and explain why resilience, a resilient 'mindset' and the 'Hardened organisations' are all vital ingredients in the protection of the capitalist system and the many freedoms taken for granted.

An example of the values which underpin our way of life is the American Declaration of Independence as follows:

> When in the Course of human events it becomes necessary for one people to dissolve the political bands which have connected them with another and to assume among the powers of the earth, the separate and equal station to which the Laws of Nature and of Nature's God entitle them, a decent respect to the opinions of mankind requires that they should declare the causes which impel them to the separation.

> We hold these truths to be self-evident, that all men are created equal, that they are endowed by their Creator with certain unalienable Rights, that among these are Life, Liberty and the pursuit of Happiness. – That to secure these rights, Governments are instituted among Men, deriving their just powers from the consent of the governed, – That whenever any Form of Government becomes destructive of these ends, it is the Right of the People to alter or to abolish it, and to institute new Government, laying its foundation on such principles and organizing its powers in such form, as to them shall seem most likely to effect their Safety and Happiness.

While this effectively promotes a secular state, this statement of values demonstrates (at least in theory) that the Government of the US (and other governments) has certain responsibilities to its citizens. Over time this has taken, in part, the form of the construction of various infrastructures to secure life, liberty and happiness. The preservation of infrastructures designed to ensure this happens is clearly important. Resilience in such infrastructures is also important. The US Constitution states the position even more clearly:

> We the People of the United States, in Order to form a more perfect Union, establish Justice, insure domestic tranquillity, provide for the common defence, promote the general Welfare, and secure the Blessings of Liberty to ourselves and our Posterity, do ordain and establish this Constitution for the United States of America … freedom of speech, press, religion, peaceable assembly and to petition the government … right to bear arms … protection from quartering of troops … protection

*from unreasonable search and seizure ... due process ... double
jeopardy ... trial by jury ... civil trial by jury ... prohibition of excess
punishment ... protection of rights ... powers of states and people...
(American Constitution, 2007)*

This Constitution gives a clear secular statement of what the US values most and
what their society is built upon. The infrastructures which enable and sustain
both the Declaration of Independence and the Constitution are those which
need to be protected and defended. And it is worth remembering that most of
the critical information infrastructure in regard to space and the Internet is in
the hands of the US and allies.

The Church leads on the defence of personal conscience in the US so the
Ten Commandments are relevant. More importantly in the US has been the rise
of Neo-conservatism aligned with the Christian Right. This has been the basis
for export of democracy under Reagan and both Bush administrations. In Latin
America and Europe the Christian Democratic movement is also important
and its effect and influence can be summarised in similar terms.

It is recognised that this is a fairly simplistic approach but it is a model,
particularly as almost all the Organisation for Economic Co-operation and
Development (OECD) countries subscribe to these 'ideals' in one way shape
or form. It is important to be simplistic in these days because the North and
West faces a simple enemy in the form of Fundamentalism, from both within
and without. Single-issue politics have also become more important. These are
often aligned with Fundamentalist positions. These 'squawks' are important
and are looked at again in Chapter 5 in the discussion about risk. Practically and
philosophically a way of life must be defended. Organisations, as members of
society, need to protect stakeholders, shareholders, supporters, services, markets
and the needy – and Infrastructure. To do so the values upon which society is
built must be both clear and understood. Once understood they must be refined
to give arguments in the armoury to counter the Fundamentalist argument.

Another way of defining the Northern, Western and, increasingly, other
societies' way of life is through capitalism:

*Although nowadays there are ideological capitalists – people who
support a set of ideas about the economic benefits and importance of
'free markets' – the term capitalism was first used to describe the system
of private investment and industry with little governmental control*

> *which emerged, without an ideological basis, in the Netherlands and Britain in the 17th and 18th centuries. A 'capitalist' was an individual who invested money (or capital) in a given business venture. The 'Classical economists' (Adam Smith, David Riccardo, etc.), aided by Karl Marx were responsible for positing this de facto set of business arrangements as an ideology. In the United States, thinkers as diverse as Hayek, Friedman and Ayn Rand, have promoted 'Capitalism' as every bit as much an ideology as Marxism. In practice, many modern western economies developed under heavy government support and subsidy. (Brooklyn College, 2007)*

The link between government, Christianity (or Christian values) and the success of Capitalism is as old as Capitalism itself.

Today the basis of our way of life and our way of doing business must be continually clarified and communicated to ensure it has a resonance with those who appreciate it's tolerance but are faced with being outcast for embracing it within a Fundamentalist context. If this seems a little extreme, and for many in this secular and liberal world it may seem to be, as it does to the author from time to time, the really important point to make is that some oppositions see it like this.

The importance of this for the organisations and Infrastructures is demonstrated by the dilemmas posed not only by engaging with the Middle and Far East, but the Shell and BP experiences in Russia, and the challenges faced by a number of companies in dealing with certain African regimes. It is ironic, perhaps, that so-called global companies, in the end, fall victim, in these instances, to their original cultural and philosophical base, and associated infrastructures. They cannot escape the political context of their origins or beliefs.

The term 'Asymmetric Military Balance' sounds like an oxymoron. It is not. It is a way of describing the state of affairs that needs to prevail in order that the export of democracy and globalisation can flourish within a relevant military doctrine.

There is an avowed assumption gaining momentum in military and non-military circles, that threats of an asymmetric nature, and by association asymmetric campaigning, is something new. This is misleading and true of neither. Both asymmetric threats and asymmetric campaigning have always been part of conflict and struggle. The nature and practice of asymmetry is 'as old as warfare itself' (Metz and Jonsson, 2001).

If we accept Sun Tzu's (Chung, 1995) premise that:

> *All warfare is based on deception, and that when confronted with an*
> *enemy one should offer the enemy a bait to lure him…*

Then for its success it is reasonable to conclude that a measure or degree of asymmetry may be necessary to avoid a prolonged stalemate, much as 'mutually assured destruction' offered symmetrical if happily unproven assurance! For successful asymmetric campaigning, and the threat of its consequences by opponents asymmetric or otherwise, exploits the differences between opponents rather than the similarities.

This is the key to understanding the nature of so many of today's threats. What appears best, most effective and most efficient is often not the case for in strategy, contends Luttwak (1987), actual or possible conflict between thinking human beings – whether it is played out in political, economic, social, technological or military contexts – is dominated by 'a paradoxical logic based on the coming together and even the reversal of opposites'. This is the essence of asymmetry.

In situations of unmatched capabilities, tactics, strategic aims and objectives between, for example, inter-state and increasingly non-state players, then tensions and frictions arise. For convenience, in what is increasingly an engagement between the haves and the have-nots (many current and disenfranchised opponents), the emerging and enduring lesson is that an asymmetric approach levels the score card.

An example is Mogadishu in October 2003 – an urban environment proved the temporary undoing of a superior army-of-the-field in a contest where the perceived advantages of US forces were rudely undermined. This was a tactical success which met its tactical objectives. The strategic implications, a withdrawal of US forces from Somalia, only became clear once the dust of a little local difficulty settled. What is certain is often not and what is uncertain often prevails. This is the lesson of asymmetry.

In these sorts of terms an 'Asymmetric Military Balance' is not an oxymoron. Rather than just use effects-based operations to attempt to induce the desired effects in an enemy's society or infrastructure it is important to understand that from the enemy's point of view an asymmetric approach may well neutralise any effects-based strategy. As a consequence there needs to be a re-balancing of effort on behalf of the West between effects-based operations and the asymmetric approach required to defeat an enemy of a completely different political, economic, social, technical and military persuasion.

Modern Western military strategy is still based on rules of engagement, treaties, values and equipment that were relevant to the first half of the twentieth century. The major battle ground of the first half of the twenty-first century is largely a virtual battleground. It is between the states and stateless, rather than between states. It is between democracy and Fundamentalism, not between democracy and dictatorship. The military doctrine required is akin to a see-saw – not too much force to launch the other side off the see-saw – but enough of a combination of both effects-based operations and appropriate asymmetric techniques to tip the balance in favour of the North and West while being ready to re-establish equilibrium in any event.

While a new world order has generated more-than-enough print to capture, if not wholly explain, the paradigm shift (about which there is still much debate), the concept of asymmetric campaigning and its enduring legacy has not. What has changed, however, is a widening of the range or spectrum of threats faced today and this has significant implications for how risk, information infrastructure, continuity professionals and organisations generally might respond.

Asymmetric threats (increasingly referred to as virtual, genetic, biological, informational, chemical and so on) should not be considered especially different from those threats which are considered germane to convention or tradition. All threats, whatever they are and however disproportionate they may seem, are contingent on a range and combination of political, military, economic, social and technical axes at strategic, operational and tactical levels, and exist, feed and flourish on the exploitation of vulnerability and weakness – real, virtual, perceived or otherwise.

Organisations, risk doctrine, information infrastructure and value systems need to be structured to cope with the widening spectrum of threats of those who seek to undermine organisational commercial capabilities, democratic freedoms and cultural values.

To look but briefly at this we should consider the nature of, and relationship between, threats. There are an increasing number of inter-related factors all of which are 'contingent on the situation': tasks, doctrine, training, values, culture, ethos, structures and leadership-style – our own and those of our opponents. The nature and relationship between these needs to be considered, as does the perception of what really constitutes risk and uncertainty in this climate and how this might be managed in the future.

> *Our advantage must come from leaders, people, doctrine, organisation and training that enable us to take advantage of ideas, techniques and technology to achieve superior effectiveness in our decision-making, in our strategic options, and, when things go wrong, in the speed and quality of our response measures. (Blank, 2003)*

History demonstrates the need to be tuned to uncertainty and the asymmetrical approach however uncomfortable the outcome. The shifts inherent in thinking humans in terms of our values, expectations, beliefs, aspirations and needs drive the process. Technology alone cannot mitigate uncertainty. Nor can history. So what we need is to continue to re-evaluate our mental frameworks to allow us the space to develop ideas in an attempt to eschew the paralysis of risk-aversion in order to improve our risk-awareness.

The importance of this from this book's perspective is that, much like the impact of 'Christian' values, global organisations become targets in a politically motivated asymmetric campaign. The evidence of this is in the attacks on banks, large corporations and institutions at the beginning of both Gulf Wars and at the time of the attack on the World Trade Centre and Pentagon.

International law regarding both critical infrastructures and information infrastructures is sparse. Indeed Dunn and Wigert (2004) go so far as to comment:

> *Due to the inherently transnational character of Critical Infrastructure and Critical Information Infrastructure there is a need to harmonize national legal provisions and to enhance judicial and police co-operation. However, so far, the international legal framework has remained rather confused and is actually an obstacle to joint action by the actors involved.*

In the EU the European Commission has started to make an effort to deal with the problem. The author has been both a Director for the Commission's eJustice project and a member of the eDemocracy-focussed Politech Institute in Brussels. Both bodies have made substantive recommendations on various approaches to solving the problem.

eJustice succeeded in its aims of:

- going beyond the state of the art in several trust and security technologies;

- convincing key representatives of civil society that these technologies, and in particular biometry, do not represent a threat to the privacy of citizens when used within well-defined guidelines;

- convincing major public authorities to adopt the results for their own use.

But the project could not, on its own, make these things happen.

The Politech Institute, amongst other things, seeks to consult the different stakeholders in the development of electronic strategies and policies in the converging domains of political technologies. This includes law. But it cannot make things happen.

There is a huge vacuum in international law in regard to critical infrastructure and critical information infrastructure protection. Elsewhere thought leaders in the subject of resilience in critical infrastructure and critical information infrastructures have been identified. In the international context it is important to have structures that have reach, respect and resources. This gives a number of problems in regard to the US and Europe in particular. This is because both are regarded has having vested interests, particularly in regard to critical information infrastructures. It also gives a problem in regard to the so-called neutral countries of Sweden and Switzerland. These countries may well be neutral in a political sense, and they may be neutral in a critical infrastructure sense, but they are not neutral in a critical information infrastructure sense.

The OECD plays a prominent role in fostering good governance in the public service and in corporate activity. It helps governments to ensure the responsiveness of key economic areas with sectoral monitoring. By deciphering emerging issues and identifying policies that work, it helps policy-makers adopt strategic orientations. It is well known for its individual country surveys and reviews. The OECD produces internationally agreed instruments, decisions and recommendations to promote rules of the game in areas where multilateral agreement is necessary for individual countries to make progress in a globalised economy. Sharing the benefits of growth is also crucial as shown in activities such as emerging economies, sustainable development, territorial economy and aid. Dialogue, consensus, peer review and pressure are at the very heart of OECD. Its governing body, the Council, is made up of representatives of member countries. It provides guidance on the work of OECD committees and decides on the annual budget.

It is recommended that the OECD takes on the international strategic responsibility for resilience in critical infrastructures and critical information infrastructures. It's approach to resilience should include direct liaison with the international thought leaders – particularly those in the UK (National Information Security Co-ordination Centre), Australia (Attorney General's Department), New Zealand (Centre for Critical Infrastructure Protection) and the US (Department for Homeland Security).

Sitting in the background of the context model is organised crime, possibly the biggest threat to organisations and business continuity. Organised crime has some parallels with Asymmetric Warfare, and indeed is often used as a proxy in fighting an Asymmetric War. In the year 2000, according to IBM research, both the numbers and value of virtual crimes exceeded those of physical crimes. According to the Bank of Canada 'phishing attacks' have increased 12-fold in a 24-month period – and are set to continue. After a lull since 2004, 2007 saw an increase in malware attacks and distribution, according to Symantec and others, and this has continued.

Galeotti (2001) notes that in 2000 organised crime was estimated to have a global turnover in excess of $1 trillion. It cost, then, the OECD over $120 million per annum. It is continually evolving and globalising and has an increasing political impact, particularly in new, emerging and transition states – thereby blurring the boundaries between crime, business and the state. In its purest form it has an impact on national resources, political stability and legitimacy. It is an agent of instability and insecurity and often creates 'free criminal zones' (geographical, social, ethnic and technological).

Kroll (2000) would say that the organised criminal is probably ahead of most governments and international businesses. He knows no boundaries, has no jurisdictional issues or budget problems to contend with. He can operate in one country, bank in another, live in another, spend his money in another and travel at will between all of them. There will be no bar to him jumping on an aeroplane at a moment's notice and escaping from one country to another, assuming a false identity with any number of 'legitimate' passports. The businesses he runs and the bank accounts that he uses are probably all fronted by notional trusts with almost impossible to identify beneficial ownership.

This is a bleak picture. It is because such criminals will be major suppliers in the narcotics industry, international banking fraudsters, those engaged in illegal immigration and trading in human beings, illegal arms dealers and various individuals breaking United Nations sanctions and embargoes. Their ability to succeed is based on a number of basic conditions: they see a gap in the market, they have an undisputed ability to organise, they lack those morals which would restrain them from criminal activity and they would make excellent businessmen in a legitimate environment.

They are helped in the success of their businesses by the inability of governments and international businesses to organise in the same way that they do. Governments and international treaties require far too much red tape to be quick and effective; and big businesses do not have the will to take up the fight unless there are indicators that they might recover losses in excess of the perceived investigation cost requirement.

Some countries will give only lip service to the international treaties that they are signed up to. They make little or no resource available to follow up on anything but the most severe threat to their own countries laws and threats to their own citizen's well-being. Altruism does not exist in this environment. The rules of like offences and mutual legal assistance often gets bogged down in internal wrangling, lack of resources and sheer bloody-mindedness on some occasions.

Big businesses – when they get caught up in large-scale frauds or criminal activity where they are either the victims or the unwitting vehicles through which criminal activity is effected – have a recognisable selfish attitude. As will be seen, their problem is bigger than they publically acknowledge.

The public interest as far as big businesses are concerned is, 'How much will it affect our turnover or our P&L?' Never, 'What can we contribute in this situation to the public good?' Donations to various charities and support to various international bodies against global crime are the visible signs that they care or more probably that their image demands. Very few major companies realistically contribute willingly in the interests of the societies from which they earn their large profits.

All this activity is now aided, abetted and largely conducted over the Internet. Unless there is a mind-set change of attitudes and understanding of the damage being done to the very fabric of society, and unless governments and big businesses decide to undertake radical changes in their thinking and approach, the battle will be lost.

The importance of organised crime to organisations, information infrastructure and critical infrastructures is immense. From ensuring compliance with a range of governance requirements designed to outlaw money-laundering through ensuring IT systems are not hi-jacked for illicit purposes to ensuring executives are protected abroad – there is clearly a profound impact on how organisational professionals go about their work.

IT threats (that is, threats which do not include physical attack) to organisations and critical infrastructure may be categorised both by the motivation and resourcing of the attacker or other threat agent, and by the means of attack.

Threat agents could be:

- staff making mistakes;

- disaffected staff or contractors;

- recreational hackers;

- individuals seeking personal gain, for example through theft or extortion;

- agents of organised crime, competing commercial interests or issue groups; or

- agents of foreign governments.

The types of IT-borne attack include:

- denial of service attacks via the Internet;

- hacking or cracking, whether leading to systems damage or breach of confidentiality;

- malware – programs with covert malicious intent, including viruses, worms and so on;

- malicious or inadvertent damage by insiders;

- the unlawful interception of messages (or actual theft of laptop or other computers).

The Internet has become ubiquitous in developed nations, so most IT-borne attacks have been carried out over the Internet. Internet-based attacks have certain characteristics which explain their prevalence and impact. Internet attacks involve action at a distance – regardless of time zones – and in many cases crossing national borders. This set of conditions offers the attacker a degree of anonymity and reduces the likelihood of punishment and the deterrent effect of legislation. Like other IT-borne threats, Internet attacks often involve the use of computers for automatic repetition of some process, such as the use of dictionary-searching tools to crack passwords or viruses that replicate themselves without limit. This factor can leverage one individual's cleverness into an attack on infrastructure that has global impact. The size of the impact in this scenario bears no relation to the quantum of resources available to the attacker. Once written, automated attack tools become widely available on the Internet and may be used by individuals who do not understand the tools or the consequences. The Internet provides opportunities for attacks on systems connected to it.

Any area of infrastructure that uses IT-based control systems is vulnerable in principle. The greatest area of risk, in terms of the adverse consequence that could result, is any potential for unrestricted access to IT systems used to manage infrastructure networks. Where access is restricted to secure locations, the vulnerabilities are those of physical security and the risk that staff will do something malicious or mistaken.

Access through telecommunications (that is, dial-up/Internet) to unstaffed network management facilities (for example, electricity substations) is used by some infrastructure providers for efficient and prompt fault resolution. This introduces a new range of vulnerabilities since there is a need for authentication of callers to the facility. The authentication system needs to be of strength commensurate with the risks posed by unrestricted access. The authentication system itself needs timely maintenance to ensure that, for example, resigning employees have their access revoked.

Interconnecting systems with the Internet provides benefits in terms of cost savings and functions that can be offered. Large infrastructure providers typically have their corporate business networks connected to the Internet and have some kind of links between these and their network management systems. While awareness of Internet threats is high in many providers, it is hard to guarantee that unrestricted access to network management facilities is impossible.

Over the last decade the diversity of IT in wide use has decreased. This has happened because of: a desire for common open standards on the part of IT purchasers, partly as a measure to prevent vendor lock-in and monopoly pricing; the overwhelming success of the Internet, due in part to the quality and openness of the engineering on which it is built, effectively displacing other ways of connecting computer systems; and the withdrawal of smaller computer manufacturers with unique equipment from the market (mainly for the reasons above) and the trend for specialised equipment to increasingly be based on off-the-shelf computers and operating systems.

These trends have led to a situation in which almost all computer networks use Internet protocols, almost all Internet routers are made by Cisco, most server computers use a version of Microsoft Windows or a flavour of Unix, desktop computers almost all use a version of Microsoft Windows, and where specialist machines such as those in the power grid are increasingly controlled through widely available and technically-understood machines of the types above. This is not meant to imply that these products are inherently less secure than alternatives. However, while homogeneity of systems leads to benefits in terms of efficiency and ease of use, it also makes all computers more vulnerable to attack. This is because having a large number of users increases the chance that lurking security problems are discovered and exploited, and because of the number of machines that can be compromised when problems do come to light.

The process of convergence to common IT standards may not be complete. Telephony, which is already dependent on digital technology, may move to use Internet protocols and Internet-style routers instead of the specialist switches and PABXs currently used. In New Zealand, the Ministry of Social Policy has recently installed just such a system across all Department of Work and Income branches. This does not imply such a move is inherently risky, indeed it should pay dividends in terms of efficiencies and greater effectiveness. However, it is part of the general convergence away from many kinds of technology to a few types whose details are very widely known.

Technological development involves increasing complexity. Although the diversity of building blocks of IT systems is decreasing, the complexity of the blocks themselves is increasing very quickly. Each generation of computer chips has several times more transistors than its predecessor, and each new version of Microsoft Windows adds millions of lines of program code. More and more of these elements are interconnected in novel ways to offer greater levels of automation and control.

In this environment it is hard or impossible to test every possible combination of circumstances and user input. Commercial pressures tempt developers to ship products with known problems (some of which are security related), leaving solutions to the problems for product updates. Consequently problems, including security problems, are often found with widely used systems.

Securing computer systems and maintaining their security requires considerable expertise. Retaining staff with this expertise is difficult. Because of the premium these people can attract, they are often contractors or consultants. Anecdotal evidence suggests that IT skills in general, and IT security skills in particular, are becoming generally scarce. In an attempt to address this shortfall the Australian Commonwealth Government is considering promoting specific centres of excellence in some universities. Elsewhere there are international moves to agree definitions of cyber-crime and to facilitate pursuit of offenders across international boundaries. The EU is attempting to negotiate such a treaty among its members.

Gathering reliable numbers about incidents of this nature is hard since companies are understandably reticent about making disclosures that might harm customer confidence or shareholder value. There is sometimes a public perception that the public sector is more susceptible to IT-related attacks than the private sector, but this may be due to the greater requirements for information disclosure in the public sector.

Without reliable figures planning protective strategies is difficult. A solution to this might be some trusted group that maintained an incident database in a suitably anonymous form.

Companies that own infrastructure would be unlikely to be liable in a legal sense if their infrastructure failed, unless it could be shown that they had failed to operate in accordance with widely accepted relevant standards.

An exception is the banking industry. As a condition of a banking licence, the directors of a bank are required to attest to prudent operation of their bank. This may make them personally liable in the event of failure (New Zealand Government, 2006).

The importance of this to the business continuity profession lies not only in the legacy of methodology from the 'data retrieval' days but also in the need to look forward and create what we might call an American Petroleum Institute/Energy Institute/Institute of Petroleum environment. The oil and gas industry has, worldwide, managed to introduce a set of standards that apply to an 'intrinsically safe' electric/electronic environment. This is the challenge for the business continuity profession in terms of IT.

Eisenhower described the relationship between the US military and US industry as the Military–Industrial Complex. If we look at any military encounter since 1066 in which Northern and Western powers have been involved then they almost always proclaimed their belief in God as a major factor. Particularly if they won.

In today's world, industry has probably been replaced, in Eisenhower's context, by the information society. It is the information society that underpins globalisation, the export of democracy based on Christian values, and both effects-based operations and Asymmetric Warfare. The North and West of the world can therefore be described as a 'Christian Military Information Complex' (a new term). This complex needs to finesse its approach to the world at large. At the same time, despite this being a primarily North and West audience, it is important for the South and East of the world – dominated by Islam, Hindu, Buddhist and Chinese communities – to be equally clear about how they should respond within their own value systems. This is important because the threats can be similar – in that they are often non-state based and atheistic.

The North and West victors of the Cold War have been proclaimed Christians. In the religious battlegrounds of our prevailing times the main opposition has been Islam. In both religious philosophies there is a significant difference between the mainstream views and those of the Fundamentalists of both sides. Mainstream is tolerant, Fundamentalist is intolerant. Generally mainstream supports states, international law and diplomacy. Fundamentalists (on both sides) tend towards being religion, not state, based – of a belief in religious law as interpreted by Fundamentalism as opposed to being governed by international law or the appropriately interpreted religious law – and frequently use terror as a weapon of persuasion as opposed to diplomacy.

It is always difficult for the tolerant to compete with the intolerant – hence why single-issue politics tend to be more successful than broad-based approaches. However, it is important to realise the challenge. It is necessary for the Church, the body politic, the military, business and the information society to take the threat of Fundamentalism seriously. All must continue to refine arguments in support of the principles of the North and West's way of life. In the largest companies and their supply chains this is already an issue. It is likely to become an issue of business continuity for all organisations in due course. In what we might call truly global companies we see these issues writ large – whether they are from North, West or, increasingly, South and East. Shell and BP are obvious examples already noted, the same issues face Tata (India), GoodBaby (China) and sovereign wealth funds: although they may not yet have registered the position fully.

In the military context effects-based operations have their place. Their nemesis has been asymmetric war-fighting techniques. As all war is a dialectic of previous war-fighting experience it is incumbent to find a balanced approach to the winning of wars in a modern context. The Malayan campaign fought by the British in the 1950s and 1960s is possibly a model. Here military effectiveness combined with (a) a successful hearts and minds campaign and (b) a period of appropriate reconstruction, to defeat a communist insurgent enemy. The period equivalents of effects-based operations and subtle counters to Asymmetric Warfare were used throughout to great success.

In the modern era it is important to learn from this and similar examples in order to strike an appropriate balance between effects-based operations and its asymmetric counter so that a form of balance is attained. This balance must recognise that absolute military power is not necessarily the answer. This new approach is termed the Asymmetric Military Balance. Such an approach is a requirement for future campaigns. Business continuity professionals need to be aware of the new military context of the model because it represents a significant risk to their organisations under some circumstances.

In the economic context the globalisation ambitions of the North and West must take account of those Obstructive Marketing initiatives they will face in their efforts to advance. Obstructive Marketing is the corollary of Asymmetric Warfare in the economic context and similar approaches are required.

Business tends to be very pragmatic so local social improvement programmes frequently run parallel to tobacco, soft drink and similar expansion efforts. Thus a balance of sorts is achieved. This is the sort of balance to be achieved in a military campaign too. Because of the times, both economic and military campaigns may run side by side. They are very infrequently co-ordinated to any great extent. Business continuity professionals are often aware of these attributes of the model, but need to understand how their organisation responds to the threats. Raising awareness and changing the corporate mind-set are key.

Underpinning all efforts is IT. This provides the means of delivery for political, economic, social, technical and military thought, campaigns, products and services. In this context the protection of IT Security, and more importantly information security, is the most important single task facing the business continuity professional. It is important to remember that this is not just about servers, but usually about people. And do not confuse information security and information technology security with secure technology. It is much more about secure people.

Insidious to all business continuity discussions, these, days is organised crime. The successful use of IT by organised crime and their links to Fundamentalists, their rule of the 'grey' economy and influence in all war zones means that they are an omnipresent threat. Countering this threat is a challenge on its own, let alone when placed beside the others in the model.

So it is the task of business continuity professionals in the North and West, to protect this 'Christian–Military–Information' complex. The 'Godfearing' model demonstrates that this is, perhaps, rather more complex a task than has traditionally been accepted by the business continuity community. This is heartening as it gives the profession both an opportunity to develop and an ongoing challenge. In the South and East the challenges are similar, but there are a range of factors to be considered, not least the different approaches to cost, productivity, labour and family. The basic issues remain the same, and the development and challenge is of the same, if not greater scale.

Organisations operating in such an environment clearly need an approach to deal with the issues. This approach is what will be looked at in Chapter 9.

This chapter started by introducing the 'Godfearing' model. The term was happenstance, but the context challenging. This model represents a credible interpretation of the strategic and operational backdrop against which a growing range of themes (not always conveniently linked together) are defining what is relevant for businesses, organisations and in business continuity today. It is always important to consider and challenge what may present itself as any prevailing orthodoxy, one of the enduring rights of free speech, and there is no bold claim to the originality of any theme. What has been attempted is to weld them together to produce a relevant context for justifying continued investment in responding to the threats to organisations, business continuity discipline and raising the strategic importance of both.

The context identifies:

- a stage beyond resilience that can be used to 'counter' Obstructive Marketing;

- that developing a response to Obstructive Marketing is appropriate now for certain types of organisations, and is likely to be important for others in the future;

- that globalising companies suffer from an antithesis of Obstructive Marketing;

- that democracy suffers from an antithesis Fundamentalism;

- that military effect-based operations suffer from an antithesis called Asymmetric Warfare;

- that these exist against a backdrop of pervasive IT and insidious organised crime.

This approach has been generally supported by other writers. In particular *The Times* (2011a) carried a model with a number of similarities to this model.

It is proposed that to counter the antitheses and Obstructive Marketing elements to these three key aspects of North and Western development, and their pervasive and insidious companions, is of relevance to organisations and the business continuity profession. It is of such relevance that there is both a route forward for the profession that needs to be further explored and a continuing challenge to the profession that goes beyond current boundaries. It is appropriate to create a truly 'Godfearing' and protected organisation and business continuity profession to counter Obstructive Marketing.

5

Risk and Dependency

Obstructive Marketing and more particularly the response to Obstructive Marketing, is very much to do with not just context but also risk and dependency. In this chapter the key issues around risk and dependency are further examined.

The recent crises in the banking industry and elsewhere have demonstrated that there have been shortcomings in the description, measurement and management of risk. A well-defined and holistic approach to risk was written in the 1970s (Rowe, 1977) and is still relevant today. It deals with the description and measurement of risks plus consequences. This is a good starting point to compare the winners and losers in the recent crisis as described by Augur (2009), Cable (2009) and others, and more recent organisational approaches to risk, such as those seen in the NHS. The models suggested by Wood (2000) and Gordon (1996) can also be reviewed against a strong disciplinary background. Knight and Pretty's (2000), and Pretty's (2008) work confirms the risk in some corporate activities.

This chapter suggests there is some commonality between Rowe (1977) and Soros (2009) and that there have been, indeed, some shortcomings in the management of risk. Following suggestions from Smith and Fischbacher (2009), and building on the work of Rowe (1977), a new model of risk description and measurement might help organisations manage the subject more successfully. By so doing they would become less vulnerable to Obstructive Marketing. Young (2011a; 2011b) confirms the requirement for a new approach to risk in a two-part analysis of the failure of risk management for the Business Continuity Institute. Parker (2012) and Goodwin (2012) have both described how their organisations (UBS and Goodwin plc.) were deficient in the description, measurement and management of risk. Sjuve (2010) has described well-managed risk in the National Australian Banking Group.

Goodger (2011a; 2011b) and Gall (2010) view the world as volatile, uncertain, complex and ambiguous. They state there is no clear predictive design mechanism(s) for understanding emergence within the complex adaptive information ecosystem that is today's world. They suggest a need for a predictive dynamic risk framework. They also complain that most are unable to comprehend or explain risk in logical terms. Goodger and Atkinson (2011) see the biggest risk to society as a lack of an integrated approach to the virtual and physical worlds. As stated elsewhere there is little research into this subject. Davis (2012) explained how the risks businesses and banks run are still not properly managed some four years after the banking crisis. A new approach to risk is clearly required.

Dependency in the context of this book is related to risk. It is how one part of an organisation depends on any other part. A dependency model brings together all parts of an organisation into a model that shows how to minimise risk and be successful. Of interest in the context of 'Hardening' is that although, according to Gordon (2010) and others, dependency modelling is a scientific approach to handling the implications of risk in any organisation it is not well-used. Deployed, primarily, in support of managing risk in banks in the 1990s it seems to have hit three key barriers:

- the belief that judgement, particularly in CEOs, counts for more than rational and scientific-based thought (Gordon, 2010);

- the view that some risk management issues need to be deliberately avoided to preserve 'competitiveness' (Walter, 2010);

- perceived cost and effort (Stennett, 2009).

In the light of subsequent events in the banking industry these issues do not stand up to close scrutiny as barriers to use. Dependency modelling is to risk as a spreadsheet is to finance. It is the tool that enables risk to be managed.

To look at risk in a holistic perspective it is necessary to go back to first principles. First principles on risk are probably best described in Rowe (1977). Rowe (1977, p.ix) starts by saying:

> *A few years ago, as a member of a federal regulatory agency, I became aware of the degree to which many regulatory decisions are based on assessments of risks, and of the inability of bureaucratic organisations*

to deal with such assessments. My work forced me to take risks into consideration in regulatory decisions, and I undertook to determine what we meant by 'risk' and what means were available to analyse it. I found a surprising diversity in definitions of risk and risk acceptance and a singular lack of understanding of the means to assess risks. Unfortunately, the concept of risk was so little understood that it was often misapplied, resulting in the erroneous use of risk concepts. Thus clarification and better understanding of the concepts involved in risk assessment appeared necessary.

Rowe's (1977) analysis is as pertinent today as when written. Any review of the banking industry over the last two to three years is testament to this. All countries, banks, bureaucracies, most companies and other organisations have risk registers. Not all understand risk. A summary of Rowe's (1977) main points is as follows.

The only certainty in life is death. Consequently, there are many examples of how societies dignify death, suggest ways to avoid it, or promise something after it. Most religions are based in part on man's fear of the unknown. These tend to minimise the negative value of the final event. Since the Renaissance people have become increasingly aware of the possibility of controlling their environment. As a result the array of risk covers a wide spectrum of human experiences from premature death to loss of financial and aesthetic values.

Maslow's (1954) hierarchy of needs categorises and ranks individual and group human needs into a conceptual hierarchy. This concept is particularly pertinent to the study of risk, since it provides a basis for considering man's action in risk-averse situations where mortality, pain or suffering is not involved. A perceived threat to a perceived need is very real, and resulting human behaviour to react to such threats involves attempts to adjust one's environment to meet needs.

There are essentially two types of uncertainty:

- descriptive uncertainty: this means the absence of information relating to the identity of the variables that explicitly define a system;

- measurement uncertainty: absence of information relating to the specification of value assigned to each variable in the system.

To reduce uncertainty information is needed.

In a process that entails the behaviour of an intelligent opponent, the skill of the opponent in relation to the skill of the proponent is the matter of uncertainty. Most people are fallible and there is no guarantee that optimum strategies will be played. The whole field of game theory, as originally developed by von Neumann and Morgenstern (2007/1944) and extended by many others, such as Luce and Raiffa (1959), deals with situations in which players are rational opponents. Thus should the opponent act as a rational economic man a whole process to describe how man operates under economic conditions can be derived. Many decisions, however, are emotionally based or use value systems different from 'economic man'. Thus risk arises from uncertainty in man's behaviour as well as from natural processes. This is important to note in the context of recent and current economic events, and later commentators.

Processes involving natural phenomena are of two types:

- processes that operate on the basis of empirical, natural laws;

- random processes that imply statistical operations.

These processes are concerned with the method of scientific empiricism, which is the basis of natural science. Underlying processes may be statistical, for example the whole body of quantum theory is based on such evidence. There is in such theory an implication that the descriptive uncertainty of the universe can be reduced to a value approaching zero. This may not be achievable, but the process of understanding natural laws reduces uncertainty and does lead to a potential ability for man to control the environment.

The existence of measurement uncertainty is prescribed by scientific theory, especially at the quantum theory level. The actual measurement process at the limits of measurement precision involves errors that contribute to the inaccuracy of the measurement. Inaccuracy and its converse, accuracy, often involve a statistical process, although bias and systematic errors may come into the picture as part of the measurement error. Since the statistical processes are random, this statistical approach to measurement, like many other processes, involves random behaviour.

Table 5.1   Reduction of uncertainty

Process	Descriptive	Measurement
Behavioural	Limited by the ability to define all variables by which people behave in given situations	Limited by the degree of rational behaviour of people as opposed to other types of behaviour
Natural deterministic	Theoretically unlimited, but limited by practicalities	Limited only by precision of a measuring system down to the absolute limit of the uncertainty principle
Natural random	Theoretically unlimited, but limited by practicalities	Cannot be reduced by any method presently known and demonstrated for future events

In statistical testing systems, random processes serve as inputs into an experiment, where resulting observations on the system under test establish patterns from which hypotheses of system behaviour are developed and tested. Such experiments reduce the descriptive uncertainty of the system but do not reduce measurement uncertainty. A process that obeys some statistical (probability) distribution provides an estimate of the most likely probabilities of occurrence for the next trial, but this trial can result in any possible value. Descriptive and measurement uncertainty limits for system processes can be stated as in Table 5.1.

These concepts are important because the increasing concern with risk and risk systems is aimed primarily at the control of risks, especially at the societal level. This is a relatively new concept in the history of man, concurrent with the scientific revolution.

Risk at the general level involves two major components:

- the existence of a possible unwanted consequence or loss;

- an uncertainty in the occurrence of that consequence which can be expressed in the form of a probability of occurrence.

Risk is therefore the potential for the realisation of unwanted, negative consequences of an event. Risk management is action taken to control risk. The array of risks covers a wide variety of human experiences involving risks – personal or societal, man-made or natural – with consequences ranging from financial involvement through premature death.

Otway (1973) identified two aspects of risk assessment: risk estimation and risk evaluation. Risk estimation may be thought of as the identification of consequences of a decision and the subsequent estimation of the magnitude of associated risks. Risk evaluation is the complex process of anticipating the societal response to risks – this could be termed the acceptability of risk.

Kates (1976), however, used the term of risk identification as follows:

- risk identification involves reduction of descriptive uncertainty;

- risk estimation involves reduction of measurement uncertainty;

- risk evaluation involves risk-aversive action, which can result in risk reduction or risk acceptance.

This can be shown diagrammatically in Figure 5.1.

Risk Identification	Risk Estimation	Risk Evaluation
Reduction of Descriptive Uncertainty	Reduction of Measurement Uncertainty	Risk-aversive Action
Research	Revelation	Aversive
Screening	Intuition	Balances
Monitoring	Extrapolation	Benefit – Risk
Diagnosis		Cost – Benefit

Figure 5.1   Risk identification, estimation and evaluation

There are five steps of risk estimation:

- causative event;

- outcome;

- exposure;

- consequences;

- consequence value.

The first four of these determine probability, and the last one determines value.

Thus risk is a function of the probability of the consequence and the value of the consequence to the risk taker.

$$R= f[p_c, C(v)]$$

Natural science through positivism deals primarily with objective risk. In the latter part of the twentieth century, the idea of synthesised probabilities developed extensively, and in the behavioural sciences the treatment of observable consequences as opposed to objective ones has assumed major importance. However, subjective risk is perceived to be reality. In our society Aristotelian truth is dominant, as procedure dominates over the Socratic truth of substance. Objective and subjective risk behaviour have been widely studied. Practical implementation has often been found wanting and therefore a different approach to overcome problems would be helpful to protect against Obstructive Marketing.

The role of the risk evaluator is to ameliorate risk inequities in society often through regulation. The amelioration of these risk inequities by regulatory bodies implies the existence of some acceptable levels of risk. If these levels are achieved, the inequities are deemed small enough to be allowed. Otherwise, risk-aversive action in the form of control is required.

Risks are controlled either by reducing the probability that a causative event will occur or by minimising the exposure pathway should an event occur. In the case of a causative event, an activity that may have some beneficial aspects may be curtailed, banned or eliminated to prevent or reduce occurrence. The philosophical question of whether risks and risk-causing activities should be regulated is one that requires an understanding of the relative costs and balances.

It is well known by behavioural scientists that there are great differences between an individual's behaviour and the influences on his actions of the groups to which he belongs. The court system and the electoral process have classically dealt with the balancing of risks at individual and institutional levels after the damage from hazards has occurred. However, evaluation of anticipated risks is relatively new in government and is practised in some regulatory agencies. Regulatory bodies are either permissive, restrictive or both.

Recent events in the banking industry have highlighted the symbiotic relationship between regulators and the industries they regulate. This is a relationship that is as old as capitalism itself. There is a pendulum swing of regulation depending on perceived and actual performance. Regulation was light in the banking industry during the period up to 2007/2008. Since the revelations over various forms of derivatives a much tougher line has been proposed by most regulators. In the UK this has been epitomised by the three-way public debate between the Treasury, the Bank of England and the Financial Services Agency on how the banks are to be regulated in the future. This debate (*The Economist*, 2009), has yet to be fully resolved with arguments for and against more regulation continuing. The International Monetary Fund (IMF) (2009) encouraged additional regulation following the Turner (2009) review. In 2011 there was general agreement to implement the Vickers Report (2011) (but not for some time yet). In 2013 the Alternative Investment Fund Managers Directive comes into operation across Europe, regulating the previously unregulated hedge fund sector (EU Directive 2011/61/EU, 2011).

One value group may attempt to influence other value groups when an issue can be promoted into one of national public concern. Because of the prevailing system of instantaneous communication and total press coverage, a potentially controversial issue is subject to magnification out of proportion to its importance. However, it provides a vehicle to sway others. This is a particularly critical condition in present society. Since societal risks are one of the subjects for which 'squawks' are often generated, information and judgement must often be qualitative and subjective, but the process of making decisions can be made visible and traceable. 'Counter marketers' take advantage of these 'squawks' – particularly if they were likely to have an implication on share prices or reputation.

Risk evaluation is a relatively simple concept, often difficult to implement. There are four basic steps:

- establish a risk referent level: Establish a level of risk for each category of risk consequences involved that is deemed acceptable on some basis. This 'reference level of acceptable risk' is determined independently of the activity to be evaluated;

- determine the level of risk associated with the new programme and alternatives;

- compare the risk with the referent within the limits of error of the estimate and referent;

- risk-aversive action. Two particular cases are important:
  - risk is controlled – find an alternative at or below the referent level or abandon the project;
  - risk is uncontrollable – find the lowest practicable risk exposure alternative.

Systemic control of risk requires a plan and its implementation to control risks, which involves the following:

- a philosophy of controlling and minimising risk as a major emphasis in the design and operation of the system involved;

- a means of regulation of the total system to assure maximum safety;

- a system design that includes the following:

  - quality assurance;

  - redundancy for critical systems;

  - training, licensing and certification of personnel;

  - inspection of equipment and operations;

  - licensing and registration of operation;

- ongoing review of system performance to meet goals;

- enforcement and auditing system.

There are five key problems in risk assessment:

- Who evaluates risk? Why? What biases are introduced?

- What is meant by value and utility?

- Can consequence values be assigned to both tangible and intangible consequences?

- How do cultural, situational, and dynamic considerations affect consequence value assignment?

- What factors affect the assignment of value?

Such is a perspective of some years standing. It could be expected that the theory and lessons of such an approach would be commonplace.

In real life there are always winners and losers. A loser in 2008 was Lehman Brothers. Thomson (2009) notes that Lehman Brothers filed for Chapter 11 protection on 15 September 2008. Lehman was, and largely remains, the subject of 76 global insolvency procedures, presenting unique challenges for administrators given the complexity of the organisational structure and its tangled web of assets. It emerged early in the administration of Lehman Brothers that a major problem across the Group was a lack of transparency.

Cairns (2009) (Managing Director of Alvarez & Marsal's European Financial Industry practice, overseeing the European aspect of the Lehman Brothers Holdings International bankruptcy case) commented that there was no clear understanding as to who the key people were, who booked the trades, who knew the systems, or who fully understood the structures. She said:

> We need to be able to deal with things next time a highly complex business with a truly global business model finds itself struggling to survive.

Barclays bought the core brokerage business for $1.75 billion, a fraction of its worth some months before. Nomura picked up the Asian business plus 3,000 skilled personnel for 'a song'. These sales confirmed that, according to the PwC administrator, Tony Lomas, that no part of Lehman had sufficient systems to track or manage risk. It was also very CEO-centric with many of the traits Dixon and Dixon (2011) noted in Chapter 4.

A winner was the National Australia Bank Group. Sjuve (2010) stated that unlike their rivals the group did not invest in the high-risk products that caused so much trouble with other banks. This is confirmed by Grimshaw (2009):

> We have been around a long time and are probably seen as a no-nonsense bank with traditional values We have not been involved in all the exotic derivatives that have wreaked havoc with the market and have talked about ourselves in recent times as 'boring is good'.

Murden (2008) interviewed Lynne Peacock, CEO at Clydesdale, and she commented as follows:

> We have taken a consistently prudent and disciplined approach to liquidity and funding.

Thus risk, even for those who lived and breathed risk in the banking industry, is clearly not so simple. All banks had some sort of risk approach. There are wide-ranging methodologies involved in capturing risk appropriately, not all used correctly. Some, the winners, made clear and accurate risk assessments, some, the losers, did not.

Risk scorecards have gained much credence in recent years. One such is based on the ideas of Wood (2000). Another is based on current Australia/New Zealand Government systems.

Wood's (2000) business risk scorecard would look to include:

- leadership;

- business design;

- business ecosystem;

- business environment;

- performance measures;

- knowledge management;

- management processes;

- organisational values.

In an eight-category score card that builds a risk profile of the organisation, Wood (2000) demonstrates one way of managing risk. He also sets the scorecard against a 'business wheel' or 'balanced scorecard' to give a more general view of where an organisation might sit within an environment or context or system. The scorecard would look something like that displayed in Figure 5.2.

SCORECARD AND RISK REGISTER

Risk – the uncertainty of outcome, whether positive opportunity or negative threat, of actions

and events

I – impact   L – likelihood (within a three-year period)

1	LEADERSHIP (Category) (Governance and Board)			SCORECARD:			External Risk (Red, Amber, Green)	Internal Risk (Red, Amber, Green)
Date	Risk Identified	I	L	Risk Factor	Response (Track or Treat)	Action Agreed	Responsible Officer	Timescale for Action

Figure 5.2   An example of a risk scorecard and risk register
Source: Wood, 2000.

This works well if linked to the Wood (2000) business wheel and balanced scorecard approach. Unfortunately many organisations miss out the context issues. For example: an NHS (2010) risk register summary looks as in Figure 5.3.

TITLE OF REPORT: Risk Register Summary Report – December 2009				

DIRECTOR RESPONSIBLE: Deputy Chief Executive

PRODUCED FOR: Risk and Clinical Governance Committee 10 December 2009
DATE PRODUCED: 2 December 2009

PURPOSE OF REPORT: To provide Risk and Clinical Governance Committee with a summary of the additions, requests for closure and key changes to the risk register.

SUMMARY OF CHANGES TO RISK REGISTER

Month	September 2009	October 2009	November 2009	December 2009
Total Number of Risks on the Register	95	99	95	92
Risks scoring 25	0	0	0	0
Risks scoring 15+	42	44	41	43
Risks scoring 8–12	43	44	42	42
Risks scoring 2–6	10	11	12	7

NEW RISKS
145: (pg9) Failure to collect income from Hospices (16).
146: (pg12) Failure of Procurement Hub to cover its running costs in 2010 (16).
81: (pg8) Locality Podiatry Service (16).

RISKS FOR APPROVAL OF CLOSURE BY RISK AND CLINICAL GOVERNANCE COMMITTEE
27: (pg23) Continuing care – risk has been superseded and new risk to be drafted.
36: (pg25) Risk merged with number 35(pg 24).
84: (pg34) Risk resolved.
60: (pg34) Risk now captured within risk number 63 (pg 33).
114: (pg37) Productivity risk now encompassed within risk number 139 (pg38).
75: (pg35) Project X – risk score reduced to 12.

RISKS INCREASING TO 15+
None

25 SCORING RISK
None

TOP PCT RISKS (those scoring 20+)
82: Seasonal pressures.
90: Learning disability home inspections.
35: HRG4 funding – changes in payment by results.
26: Devolvement of infrastructure resource/personnel to support locality working.
113: Commissioned services funding.
114: Delivery against the productivity plan.
127: Loss of capital funding from a the impact of a delay in Y programme.
117: Future sustainability of the financial position of NHS.
58: Pandemic flu.
133: Loss of IT facilities at Villa 22 ASPH.
102: Implementation of NHS Health checks.
A summary of key performance measures relating to the risk register is attached with this report.

REVIEW PROCESS: The Risk Register will be updated following review at the Risk and Clinical Governance Committee. The revised document will be sent to all directors for information and review within their team and placed on the Staff Portal. The Risk Strategy Development Manager will arrange to meet with Directors to update all risks due for review. A summary report and the Corporate Risk Register (risks of 15+) will go to EMT and to Board on a quarterly basis.

RECOMMENDATION: The Risk and Clinical Governance Committee are asked to note the additions and changes to the Risk Register and to approve closures of risks as outlined above.

Figure 5.3   An NHS PCT risk summary

In Figure 5.3 scoring is against a 5 x 5 matrix for impact and likelihood. So a score of 25 is very high risk. Scores over 20 get aired at executive meetings. This summary, and entry, is from an organisation that manages over £1.7 billion pounds of public money, five acute hospitals consuming £200 million plus per annum, various community hospitals and over 15,000 staff. There is a new risk for hospices, rated at 15. These account for less than 0.1 per cent of financial commitment – at the same time there is no risk against acute hospitals, one of which lost £2 million in the month reported, and no risk against the likelihood of the organisation failing to meet its statutory financial balance (which it failed to meet and was therefore a very high risk indeed). There is clearly a systemic problem of description and measurement, and an organisational confusion about what risk really is. It is worth noting that this paragraph is a very short summary of a range of NHS issues reviewed for this book that identified not only the root and key problems with risk but also with A&E management, business continuity planning, discharge processes, IT, hygiene, infection control, management processes and security.

As an aside one interesting way in which the author could identify failing hospitals was the 'barefoot' test. Take off your shoes and socks and walk barefoot round a hospital – if you end up with clean feet, as the author did at places like Frimley Park and Newcastle's Freeman and RVI, you know you are in a first-class hospital. If you don't, you are not. Another indicator is if people are allowed to smoke outside the front entrance – this seems to have an anecdotal correlation with Noro Virus and Diarrhoea and Vomiting outbreaks.

An Australian Attorney General (including New Zealand) (2006) model on risk takes a further, but similar, approach. Given the concerns expressed over the adequacy of commercial incentives in respect of infrastructure security, government needed to consider how it could assure itself that sufficient risk management was being undertaken. A reasonable way forward was to establish the extent to which infrastructure owners use risk management methods. New models of risk and mitigation were designed. These models use a similar approach to the NHS model described but it is more sophisticated and looks at a system approach. The NHS uses an Australian/New Zealand based 5 x 5 approach but has not described the system appropriately. Both the NHS and the Australian and New Zealand 5 x 5 approaches have a difficulty in appropriate measurement and exposing a range of 'known unknowns' and 'unknown unknowns'. Others have looked at how risk may be looked at differently from such a relatively simple 5 x 5 approach.

Soros (2009) comments that financial institutions depend on confidence and trust to do business. A decline in their share and bond prices can increase their financing costs. That means that bear raids on financial institutions can be self-validating, which is in direct contradiction of the efficient market hypothesis – Rowe (1977) and others' rational man. It is consistent with the views of Taleb (2007) and Soros (2009). The prevailing paradigm acknowledges only known risks and fails to allow for the consequences of its own deficiencies and misconceptions.

Soros (2009) contends that social events have a different structure from natural phenomena. In natural phenomena, he says, there is a causal chain that links one set of facts directly with the next. In human affairs the course of events is more complicated. Not only facts are involved but also the participants' views and the interplay between them enters into the causal chain. There is a two-way connection between the facts and opinions prevailing at any moment in time: on the one hand participants seek to understand the situation (which includes both facts and opinions); on the other, they seek to influence the situation (which again includes both facts and opinions).

The interplay between the cognitive and manipulative functions intrudes into the causal chain so that the chain does not lead directly from one set of facts to the next but reflects and affects the participants' views. Since those views do not correspond to the facts they introduce an element of uncertainty into the course of events that is absent from natural phenomena. That element of uncertainty affects both the facts and the participant's views. Natural phenomena are not necessarily determined by scientific laws of universal validity. For instance, Heisenberg's (1927) uncertainty principle does not determine the behaviour of quantum particles or waves, it merely asserts that their behaviour cannot be determined. There is a somewhat similar uncertainty principle at work in social events.

Thus Soros (2009) describes his reflexivity theory as a two-way connection between the participants' thinking and the situation in which they participate. This theory is used by Soros (2009) to explain the reasons for recent bubbles in the finance and housing markets and to debunk the view that economists can produce theories that explain and predict the behaviour of financial markets in the same way that natural scientists can explain and predict natural phenomena. In so doing he also calls into question Popper's (1935) declared view of the unity of method. He states that misinterpretations of reality and other kinds of misconceptions play a much bigger role in determining the course of events than generally recognised.

Soros (2009) is very aligned to Rowe (1977). Indeed his reflexivity theory matches Rowe's (1977) views in many areas. The comments also resonate with the Marsh Inc. survey on business continuity which noted a gap between perception and reality in those who undertook business continuity plans. It resonates with general research findings. The demise of the rational person also resonates with other comments in this book.

Dr Deborah Pretty, of Oxford Metrica, has made something of an academic and business career tracking risk in major financial and corporate institutions. In early work, Knight and Pretty (2000), she identified the links between catastrophes, reputation and shareholder value. This was much about risk management.

The conclusion from the foregoing is that despite years of focus risk is still not well managed. This seems to be a combination of a lack of understanding and a lack of application.

Smith and Fischbacher (2009) contend that there has been a state of evolution in risk management and challenges over the last decade. They point out the importance of Black Swans, after Taleb (2007), events of low probability with high consequences. They note the borderless nature of risk and the issue of resilience in both spatial and temporal domains. This researcher would add the virtual domain to this. They use the examples of the recent banking crisis, swine 'flu and terrorist activity. They identify 'spaces of vulnerability' and 'spaces of destruction'. In drawing on a range of work they support, implicitly, the need for the 'Hardening' of organisations.

A related, and equally important aspect of the treatment of resilience, is the notion of vulnerability and the way in which the process operating within space and time is conceptualised. The 'landscapes' in which organisations operate are invariably fractured and pitted. There are 'spaces of vulnerability' that exist both within and between organisations and these have the potential to expose weaknesses in organisational controls and thus impact upon the limitations of strategies to develop resilience. Inevitably, gaps in defences emerge, weak signals and early warnings are ignored, and there is a high degree of likelihood that managerial assumptions and beliefs will lead to an erosion of organisational capabilities around control. There are many service design issues associated with this process. For example: there are new challenges to the way in which organisations are designed to provide both a seamless service to 'customers' and to maintain a level of security that is effective, and minimally intrusive.

The interaction between these, and other elements, will serve to create and sustain 'spaces of destruction' (Smith and Fischbacher, 2009) in which the interplay between resilience and the search for equilibrium by organisations will create fractures within the defences which organisations establish to ensure stability in the first place. Managers may then ultimately become the authors of their own misfortune as they seek to create rigid systems of control that maintain a particular point of equilibrium in situations where, in fact, the dynamics of the system mitigate against such rigid attempts at control. These controls may inhibit the required levels of adaptation to environmental changes and may, therefore, result in a shift in the very equilibrium that the controls were designed to protect in the first place. This raises a question on how organisations can develop the dynamic capabilities that are required to cope with such challenges – a challenge that also faces the academic and research communities in terms of the ways in which they train and educate managers. This is an area of study also being looked at by Goodger (2011a). The need for flexibility, after Borodzicz (2010), within an Obstructive Marketing context becomes apparent.

If the MBA, for example, is to provide the means of developing these capabilities, and become more than a composite of the functional areas of management, then it will need to ensure that it also evolves to meet the future needs of organisations around the creation and maintenance of these dynamic capabilities. It needs to encourage future generations of managers to reflect upon the lessons that emerge from the various crises facing organisations and give them the skills to learn from those mistakes and, perhaps more importantly, to reflect upon the limits of their own knowledge and thereby help to prevent future events. By failing to do so, we will simply be destined to repeat the problems of the past (Smith and Fischbacher, 2009).

In the period 2009–2012 much has changed in the regulatory field. This has resulted in changed risk profiles but not necessarily a changed view on risk.

Clearly the corner shop does not need the same sort of risk management as the global corporation. However, as this book looks at Obstructive Marketing, and a response to it, in organisations it is appropriate to suggest a way of managing risk in organisations that need to respond.

It is suggested (Hyslop and Collins, 2013) that risk can and should be looked at as a function of:

- context as a precursor: 'Godfearing' model, see above.

Then:

- description: Hyslop (2010) and Wood (2000);

- measurement: Rowe (1977) and Gordon (1996);

- critical information infrastructure resilience: Anderson and Moore (2006) (design of critical information infrastructure) and Hyslop (2007) (resilience and protection of critical information infrastructure);

- critical infrastructure Resilience: Boin and Smith (2006) (issues of critical infrastructure);

- spaces of vulnerability: Smith and Fischbacher (2009);

- spaces of destruction: Smith and Fischbacher (2009).

This gives rise to a potential new model/index for risk. For the sake of brevity this will be called the General Risk Analysis model or the 'Gray' model for short.

In this model risk could be said to be a function of description and measurement certainty plus financial and reputational exposure plus a view on virtual form and physical form and vulnerability (known and unknown) to cultural, criminal, casual and competitive threats and a potential for destruction (known and unknown) by cultural, criminal, casual and competitive threats. To begin with this will be developed against a nominal scale from 1–10 for each variable, objectively assessed if possible but nevertheless with some subjective and common sense interpretation. The value 0 cannot realistically be used because there is some exposure to all these variables by all organisations.

This can be expressed as follows again after Hyslop and Collins (2013):

$$R = f (D + M + F + R + P + 5CV(K) + p5CV(NK) + 5CD(K) + p5CD(NK))$$

R = Risk.

f = Function.

D = Description: a range of values from complex (10) to simple (1). For example: The NHS is a highly complex organisation, the corner shop a very simple organisation.

M = Measurement: a range of values from complex (10) to simple (1).

F = Financial risk: interpreted from either exposure or annual report, with high risk (10) or low risk (1).

R = Reputation risk: interpreted from size and/or quality, with high risk (10) and low risk (1).

V = Virtual: a range of values from highly virtual (10) to not virtual (1).

P = Physical: a range of values from highly physical (10) to not physical (10). (Note: physical is not the same as virtual).

p = Probability.

5CV = 5C Vulnerability: vulnerability to cultural, criminal, casual, competitive and critical infrastructure threats expressed as known and a probability of unknown. These risks can be interpreted from various sources.

5CD = 5C destruction: exposure to cultural, criminal, casual, competitive and critical infrastructure threats expressed as known and a probability of unknown. These risks can be interpreted from various sources.

K = Known.

NK = Unknown.

This is a relatively simple model, as with the 'Godfearing' model, but it does require an understanding of context and risk. The model generates a risk score that ranges from a relatively high number to a relatively low number out of 100 to rate the overall risk exposure of an organisation. This is a fairly crude way of describing the overall vulnerability of an organisation – but straightforward and simple to use with the 'Godfearing' context scorecard.

Examples:

Table 5.2   'Gray' risk model examples

Org	D	M	V	P	F	R	5CV (K)	P5CV (NK) X 10	5CD (K)	P5CD (NK) X 10	Total
Amazon	4	4	8	8	8	8	5	5	5	5	60
NHS	8	8	5	8	8	8	8	8	8	8	77
Corner store	1	1	1	5	5	5	1	1	1	1	22
Global market bank	9	9	9	9	9	9	9	9	9	9	90

Amazon.com can therefore be described in the following terms:

- context score (using the scorecard discussed earlier) still broadly confined to the West and therefore = 5.

Then on risk:

- description: relatively simple business system = 4;

- measurement: easily measured = 4;

- highly virtual organisation (online booking) = 8;

- highly physical organisation (uses warehouses and physical distribution) = 8;

- financially vulnerable: for example, profit warnings = 8;

- reputationally vulnerable: for example, Christmas deliveries going awry = 8;

- 5C vulnerability (has a number of vulnerable areas) = 5;

- 5C destruction (has a number of destruction zones) = 5;

- unknown 5C vulnerability (virtual organisations and extended geographical organisations score high) = 5;

- unknown 5C destruction (virtual organisations and extended geographical organisations score high) = 5.

The example shows Amazon. In Table 5.2 banks are highly risky organisations, and the corner shop a much less risky organisation. (Unless banks are underwritten by taxpayers and then they become very low-risk entities.)

It is suggested that risk needs to be looked at in a completely different way. Such a way can be summarised by the formula expression noted above. The expression should enable organisations such as ...

- the country;

- the banks;

- the globalised company;

- the public sector;

- national companies;

- local companies;

- the international charity;

- the business continuity profession

... to be looked at in context, described and measured from a slightly different but holistic perspective. Such a perspective should be proportional to their overall position in a 'Godfearing' context, and their 'Gray' risk index. High contextual visibility and a high-risk index would warrant some protection against Obstructive Marketing.

Thus at this stage in developing a response to Obstructive Marketing there is a new contextual model, the 'Godfearing' model, and a new risk model, the 'Gray' risk index. If organisations need to protect themselves against Obstructive Marketing then it is necessary to understand 'what' needs to be protected in the organisation to mitigate context and risk. This requires an understanding of dependencies.

Over the last 15 years the author has worked with dependency modelling on various projects. The dependency model described here was initially developed by Professor John Gordon. Relevant software supports the model.

The 'Gordon' model is a tool for analysing risk to any system, be it an organisation, endeavour, enterprise, infrastructure, business, factory, machine, plan or idea – anything of which a suitable model can be built. It works by statistically analysing the model. The 'Gordon' model for this chapter is concerned with organisational objectives and whether they can be achieved. An organisational objective can be anything from avoiding disasters to successfully launching a new enterprise.

The 'Gordon' model:

- finds the probability of achieving organisational objectives;

- finds the true risks to those organisational objectives;

- finds those dependencies which are most pivotal to organisational objectives;

- finds the best ways to deploy resources for maximum benefit;

- finds the cost-effectiveness of countermeasures;

- finds the most likely causes of success and failure;

- finds the most critical uncertainties;

- finds single and multiple-point failure modes;

- measures risk;

- finds ways to reduce risk;

- finds ways to reduce risk at least cost or reduce costs at least risk, or both.

It does this through the use of a Bayesian engine and Monte Carlo simulations.

The 'Gordon' dependency model represents the organisational objective plus those things the objective depends upon, plus the things those things depend on, and so on. An example is the relationship between various entities in a home as in Figure 5.4.

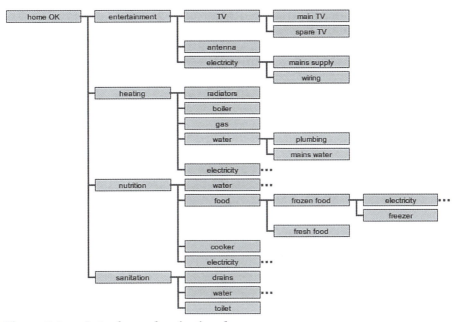

Figure 5.4   Interdependencies in a home

There is a main organisational objective, called *home OK* and it depends upon the provision of *entertainment, heating, nutrition* and *sanitation. Entertainment* (by which is meant the ability to watch TV) in turn depends on the availability of *TV*, an *antenna* and *electricity. Electricity* in turn depends on *mains supply* and *wiring*. (Notice that after its first appearance *electricity* is shown with three dots, meaning that the dependencies of *electricity* are the same as before but for brevity are not repeated.) The rest of the diagram should be self-evident.

Only the names of the interdependent entities are shown, not their nature or the types of relationships, but nevertheless these details are present in the model and can be viewed and changed. Notice that all the entities in the boxes are *organisational objectives* in some sense, in other words they are something the home needs. None of them represents a problem. Problems, in the sense of this model, are merely unsatisfied organisational objectives.

The following model looks at how to organise a garage filling station as in Figure 5.5. It shows two ways of organising a garage filling station. Each of the ways is shown as a different objective.

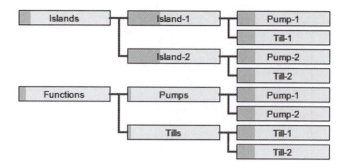

Figure 5.5   Two ways of organising a filling-station forecourt

The *garage* has four appliances – two pumps and two pay-points (tills). The first setup is called *islands* where the appliances are organised as two islands each with a pump and a till. Each island is an AND-relationship of a pump and a till, while *islands* is an OR-relationship of the two islands.

In the second setup, called *functions*, the plumbing and wiring is slightly different so that either till works with either pump. It's organised by functionality, and there are two function called *pumps* and *tills*. *Pumps* is satisfied if one or more pumps is working, so it's an OR-relationship of the two pumps, and *tills* is similar for the tills. However *functions* is an AND-relationship of *pumps* and *tills*.

As the diagram shows, *functions* is more likely to succeed than *islands*, which may be surprising. A good way to help understand why this happens is to show the failure modes. These are the four failure modes for *islands*, as shown in Figure 5.6.

The entities with red borders fail. The failure is caused by the uncontrollables failing on the right. For instance the first failure mode is caused by *pump-1* and *pump-2* failing. As a result both islands fail, and hence *islands* fails. These are the two failure modes for *functions* as shown in Figure 5.7.

The difference is that *islands* have more failure modes than *functions*. Moreover every failure mode of *functions* is also a failure mode of *islands* and so those occur with the same probability in both models.

The fact that *islands* has more ways to go wrong is convincing as an explanation, even for someone with a non-technical background.

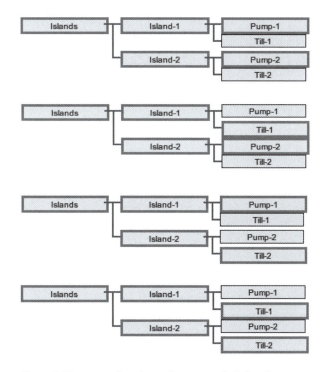

Figure 5.6   Four failure modes for a forecourt's *islands*

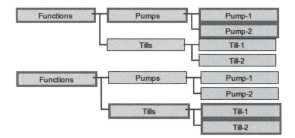

Figure 5.7   Two failure modes for forecourt *functions*

Turning to the theme of this book, Obstructive Marketing, a model could be constructed identifying what is needed to prevent an Obstructive Marketing attack. This could have a high-level 'No perpetrators of Obstructive Marketing' or that there is some sort of plan as a counter-measure to known perpetrators. In addition, timing a market development

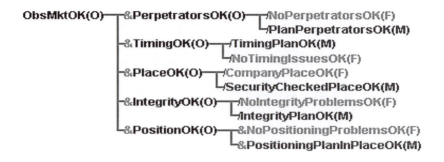

Figure 5.8   Obstructive Marketing headline dependency model

to mitigate Obstructive Marketing, getting the right place, having integrity (in the sense of the operation being secure) in an overseas market and having the right product or service positioning plan are all important to countering Obstructive Marketing. A headline dependency model may therefore look something like Figure 5.8. Different headlines could, of course, be chosen, these are simply representative. Further the 'leaves' could be extended to the right down to individual pieces of equipment with their mean time between failure performance being included as a probability for equipment failure.

Measuring and managing risk by dependency modelling works. It is not common, even amongst banks and other high-risk organisations. It is a formal approach to the subject. It remains something of a mystery as to why it is not more commonly used as a tool to aid the management of risk and the management of organisations. In practice this model is encapsulated in a software tool that can be deployed for any type of organisation. The dependency modelling tool is to risk as a spreadsheet is to a business plan. An organisation that lacks such an approach is exposed, with structures vulnerable, to Obstructive Marketing.

This chapter has dealt with the description, measurement and management of risk, starting with an understanding of context and concluding with why dependencies are important. It has noted how organisations do not look at these subjects properly. Two models have been devised to address the deficiencies – one for context and one for risk and dependency. The issues described here are often related to 'external' issues, but they clearly also have internal implications.

6

Asymmetric Warfare

The concept of Asymmetric Warfare has been around for millennia. It is the basis of the David and Goliath story; Sun Tsu commented on it, Machiavelli commented on it and various philosophers and military commentators since have commented upon it too. However, as this chapter will show there are three disturbing issues:

- there has been much commentary on the issue in Western military circles over the last two generations but no real consensus;

- not a lot has necessarily changed in military circles in that time;

- the world has changed in the meantime from a bi-polar world to a multi-polar world.

To begin this chapter it is useful to have some definitions of war and the laws of war. This helps us with a basic understanding of the differences between different types of warfare and the changing nature of the rules of war. Following that two separate perspectives on Asymmetric Warfare will be given from 1997 and 2011. The purpose of this is to demonstrate that thinking on these issues has been continuous for a period of time, and that not a great deal has necessarily come of it. There is little that is new – except many of the required counter-measures are not in place. To demonstrate this see Chris Donnelly's views from 2003, quoted in Chapter 2. This shows how important the role of the corporate sector can be in countering any asymmetric threat.

Total war is a war in which a belligerent engages in the complete mobilisation of fully available resources and population. In the mid-nineteenth century, 'total war' was identified by scholars as a separate class of warfare. In a total war, there is less differentiation between combatants and civilians than in other conflicts, and sometimes no such differentiation at all, as nearly every human resource, civilians and soldiers alike, can be considered to be part of the belligerent effort. Total war played a major part in conflicts from the French Revolutionary Wars to the Second World War, but has been replaced in the modern era by cheaper, quicker and more effective policies including guerrilla and Asymmetric Warfare and the adoption of weapons of mass destruction.

Regional and civil wars have been a feature of the world order since human societies developed the capacity to organise combatants to wage war. The implications of these wars for political, economic and social development have changed dramatically with the emergence of new military technologies that permit greater and far-reaching damage. The rapid emergence of these new technologies in the nineteenth century ushered in new forces that facilitated the circulation of weapons and the capacities to wage and sustain regional wars. With further advances in warfare technologies, the potential for regional and civil conflicts to evolve into global ones has dramatically increased and has made the need for conflict resolution ever more pressing.

The end of the Second World War led to the decline of colonialism and the realignment of the world in the context of Cold War rivalries. While the Cold War exacerbated regional wars, it did not necessarily cause them. Regional wars typically grow out of local and regional grievances and conflicts. However, given the continued easy access to weapons, both small arms as well as weapons of mass destruction, regional wars increasingly have global implications. Failures to resolve these local conflicts before they evolve into regional wars can potentially have devastating effects. This reality makes regional and civil wars an international security concern more than ever before.

An insurgency is an armed rebellion against a constituted authority (for example, an authority recognised as such by the United Nations) when those taking part in the rebellion are not recognised as belligerents. An insurgency can be fought via counter-insurgency warfare, and may also be opposed by measures to protect the population, and by political and economic actions of various kinds aimed at undermining the insurgents' claims against the incumbent regime. The nature of insurgencies is an ambiguous concept.

Not all rebellions are insurgencies. There have been many cases of non-violent rebellions, using civil resistance, as in the People Power Revolution in the Philippines in the 1980s that ousted President Marcos and the Egyptian Revolution of 2011. Where a revolt takes the form of armed rebellion, it may not be viewed as an insurgency if a state of belligerency exists between one or more sovereign states and rebel forces. For example, during the American Civil War, the Confederate States of America was not recognised as a sovereign state, but it was recognised as a belligerent power, and thus Confederate warships were given the same rights as US warships in foreign ports.

When insurgency is used to describe a movement's unlawfulness by virtue of not being authorised by or in accordance with the law of the land, its use is neutral. However when it is used by a state or another authority under threat, 'insurgency' often also carries an implication that the rebels' cause is illegitimate, whereas those rising up will see the authority itself as being illegitimate. Criticisms of widely held ideas and actions about insurgency started to occur in works of the 1960s – they are still common in recent studies.

Asymmetric Warfare is war between belligerents whose relative military power differs significantly, or whose strategy or tactics differ significantly. Asymmetric Warfare can describe a conflict in which the resources of two belligerents differ in essence and in the struggle, interact and attempt to exploit each other's characteristic weaknesses. Such struggles often involve strategies and tactics of unconventional warfare, the weaker combatants attempting to use strategy to offset deficiencies in quantity or quality. Such strategies may not necessarily be militarised, and this is important in the context of Obstructive Marketing. This is in contrast to symmetric warfare, where two powers have similar military power and resources and rely on tactics that are similar overall, differing only in details and execution. The term is frequently used to describe what is also called 'guerrilla warfare', 'insurgency', 'terrorism', 'counterinsurgency' and 'counterterrorism', essentially violent conflict between a formal military and an informal, poorly equipped, but resilient opponent.

The law of war is a body of law concerning acceptable justifications to engage in war (*jus ad bellum*) and the limits to acceptable wartime conduct (*jus in bello* or international humanitarian law). The law of war is considered an aspect of public international law (the law of nations) and is distinguished from other bodies of law, such as the domestic law of a particular belligerent to a conflict, which may also provide legal limits to the conduct or justification of war. Amongst other issues, modern laws of war address declarations of war, acceptance of surrender and the treatment of prisoners of war; military necessity, along with distinction and proportionality; and the prohibition of certain weapons that may cause unnecessary suffering.

The Senior Workshop on International Rules Governing Military Operations (SWIRMO) of 10 October 2012 in Kuala Lumpur, Malaysia said the nature of combat and conflicts changes constantly and the aim of the workshop was to adapt the rules accordingly. The workshop cited the example of the rules on who can be legitimately targeted which were drawn up after World War Two and suggested:

> *Formed military forces, with uniforms squaring off against each other in interstate conflict; but, the vast majority of conflicts now are within states – non-international conflicts – and often opposition forces are not wearing uniforms (they are) fighting in urban areas, hiding among civilian populations and it makes it very difficult to apply those rules in these modern types of conflicts, the workshop said.*

These definitions will be argued by some scholars but that is not the main point. The main point is that over time the rules of war have changed. No longer are they formal competitions on foreign or national soil (Crecy, Bosworth Field) and so on or campaign armies (Alexander, Napoleon), total war where the resources of countries are melded to the fight (the First World War and the Second World War) and nor is there a Cold War. These have all been superseded by economic warfare – which is where Obstructive Marketing comes in – or the new fights between small stateless groups epitomised by Al Qaeda who practice Asymmetric Warfare on their own and foreign soil. The rules of war that developed in parallel to warfare, whether they be Christian, Islamic, Hague Convention or Geneva Convention related, are not recognised by stateless or illegitimate insurgencies and have become irrelevant in many areas of the world. Recent history has required some rapid re-thinking of military doctrine. This re-thinking is has been slow to come to terms with the new realities – but some examples follow.

In his classic *Britain in the Century of Total War*, Marwick (1968) describes war as it used to be known. He quotes Marx (*The Eastern Question*, 1897):

> *The redeeming feature of war is that it puts a nation to the test. As exposure to the atmosphere reduces all mummies to instant dissolution, so war passes extreme judgement on social systems that have outlived their vitality.*

He also predicated his book on the four aspects of total war he felt were important:

- profit and loss: destruction and disruption;

- test, dissolution and transformation;

- politics;

- military participation.

Marwick argued how total war was a positive force for political and social change within a national environment depending on the level of military participation and destruction and disruption involved.

Today the military doctrines are more removed from society in many ways than they were. Not everyone is involved. Certainly in the West there is a one or two stage removal of the largely professional armed forces from the rest of society. This distance has happened as a result of a number of different military doctrines. The first of these is the Revolution in Military Affairs (RMA).

There are three basic interpretations of the RMA (Metz and Kievit, 1995). The first focuses primarily upon changes in the nation-state and the role of an organised military in using force. This approach highlights the political, social and economic factors worldwide, which might require a completely different type of military and organisational structure to apply force in the future. This is important to the consideration of Obstructive Marketing. Authors such as Edwards (2000) (advocate of 'Battle Swarm' tactics), emphasise the decline of the nation-state, the nature of the emerging international order and the different types of forces needed in the near future as a consequence.

The second interpretation, and the more usual, highlights the evolution of weapons technology, IT, military organisation and military doctrine among advanced powers. This 'system of systems' perspective on the RMA has been ardently supported by Owens (2000), former Vice Chairman of the US Joint Chiefs of Staff, who identified three overlapping areas for force assets. These are:

- intelligence, surveillance and reconnaissance;

- command, control, communications and intelligence processing;

- precision force.

Advanced versions of RMA incorporate other sophisticated technologies, including unmanned aerial vehicles (UAVs), nanotechnology, robotics and biotechnology. Recently, the RMA debate focussed on 'network-centric warfare' which is a doctrine that aims to electronically connect all troops on the battlefield.

Finally, the third concept is that a 'true' RMA has not yet occurred or is unlikely to. Authors such as Kagan and Kagan (2000), point to the fact much of the technology and weapons systems ascribed to the contemporary RMA were in development long before 1991 and the Internet and IT boom.

Renewed interest was placed on RMA theory and practice after what many saw as a one-sided victory by the US in the 1991 Gulf War against Iraq. After the Kosovo War, where the US did not lose a single life, others suggested that war had become too sterile, creating an almost 'virtual war', see Der Derian (2001). Consequently, the US failure to capture Osama bin Laden (until 2011) and the Iraqi insurgency led some to question RMA's build-up as a military panacea. US foes may increasingly resort to Asymmetric Warfare to counter RMA.

RMA assumes that civilian organisations will be targeted and expects them to respond by an undetermined 'Hardening'.

As defined by the United States Military Joint Forces Command (USJFCOM) (2008), effects-based operations are:

> *A process for obtaining a desired strategic outcome or effect on the enemy through the synergistic and cumulative application of the full range of military and nonmilitary capabilities at all levels of conflict.*

The intent and desired outcome of an effects-based approach is to employ forces that paralyse the enemy forces and minimise its ability to engage friendly forces in close combat. Effects-based operations specifically target aspects of the civilian infrastructure – Obstructive Marketing in the military sense. Therefore civilian organisations need to be protected to withstand such attacks.

Staten (1997) stated that it was of great concern that any number of what were previously considered essentially stable countries were experiencing religious, ethnic and other internal conflicts with increasing numbers of separatist movements trying to carve up larger countries into smaller and more tightly focussed ethnic areas. Some of these conflicts are ancient and have been the cause of fighting for hundreds of years. Others are more recent and the result of demographic shifts, changing political regimes or religious/ ideological shifts. Faltering economic circumstances in several parts of South West Asia, the Far-East, Africa and South America added to a combustible mix certain to fuel future conflicts in a number of parts of the globe for the foreseeable future.

Rathmell et al. (1997) forecast that by the advent of the twenty-first century, not only would it be likely that many of the conflicts facing the US and her allies would be of an asymmetrical and devolving nature, but also likely that the threats would come from diverse and differing vectors. He predicted that conventional terrorism and low-intensity conflict would be accompanied or compounded by computer/infrastructure attacks that would cause damage to vital commercial, military, and government information and confront communications systems. It is the case that the US gains tremendous advantages from its advanced information and battlefield management systems, but by virtue of this becomes increasingly vulnerable to cyber-attacks from adversaries. Infosecurity (2012) carried a story regarding Iran's view that it had to develop a cyber-army.

Gotowicki (1997), Staten (1997) and Rathwell (1997) anticipated efforts to cause widespread fear by computer-generated attacks on electrical, water, banking, government information, emergency response systems and other vital infrastructures, while simultaneously suffering terrorist tactics involving multiple conventional explosives and/or chemical/biological/nuclear devices. Even a country as large and sophisticated as the US could suffer greatly at the hands of an educated, equipped and committed group of fewer than 50 people.

> *At the present time, such an attack could realistically be expected to cause an effect vastly disproportionate to the resources expended to undertake it. (Staten, 1997, p1)*

These are not only prescient comments in the light of the later attacks on the World Trade Centre on 11 September 2001 but position organisations as targets.

Asymmetric Warfare is a military counterpart to Obstructive Marketing, and the latter is a subset of the former. The latter may even be better called Asymmetric Obstructive Marketing (a new term, original to this book), to ally it more closely to its military counterpart. In the hands of terrorists and organised crime there is often no distinction between military and economic (see below) targets. The response of organisations to withstand such attacks will become increasingly necessary as these techniques become a means of a smaller force attacking a bigger one. The Internet is a key target and conduit for both.

The intent and desired outcome of an effects-based approach is to employ forces that paralyse the enemy forces and minimise its ability to engage friendly forces in close combat. Effects-based operations specifically target aspects of the civilian infrastructure. Therefore civilian organisations need to respond to withstand such attacks. Jobbagy (2003) has written a succinct literature survey on effects-based operations.

The rules of war change over time and there is a change in the rules of war occurring now. These changes in the rules of war bring commercial organisations, the Internet and critical infrastructures much more to the fore. As a consequence there is a need for a response from a range of organisations that may not have had to think in such terms before. To demonstrate how far the 'Rules of War' have changed it is only necessary to recap the Hague Convention, see below, on the one hand and think of the headlines of attacks, as mentioned in Chapter 1, kidnaps, terrorist attacks of various kinds, cyber-warfare, attacks on other critical infrastructures to understand how far things have moved over the latter parts of the twentieth century and the first part of the twenty-first century.

The following are the traditional Hague Convention Regulations respecting the laws and customs of war on land. This version is taken by permission from and hereby acknowledges the Avalon Project at Yale University (Yale, 2013). Shown are those sections that, from a reading of *The Economist* over the last year or so, have not applied to a variety of recent conflicts.

CHAPTER I
The qualifications of belligerents

Article 1. The laws, rights, and duties of war apply not only to armies, but also to militia and volunteer corps fulfilling the following conditions:

1. To be commanded by a person responsible for his subordinates;
2. To have a fixed distinctive emblem recognizable at a distance;
3. To carry arms openly; and
4. To conduct their operations in accordance with the laws and customs of war.

In countries where militia or volunteer corps constitute the army, or form part of it, they are included under the denomination 'army.'

Article 2. The inhabitants of a territory which has not been occupied, who, on the approach of the enemy, spontaneously take up arms to resist the invading troops without having had time to organize themselves in accordance with Article 1, shall be regarded as belligerents if they carry arms openly and if they respect the laws and customs of war.

Article 3. The armed forces of the belligerent parties may consist of combatants and non-combatants. In the case of capture by the enemy, both have a right to be treated as prisoners of war.

CHAPTER II
Prisoners of war

Article 4. Prisoners of war are in the power of the hostile Government, but not of the individuals or corps who capture them. They must be humanely treated. All their personal belongings, except arms, horses, and military papers, remain their property.

Article 5. Prisoners of war may be interned in a town, fortress, camp, or other place, and bound not to go beyond certain fixed limits; but they cannot be confined except as in indispensable measure of safety and only while the circumstances which necessitate the measure continue to exist.

Article 6. The State may utilize the labour of prisoners of war according to their rank and aptitude, officers excepted. The tasks shall not be excessive and shall have no connection with the operations of the war. Prisoners may be authorized to work for the public service, for private persons, or on their own account. Work done for the State is paid for at the rates in force for work of a similar kind done by soldiers of the national army, or, if there are none in force, at a rate according to the work executed. When the work is for other branches of the public service or for private persons the conditions are settled in agreement with the military authorities. The wages of the prisoners shall go towards improving their position, and the balance shall be paid them on their release, after deducting the cost of their maintenance.

Article 7. The Government into whose hands prisoners of war have fallen is charged with their maintenance. In the absence of a special agreement between the belligerents, prisoners of war shall be treated as regards board, lodging, and clothing on the same footing as the troops of the Government who captured them.

Article 8. Prisoners of war shall be subject to the laws, regulations, and orders in force in the army of the State in whose power they are. Any act of insubordination justifies the adoption towards them of such measures of severity as may be considered necessary. Escaped prisoners who are retaken before being able to rejoin their own army or before leaving the territory occupied by the army which captured them are liable to disciplinary punishment. Prisoners who, after succeeding in escaping, are again taken prisoners, are not liable to any punishment on account of the previous flight.

Article 9. Every prisoner of war is bound to give, if he is questioned on the subject, his true name and rank, and if he infringes this rule, he is liable to have the advantages given to prisoners of his class curtailed.

Article 10. Prisoners of war may be set at liberty on parole if the laws of their country allow, and, in such cases, they are bound, on their personal honour, scrupulously to fulfil, both towards their own Government and the Government by whom they were made prisoners, the engagements they have contracted. In such cases their own Government is bound neither to require of nor accept from them any service incompatible with the parole given.

Article 11. A prisoner of war cannot be compelled to accept his liberty on parole; similarly the hostile Government is not obliged to accede to the request of the prisoner to be set at liberty on parole.

Article 12. Prisoners of war liberated on parole and recaptured bearing arms against the Government to whom they had pledged their honour, or against the allies of that Government, forfeit their right to be treated as prisoners of war, and can be brought before the courts.

Article 13. Individuals who follow an army without directly belonging to it, such as newspaper correspondents and reporters, sutlers and contractors, who fall into the enemy's hands and whom the latter thinks expedient to detain, are entitled to be treated as prisoners of war, provided they are in possession of a certificate from the military authorities of the army which they were accompanying.

Article 14. An inquiry office for prisoners of war is instituted on the commencement of hostilities in each of the belligerent States, and, when necessary, in neutral countries which have received belligerents in their territory. It is the function of this office to reply to all inquiries about the prisoners. It receives from the various services concerned full information respecting internments arid transfers, releases on parole, exchanges, escapes, admissions into hospital, deaths, as well as other information necessary to enable it to make out and keep up to date an individual return for each prisoner of war. The office must state in this return the regimental number, name and surname, age, place of origin, rank, unit, wounds, date and place of capture, internment, wounding, and death, as well as any observations of a special character. The individual return shall be sent to the Government of the other belligerent after the conclusion of peace. It is likewise the function of the inquiry office to receive and collect all objects of personal use, valuables, letters, etc., found on the field of battle or left by prisoners who have been released on parole, or exchanged, or who have escaped, or died in hospitals or ambulances, and to forward them to those concerned.

Article 15. Relief societies for prisoners of war, which are properly constituted in accordance with the laws of their country and with the object of serving as the channel for charitable effort shall receive from the belligerents, for themselves and their duly accredited agents every facility for the efficient performance of their humane task within the bounds imposed by military necessities and administrative regulations. Agents of these societies may be admitted to the places of internment for the purpose of distributing relief, as also to the halting places of repatriated prisoners, if furnished with a personal permit by the military authorities, and on giving an undertaking in writing to comply with all measures of order and police which the latter may issue.

Article 16. Inquiry offices enjoy the privilege of free postage. Letters, money orders, and valuables, as well as parcels by post, intended for prisoners of war, or dispatched by them, shall be exempt from all postal duties in the countries of origin and destination, as well as in the countries they pass through.

Presents and relief in kind for prisoners of war shall be admitted free of all import or other duties, as well as of payments for carriage by the State railways.

Article 17. Officers taken prisoners shall receive the same rate of pay as officers of corresponding rank in the country where they are detained, the amount to be ultimately refunded by their own Government.

Article 18. Prisoners of war shall enjoy complete liberty in the exercise of their religion, including attendance at the services of whatever church they may belong to, on the sole condition that they comply with the measures of order and police issued by the military authorities.

Article 19. The wills of prisoners of war are received or drawn up in the same way as for soldiers of the national army. The same rules shall be observed regarding death certificates as well as for the burial of prisoners of war, due regard being paid to their grade and rank.

Article 20. After the conclusion of peace, the repatriation of prisoners of war shall be carried out as quickly as possible.

CHAPTER III
The sick and wounded

Article 21. The obligations of belligerents with regard to the sick and wounded are governed by the Geneva Convention.

SECTION II   HOSTILITIES

CHAPTER I
Means of injuring the enemy, sieges, and bombardments

Article 22. The right of belligerents to adopt means of injuring the enemy is not unlimited.

Article 23. In addition to the prohibitions provided by special Conventions, it is especially forbidden:

a. To employ poison or poisoned weapons;
b. To kill or wound treacherously individuals belonging to the hostile nation or army;
c. To kill or wound an enemy who, having laid down his arms, or having no longer means of defence, has surrendered at discretion;
d. To declare that no quarter will be given;
e. To employ arms, projectiles, or material calculated to cause unnecessary suffering;
f. To make improper use of a flag of truce, of the national flag or of the military insignia and uniform of the enemy, as well as the distinctive badges of the Geneva Convention;
g. To destroy or seize the enemy's property, unless such destruction or seizure be imperatively demanded by the necessities of war;
h. To declare abolished, suspended, or inadmissible in a court of law the rights and actions of the nationals of the hostile party. A belligerent is likewise forbidden to compel the nationals of the hostile party to take part in the operations of war directed against their own country, even if they were in the belligerent's service before the commencement of the war.

Article 24. Ruses of war and the employment of measures necessary for obtaining information about the enemy and the country are considered permissible.

Article 25. The attack or bombardment, by whatever means, of towns, villages, dwellings, or buildings which are undefended is prohibited.

Article 26. The officer in command of an attacking force must, before commencing a bombardment, except in cases of assault, do all in his power to warn the authorities.

Article 27. In sieges and bombardments all necessary steps must be taken to spare, as far as possible, buildings dedicated to religion, art, science, or charitable purposes, historic monuments, hospitals, and places where the sick and wounded are collected, provided they are not being used at the time for military purposes. It is the duty of the besieged to indicate the presence of such buildings or places by distinctive and visible signs, which shall be notified to the enemy beforehand.

Article 28. The pillage of a town or place, even when taken by assault, is prohibited.

CHAPTER II
Spies

Article 29. A person can only be considered a spy when, acting clandestinely or on false pretences, he obtains or endeavours to obtain information in the zone of operations of a belligerent, with the intention of communicating it to the hostile party. Thus, soldiers not wearing a disguise who have penetrated into the zone of operations of the hostile army, for the purpose of obtaining information, are not considered spies. Similarly, the following are not considered spies: Soldiers and civilians, carrying out their mission openly, entrusted with the delivery of despatches intended either for their own army or for the enemy's army. To this class belong likewise persons sent in balloons for the purpose of carrying despatches and, generally, of maintaining communications between the different parts of an army or a territory.

Article 30. A spy taken in the act shall not be punished without previous trial.

Article 31. A spy who, after rejoining the army to which he belongs, is subsequently captured by the enemy, is treated as a prisoner of war, and incurs no responsibility for his previous acts of espionage.

CHAPTER III
Flags of truce

Article 32. A person is regarded as a parlementaire who has been authorized by one of the belligerents to enter into communication with the other, and who advances bearing a white flag. He has a right to inviolability, as well as the trumpeter, bugler or drummer, the flag-bearer and interpreter who may accompany him.

Article 33. The commander to whom a parlementaire is sent is not in all cases obliged to receive him.

He may take all the necessary steps to prevent the parlementaire taking advantage of his mission to obtain information.

In case of abuse, he has the right to detain the parlementaire temporarily.

Article 34. The parlementaire loses his rights of inviolability if it is proved in a clear and incontestable manner that he has taken advantage of his privileged position to provoke or commit an act of treason.

CHAPTER IV
Capitulations

Article 35. Capitulations agreed upon between the Contracting Parties must take into account the rules of military honour. Once settled, they must be scrupulously observed by both parties.

CHAPTER V
Armistices

Article 36. An armistice suspends military operations by mutual agreement between the belligerent parties. If its duration is not defined, the belligerent parties may resume operations at any time, provided always that the enemy is warned within the time agreed upon, in accordance with the terms of the armistice.

Article 37. An armistice may be general or local. The first suspends the military operations of the belligerent States everywhere; the second only between certain fractions of the belligerent armies and within a fixed radius.

Article 38. An armistice must be notified officially and in good time to the competent authorities and to the troops. Hostilities are suspended immediately after the notification, or on the date fixed.

Article 39. It rests with the Contracting Parties to settle, in the terms of the armistice, what communications may be held in the theatre of war with the inhabitants and between the inhabitants of one belligerent State and those of the other.

Article 40. Any serious violation of the armistice by one of the parties gives the other party the right of denouncing it, and even, in cases of urgency, of recommencing hostilities immediately.

Article 41. A violation of the terms of the armistice by private persons acting on their own initiative only entitles the injured party to demand the punishment of the offenders or, if necessary, compensation for the losses sustained.

SECTION III   MILITARY AUTHORITY OVER THE TERRITORY OF THE HOSTILE STATE

Article 42. Territory is considered occupied when it is actually placed under the authority of the hostile army. The occupation extends only to the territory where such authority has been established and can be exercised.

Article 43. The authority of the legitimate power having in fact passed into the hands of the occupant, the latter shall take all the measures in his power to restore, and ensure, as far as possible, public order and safety, while respecting, unless absolutely prevented, the laws in force in the country.

Article 44. A belligerent is forbidden to force the inhabitants of territory occupied by it to furnish information about the army of the other belligerent, or about its means of defence.

Article 45. It is forbidden to compel the inhabitants of occupied territory to swear allegiance to the hostile Power.

Article 46. Family honour and rights, the lives of persons, and private property, as well as religious convictions and practice, must be respected.

Private property cannot be confiscated.

Article 47. Pillage is formally forbidden.

Article 48. If, in the territory occupied, the occupant collects the taxes, dues, and tolls imposed for the benefit of the State, he shall do so, as far as is possible, in accordance with the rules of assessment and incidence in force, and shall in consequence be bound to defray the expenses of the administration of the occupied territory to the same extent as the legitimate Government was so bound.

Article 49. If, in addition to the taxes mentioned in the above article, the occupant levies other money contributions in the occupied territory, this shall only be for the needs of the army or of the administration of the territory in question.

Article 50. No general penalty, pecuniary or otherwise, shall be inflicted upon the population on account of the acts of individuals for which they cannot be regarded as jointly and severally responsible.

Article 51. No contribution shall be collected except under a written order, and on the responsibility of a commander-in-chief. The collection of the said contribution shall only be effected as far as possible in accordance with the rules of assessment and incidence of the taxes in force. For every contribution a receipt shall be given to the contributors.

Article 52. Requisitions in kind and services shall not be demanded from municipalities or inhabitants except for the needs of the army of occupation. They shall be in proportion to the resources of the country, and of such a nature as not to involve the inhabitants in the obligation of taking part in military operations against their own country. Such requisitions and services shall only be demanded on the authority of the commander in the locality occupied. Contributions in kind shall as far is possible be paid for in cash; if not, a receipt shall be given and the payment of the amount due shall be made as soon as possible.

Article 53. An army of occupation can only take possession of cash, funds, and realizable securities which are strictly the property of the State, depots of arms, means of transport, stores and supplies, and, generally, all movable property belonging to the State which may be used for military operations. All appliances, whether on land, at sea, or in the air, adapted for the transmission of news, or for the transport of persons or things, exclusive of cases governed by naval law, depots of arms, and, generally, all kinds of munitions of war, may be seized, even if they belong to private individuals, but must be restored and compensation fixed when peace is made.

Article 54. Submarine cables connecting an occupied territory with a neutral territory shall not be seized or destroyed except in the case of absolute necessity. They must likewise be restored and compensation fixed when peace is made.

Article 55. The occupying State shall be regarded only as administrator and usufructuary of public buildings, real estate, forests, and agricultural estates belonging to the hostile State, and situated in the occupied country. It must safeguard the capital of these properties, and administer them in accordance with the rules of usufruct.

Article 56. The property of municipalities, that of institutions dedicated to religion, charity and education, the arts and sciences, even when State property, shall be treated as private property. All seizure of, destruction or wilful damage done to institutions of this character, historic monuments, works of art and science, is forbidden, and should be made the subject of legal proceedings.

Why has room been taken to reproduce this? The answer is simple: we live in such a sound-bite dominated world that the detail of this convention is often overlooked by the news organisations reporting on war. Their reporters do not bother to understand this detail so they become blasé about the conventions. They mention them, but because they have not bothered to read them they do not understand the depth to which they are being betrayed. This enables regimes to, literally, get away with murder in front of the world's news organisations. Every single article of this Hague Convention has been broken over the last year or so in conflict around the world. Civilisation has not moved forward. Although it is obviously naïve to think that conflict will necessarily be played either fairly or within the rules of the game the point is that in an Asymmetric contest that involves a conflict between either states or the stateless international law is currently and repeatedly irrelevant. Additionally, this fact is not properly reported.

This is important to organisations, not just of itself, but because international trade is also governed by a set of rules too. These are, for example, International Commerce Terms (Incoterms). These permitted trade, admittedly on Western terms, to flourish within a set of rules. However, these rules are not agreed, either, by all today. On top of this comes parallel banking systems and new approaches to international trade from China, Russia and India – not necessarily aligned to Western or each other's rules. The result is potential chaos in military and economic terms. It is important to understand this.

Chace (2011) comments as follows:

> With a clear definition the intellectual process can begin to logically and methodically incorporate asymmetric warfare into modern war fighting concepts, doctrine, and operational use. Consider the possibility that a 'clear definition' not only impedes, but also terminates the intellectual process and that 'logically and methodically' incorporating asymmetric warfare is a dangerous oxymoron. Analysts are encouraged to 'think like the enemy' in order to predict the next enemy move. Although they study our manuals and periodicals, the enemy does not use definitions or acronyms; they use imagination driven by intelligence, understanding, instinct, and deceit. To 'define' asymmetric warfare sends the wrong symbolism to an enemy that feeds off symbolism and an innate ability to exploit weakness in culture and character. Doing so would mean we have already lost. Proposing a common understanding while well intentioned, the reasons supporting a definition of asymmetric warfare apply a symmetric solution to, literally, an asymmetric problem. Without a pure definition, would use of the term run rampant, as many suggest? Maybe. But is there harm in that, or just discomfort? In his foreword to Stephen Blank's 2001 article, 'Rethinking Asymmetric Threats,' Douglas Lovelace, director of the Strategic Studies Institute, writes, 'A correct assessment of the nature of the threat environment is essential to any sound defence doctrine for the U.S. Army and the military as a whole.'

A basic militaristic understanding of Asymmetric Warfare would indeed lessen confusion and promote flexible doctrine – but not, as illustrated by *Miller vs. California*, a definition. Recognising that definitions and acronyms can sometimes only narrow scope, not open it, we must understand the laws of linguistic relativity and cognitive anthropology. Therefore, any basic understanding of Asymmetric Warfare must find harmony between explaining what is already known through instinctive judgment, or 'feeling', and tearing down the phrase so much that its meaning is lost. Asymmetric Warfare, therefore, can be understood through three basic tenets: a warfighting methodology that can be applied throughout the full spectrum of operations, aspects of national power, or actions by hostile actors; no rules – it is constrained only by the imagination; targets any real or perceived vulnerability in an adversary's holistic environment in order to gain an advantage. Asymmetric Warfare is not a new form or category of war, but a methodology applicable throughout full-spectrum operations and one of many options available to a commander charged with planning and executing a campaign.

Its philosophy is also mirrored in the political, economic and scientific communities, which often directly and indirectly affect defence strategy and combat operations. A 1998 US National Defence University study defined Asymmetric Warfare as 'a version of not "fighting fair"', a notion that carries a large ethnocentric burden avoided by the second tenet. Regardless of belief systems or behaviour, Asymmetric Warfare is constrained only by the imagination and, consequently, falls outside the realm of any rules of war (for example, The Hague or Geneva Conventions – see above for recent transgressions) or society.

This does not mean that the US military's use of Asymmetric Warfare falls outside the laws of war that the US and many others throughout the world subscribe to, but merely that the tactics and strategies of others may *not*, as evidenced by countless vignettes from Iraq, Afghanistan, Somalia, the Philippines and beyond. The absence of rules inherent in Asymmetric Warfare can also apply to cultural taboos. For instance, a pious Muslim male may be permitted to stray from very strict religious and cultural practices in the name of Jihad. Shaving his beard, failing to preach, and even undergoing plastic surgery are just a few examples.

Asymmetric Warfare targets any real or perceived vulnerability in order to gain an advantage, often ideally done without an adversary's awareness. Blank (2004) writes, 'The idea of avoiding enemy strengths while probing for their weaknesses and maximizing our own advantages is hardly revolutionary', an idea that Metz and Johnson (2001) acknowledge as a 'core logic' of all competitive endeavours, downplaying the need for a specified asymmetric branding of threat-based warfare.

Asymmetric Warfare is surgical in its focus on enemy vulnerabilities – it exists where the sole purpose of any action is to create and exploit a real or perceived weakness. While it goes without saying that any adversary prefers to avoid enemy strengths while probing for weaknesses and maximising advantages, no other brand of warfare targets vulnerabilities with such precision, focus and purpose. Rather than oppose doctrine, this argument reveals that previous efforts to provide a doctrinal definition of Asymmetric Warfare have failed not only to respect the nature of asymmetry and independent rational cognisance, but also to adhere to several principles doctrine must provide.

Doctrine must facilitate flexibility, not promote intransigence. Doctrine must embrace a philosophy of initiative and creative thinking to deal with an adaptive, cunning and typically asymmetric enemy, not create tunnel vision. Doctrine must recognise the elements of uncertainty and the unexpected, not fight them. Doctrine cannot predict the nature and form of asymmetric conflicts and enemies, but it can forecast the necessary traits and body of conceptual knowledge necessary to cope with and understand a chaotic Asymmetric Warfare environment. *Doctrine* has become synonymous with *definition* and often serves as a glossary for *what to think* rather than a philosophy for *how to think*, resulting in closed-minded approaches to abstract and complex situations.

The education process that addresses the true problem and will eventually alter this mentality begins with Outcomes-based Training and Education (OBTE) and the grooming of the intangible attributes that will propagate among the 'blink' generation and ultimately change the culture of the military. To those who believe that a definition impedes not only our intellectual process but also our ability to adapt at the same level of 'the enemy does not use definitions or acronyms; they use imagination driven by intelligence, understanding, instinct, and deceit' (Chace, 2011).

In defining Asymmetric Warfare, our enemies defy any attempt to force the concept of Asymmetric Warfare into a cookie-cutter template regimentally inserted into a catalogue of associated situations. Trying to place Asymmetric Warfare into a template reinforces a weak and unsound approach to combating the overarching methodology of rogue state and non-state terrorists, providing our enemies with the symbolism and reaffirmation that the US military is as inflexible, non-adaptive and incapable of independent thought as ever before.

The three tenets identified here illustrate the schema that enable instantaneous recognition of asymmetry, or 'asymmetric-ness' in warfare – something we do intrinsically and without the need of a definition. Asymmetric Warfare can be violent or non-violent, material or psychological, technological or primitive, criminal or judicial. It is 'black' warfare – unknown and limitless – and will continue to transform. To ensure relevance, we must do likewise. The Armed Forces need fewer chess players and more poker players.

As noted in Chapter 2 the links between terrorism, organised crime and failed states are well made.

In the military domain the action of effects-based operations (a term officially discontinued in the US military from mid-August 2008, but still in common usage) has been partly compromised by a reactive asymmetric approach to war-fighting, an asymmetric war. A new way of dealing with this is to find the Asymmetric Military Balance, a new term. This will be discussed further.

The importance of this to organisations is that any asymmetric war necessarily involves organisations. Organisations therefore become part of the Asymmetric Military Balance and thus have to respond to deal with the consequences of such a context. The term Asymmetric Military Balance sounds like an oxymoron. It is not. It is a way of describing the state of affairs that needs to prevail in order that the export of democracy and globalisation can flourish within a new military reality.

The nature and practice of asymmetry is as old as warfare itself (Metz and Jonsson, 2001). What is perhaps new for the West is that the rules that have governed warfare over the centuries are no longer as firm, or as Western focussed, as they were. The expectation has been that wars get fought by armed forces. The inclusion of the civil community and the organisations of different 'groups' is thought to be new, but is not. Napoleon (Russian campaign), Buller (Boer War), Westmorland (Vietnam), Brezhnev (Afghanistan), and latterly the campaigns in the Gulf and Afghanistan all used Asymmetric Warfare features (Dixon and Dixon, 2011). The asymmetric model has further developed through the use of the Internet and mobile phone as means of communication, a weapon and a target.

This is the key to understanding the nature of so many of today's threats. What appears best, most effective and most efficient is often not the case for in strategy, contends Luttwak (1987), actual or possible conflict between thinking human beings – whether it is played out in political, economic, social, technological or military contexts – is dominated by a paradoxical logic based on the coming together and even the reversal of opposites. This is the essence of asymmetry. An example would be Mogadishu in October 2003, another current piracy in many oceans of the world.

In these sorts of terms an Asymmetric Military Balance is not an oxymoron. Rather than just use effects-based operations to attempt to induce the desired effects in an enemy's society or infrastructure it is important to understand that from the enemy's point of view an Asymmetric approach may well neutralise any effects-based strategy. As a consequence there needs to be a re-balancing of effort on behalf of the West between effects-based operations and the asymmetric approach required to defeat an enemy of a completely different political, economic, social, technical and military persuasion. This will require both Asymmetric Warfare and effects-based operations. A failure in Iraq was not to plan for the hearts and minds or reconstruction properly. This adds a third factor to the balance. This third factor also brings centre stage those equipped to deal with disaster and development; to this can be added the impact of globalisation and its anti-thesis Obstructive Marketing.

Modern Western military strategy is still based on rules of engagement, treaties, values and equipment that were relevant to the first half of the twentieth century, if not earlier. The major battle ground of the first half of the twenty-first century is largely a virtual battleground. It is also increasingly between states and the stateless, rather than between states. It is between democracy and Fundamentalism, not between democracy and dictatorship. The military doctrine required is akin to a see-saw, not too much force to launch the other side off the see-saw ('Asymmetric See-Saw Theory', a new term and original to this book), but enough of a combination of both effects-based operations, appropriate asymmetric techniques and hearts and minds/reconstruction to tip the balance in favour of the North and West, while being ready to re-establish equilibrium in any event. Globalisation and Obstructive Marketing can also, as noted, be added to the mix. Figure 6.1 gives an idea of how an Asymmetric Military Balance is effected, and the see-saw aspect of the theory is clear.

Organisations, risk doctrine, information infrastructure and value systems need to be structured to cope with the widening spectrum of threats of those who seek to undermine organisational commercial capabilities, democratic freedoms and cultural values.

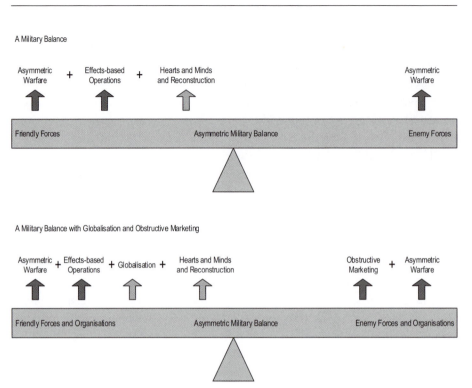

Figure 6.1   The Asymmetric Military Balance
Source: Maitland P. Hyslop, 2013, © Northumbria University.

The more frequent occurrence of what this book has so far called Obstructive Marketing could be further refined into, as noted earlier, Asymmetric Obstructive Marketing, a new term original to this book, as a consequence of the obvious and increasing use of organisations and commerce in warfare. This is a subject for further research.

The exploration of a number of themes in both Chapter 2 and this chapter has built a picture of a different world. This new world is characterised by a number of features. The certainty that existed during the Cold War has not been replaced by the hegemony of a single world superpower but has been replaced by uncertainty combined with an evolving group of developing nations and power foci all of whom have slightly different interests. Free market capitalism, the supposed dominant economic philosophy, is not necessarily dominant as Brazil, China, India, Russia, Korea and South Africa demonstrate to a greater or lesser degree.

Clausewitz (1962) commented that war is the extension of politics (policy) by other means. War has become much more complex. Many commentators have noted the need for a government–organisation partnership in order to be properly secure, including the need for a new means of communicating. This is the new security and symbology environment. This at a time when the nation-state is itself under question, when national risk registers miss key threats, when organisations are clearly disconnected from both the new reality and their own governments. This has been further exacerbated by the rise of Asymmetric Warfare, Obstructive Marketing, cyber and information warfare and the ability of organised crime to take advantage of a more fractured physical and virtual world.

Since 2007 the economic crisis has resulted in a rebalancing of the world's economies in favour of the developing countries. MBA courses meantime have not addressed organisational needs to meet this new environment, rather they are perpetuating an older model dominated by the needs of the 'Big 4' consultancy firms.

Socially, there is not only uncertainty about the nation-state but, as noted by Hyslop (2010), increasing challengers to the existing social status quo. Facebook in 2012 would be the third largest country in the world by population.

There is no hard technology infrastructure in Africa, most people are poor but most also have access to a mobile phone. The Arab Spring, the UK riots, the African revolutions were managed by social media and the mobile phone and in part driven by another Black Swan, food shortages. Socially, too, models are changing.

Technology is now dominated by the digital and data age. The need is neither for IT nor for managed data but to ensure that information is assured, intellectual property protected and that the rights of individuals and organisations have some integrity. This is extraordinarily difficult to achieve in a population where only a small proportion fully understand the implications of this information age, let alone are able to act on it. IBM (2012) note that only 16 per cent of CEOs fully use the digital tools available to them.

Environmentally the world has reached a point where if everyone consumed at a European level, three earths would be needed for the resources required, five if it was at US levels (World Population Balance, 2012). The pressure on resources from the Chinese alone is distorting the world yet again. There are few fish left in the sea (Mainelli and Harris, 2011).

Legally, there is the continuing attempt by the US to extend the territorial reach of its laws, the lack of law on the Internet, and the dismissal of laws other than religious ones by fanatical Islamicists amongst others.

In this milieu it is suggested by this book that organisations need to take a different look at the way they manage themselves in order to be operationally successful. The hypothesis is that they need new models of risk, dependency, staff, crisis and general management in order to be successful and that most of the existing models they use are reactive. This, it is suggested, has been demonstrated by both this chapter and Chapter 2. It is likely, given the breadth of some of the issues discussed and uncovered, that the changes sought by this book are not enough, particularly in regard to information assurance. How things link together is represented by the following tables, all of which demonstrate a series of common themes from this book.

In a general sense the economic case and the global drivers prevalent over the last 20 years or so are likely to be modified by recent events. Table 6.1 summarises the impact of global events on the economy from the different perspectives of 1997 and 2007.

Table 6.1   Impact of recent global events on the economy

Key Global Driver (1997)	Likely Impact Of Recent Events (2007)
Common customer needs	More differentiation
Global customers	Regional markets re-emerge
Global channels	Regional channels
Transferable marketing	More differentiation
Global scale economies	Regional economies (except china)
Steep experience curves	More measured approaches
Low transportation costs	Higher transportation costs
Difference in in-country costs	Continues – but slower
High product development costs	Higher product development costs
Need for technology transfer	Technology transfer less popular
Open trade policies	Protectionism re-emerges
Open technical standards	Continues – but slower
Open marketing regulations	Protectionism
High exports and imports	Less imports
Interdependence	More Independence
Globalised competitors	Regional competitors
Transferable competitive advantage	Held competitive advantage

Note: After Yip, 1997 and Hyslop, 2009b.

In terms of the globalising company their ambitions, as noted elsewhere, can be challenged by an Obstructive Marketing group. This challenge is summarised in Table 6.2.

Table 6.2   The globalising company and the Obstructive Marketing group

Globalising Company	Obstructive Marketing Group
Believe they are right	Believe they are right
Have lots to lose	Have lots to lose
Have money	Have some money
Have faith	Have faith
Geographically concentrated	Geographically dispersed (many, everywhere)
Perceived as strong, arrogant	Perceived as weak
Used to dominating	Used to serving
Hi-technology dependent	Technology independent, parasitic
Independent of family	Family dependent
Suffers from organised crime	Suffer from casual crime
Tends to be independent of groups	Tends to group cohesion
Lowering education – tasks carried out independently for example: checkouts in supermarkets	Rising education – multi-tasked and adaptable
'own' resources	'own' fewer resources
Use lots of resources	Use fewer resources
Believe in capitalism	Believe in different things
Has massive economic power	Has limited economic power
Visible	Not easily visible
Operate to short-term goals driven by quarterly results and shareholders	Operate to long-term goals, or have no goals

The approaches of the globalising company and Obstructive Marketing group can find an equivalent in a table, Table 6.3, looking at the Western Alliance and Al Qaeda: a classic Asymmetric contest.

The changing environment, the challenges to organisations and the asymmetric challenge offered by Al Qaeda have similar roots. The individual skills, the organisational values and the type of organisation that will be effective in the future have many similarities. To counter the challenges and develop the individual and the organisation a new response is required.

Table 6.3   The Western Alliance and Al Qaeda

Western/Northern Alliance	An Al Qaeda Type Alliance
Believe they are right	Believe they are right
Have lots to lose	Have not much to lose
Have money	Have less money
Have little faith	Have lots of faith
Geographically concentrated	Geographically dispersed
Perceived as strong, arrogant	Perceived as weak
Not used to fighting	Used to fighting
Hi-technology dependent	Technology independent, parasitic
Family in decay	Family strong
High crime	Low crime
Weak group cohesion	Strong group cohesion
Lowering education	Rising or no education
'Own' resources, especially food and water	'Own' fewer resources, especially food and water
Use lots of resources	Use fewer resources
Believe in capitalism	Believe in God
Has massive conventional military power	Has limited conventional military power
Does not use terrorism	Does use terrorism
Visible	Not easily visible
Timing: Operate to short-term goals driven by political considerations	Timing: Operate to long-term goals driven by a sense of history

It has also become clear that some organisations need to respond more than others. Large and geographically spread organisations tend to suffer more from Obstructive Marketing which is, again as noted, a good proxy for those likely to need some sort of co-ordinated response. This said the world has changed and few organisations are untouched by global forces. Therefore, all organisations, it is contended, need to be able to respond to some extent.

7

The Effect of the Capital Markets and Sovereign Wealth Funds

This chapter owes much to Millman (1995) who not only predicted the 2007/2008 events but charted their development back to the 1980s. Today the problems of the financial markets have not gone away as the ratio of world GDP to world credit to world derivatives is at least 1:3:6. With a notional derivative market eighteen times bigger than world GDP it is unlikely that the global financial problem has gone away.

Stock market prices, these days, react to a company's financial risks, and when firms act to reduce the risk, their cost of capital goes down and their stock prices should improve. In short a firm's stock price should not be at the whim of currency rates, market trends, interest changes and fluctuating commodity prices. The implications for the field of risk management and for the further development of financial science are strong. Investors now expect corporations to do something about the risks they face. Companies that do manage the financial risk they face are rewarded with better stock prices. Companies that do not manage their financial risk can expect to pay more for capital.

Corporate executives now have the means to control their financial environment. They can negotiate a financial contract that will lock in prices they pay for raw materials, interest rates and the value of their international revenues, and can even protect themselves against a wide range of taxes by moving money around the world smoothly and secretly. They can also take massive financial risks that can, in a matter of days, destroy their companies. One phone call to a banker can accomplish all this. Whether they are using financial markets to hedge a business risk or to take a speculative chance, they are casting a vote that helps to determine the direction of currency exchanges and interest rates throughout the world. By the funds they provide to bankers and investment managers, they determine what countries money will flow into and what countries it will flow out of.

When corporate managers stick to hedging risks that immediately affect their own business, risks that they know and whose effects they fully understand, the outcome is predictable – they stabilise their business and investors are likely to reward them. However, when a corporate executive becomes convinced that they understand the direction in which markets are moving well enough to predict the future, and decide to bet their shareholders' capital and their employee's jobs on their view of the markets, they step onto uncertain ground.

The bankers and brokers from whom corporate executives buy the highly leveraged swaps and options used for such bets seldom if ever take such extreme risks themselves. In fact, the real experts in risk take as little as it as they can. If they bet on a market trend, they do so carefully, backed by powerful analytic technology and constantly monitoring their positions. In fact, much of the investment in technology by banks and investment banks has been for the purpose of measuring and monitoring risk in order to prevent inadvertent or deliberate bets that could cause serious damage to the firm. This is a field of finance as demanding as astrophysics. Yet the markets remain, even for these, at times, bewildering.

In looking at the risks posed by the markets and financiers it is possible to go over, ad infinitum, the build-up to the financial crisis of 2007/2008. However, it is important to understand that many of the mechanisms that can cause disruption to organisation pre-date the most recent crisis. The following examples show some of the hidden risks of dealing in the major markets.

The first example is that of the Malaysian Central Bank. On 22 September 1985, the finance ministers and central bank chiefs of the G5 assembled in New York amid much secrecy. At this point the world was on the brink of a financial crisis. Over five years, high interest rates in the US have been increasing the value of the dollar. Commodity prices had crashed, pushing third world resource-rich countries into difficulty. The dollar had peaked and, as the G5 met, its strength was beginning to dissipate under market pressure. On the 22 September 1985 the G5 announced their intention to encourage appreciation in the non-dollar economies. Dollars were sold and the dollar price fell.

The result in Malaysia was that held dollar reserves became virtually worthless and the Malaysian central bank, in Western terms, went rogue. The Malaysian central bank began an asymmetric campaign against the world's leading currencies. Malaysia's Bank Negara became the most feared trader in the currency markets. They did this by using all the resources of a central bank – privileged information, unlimited credit and more. It is important to understand that at the time, and in the banking environment of the time, Bank Negara was committing apostasy against the creed of Central Banking. Instead of working to ensure global financial stability Bank Negara repeatedly moved huge sums of money into the most vulnerable market situations in order to destabilise exchange rates for its own profits.

By 1988, the PWC-trained Bank Governor, Jaffar bin Hussein, admitted that trading had accounted for 40 per cent of the bank's total overseas income that year, up from 20 per cent the year before. He justified this unorthodox activity by noting that 'exchange rate volatility since the G5 agreement has changed the stakes of the game'. The Governor had the support of the non-aligned Prime Minister Mahathir. Negara's currency trading made the West fear Malaysia and that did not clash with the Mahathir agenda. Mahathir had also read Machiavelli and knew it was better for the Prince to be feared than loved. US officials criticised this trading only for it to be denied, as major plays were being made in the markets with huge transactions moving currencies as the bank placed speculative trades. The Western banks were often complicit in dealing with Negara to attempt their own profits in piggy-back operations.

Market sources said that Negara specialised in exploiting these rules – selling a currency short in large enough volumes to trigger panic selling and then buying back the currency to lock in the profit. Piggy-backers also made a profit. This meant a wave of support from Western traders for Negara's actions. When Negara attacked the pound five years after the 1985 meeting, and just prior to the UK's entry into the exchange rate mechanism, sterling lost 4 cents on the day and caused heavy British bank losses. Defending themselves by creating a cartel, the British banks became the focus of the regulators, not Negara. The market manipulation was so obvious and general that the Americans said that normally such traders would go to jail. However, the international currency markets were unregulated so Negara could 'do well in an area of the financial market which had previously been the preserve of western banks for so long'. Negara lost what it had gained when the UK came out of the European Exchange Rate mechanism in 1992.

Bank Negara had used finance as a weapon. It conquered the core of the financial system, the interbank currency market, and held a commanding position until the weapon blew up in its own face. The risk represented by Negara is the risk that a major well-capitalised entity could pursue a deliberate strategy to achieve certain political objectives through the equivalent of financial terrorism. The political objectives could be as simple as commanding attention and respect, as in Malaysia's case, but they could be much more sinister.

By the mid-1990s, the Negara type action was being replaced by the amount of capital in hedge funds, and the massive movement of funds by banks, pension funds and insurance companies. The investigations into derivative markets that began as early as the mid-1990s identified flaws in governance and regulation. These flaws allowed traders to trade with no respect for geography. Because of this the legal jurisdiction boundaries to trades became blurred, and hence trades unregulated. Traders had known for years that the regulatory barriers were, to all practical purposes, meaningless.

A much earlier, and relatively simple, example of this was the invention in 1982 on the Chicago Mercantile Exchange of a stock index futures contract on the Standard and Poor's 500 – a list of 500 stocks. A trader who wanted to buy these stocks could either place an order to purchase them on the New York Stock Exchange or buy the futures contract in Chicago and receive an economic return equivalent to that of stocks in the index. The future contract cost only 5 or 10 per cent as much as actually buying the stocks but the price of the futures contract and the price of the stocks in the index had to be mathematically related. If the stocks were much more expensive on the stock exchange than the ideal mathematical relationship suggested they ought to be, people could buy the futures contract, sell the stocks themselves and pocket an immediate profit. If it was easier or cheaper to buy and sell futures than to buy and sell stocks then business would move from the stock exchange to the futures market. This is exactly what happened during the great stock market crash of 1987. The phenomenon is not limited to stocks. Currency futures in Chicago, currency options in Philadelphia and currency forward on the interbank market all moved up and down together for the same reason. This is the law of one price in action. This type of trading developed over the years in silver, soya beans, gold, treasury bond futures and was eventually mainstream for the seven largest banks in the US. Until the late 1990s and the 2000s no US bank had lost money trading, only by loose lending. However, regulators began to point out that as financial institutions moved aggressively into the trading business they increased the linkages between markets, and consequently, the risk that a major shock in one market could reverberate dangerously through the entire financial system – as it did of course in 2007. In fact, trading had changed a familiar old workhorse of a system into a racehorse that was certainly faster and more streamlined but might also be much more fragile.

In 1992, 15 years before the 2007 problem, bank regulators in the US and Europe began to speak publically of their worries. In a prescient statement in January 1992 the president of the Reserve Bank of New York addressed a congregation of top executives of New York banks. In strong language, he suggested that perhaps their trading in derivatives did not serve a legitimate hedging purpose but merely fuelled speculation. In March 1992, Alexandre Lamfalussy, General Manager of the Bank of International Settlements, was even more explicit. In a lecture at City University in London, UK, he said that the growth of trading in futures and swaps 'makes it increasingly difficult to assess the direct credit, liquidity and interest rate risks assumed by any individual financial firm'.

In addition the growth of trading in such instruments had created new links between sectors of the financial industry that used to be separate. 'We simply do not know the size of the indirect risks for the individual institution generated by interdependence. These risks cannot be easily captured even through very sophisticated risk assessment techniques.' Later in 1992 the Bank of England admonished the International Swap Dealers Association by focussing on the dubious legality of certain trades and the questionable enforceability of contracts, both sources of risk. He noted that accounting standards could not cope with the new businesses, as accountants disagreed among themselves about how to measure the gains and losses on trading. It said that institutions depended heavily on a few, highly skilled specialists who built risky portfolios their managers did not understand. These specialists were in short supply, highly paid and fervently courted. Sometimes they left suddenly and the problem of managing the risk they left behind was a troubling one.

In 1993 the prestigious Group of Thirty, a Washington-based think tank, issued a ground-breaking report that was the first major attempt to categorise and assess risks of the new markets. The report identified four major categories of risk: credit, market, operational and legal. In order to understand why regulators worried about the new hidden world of these markets, it helps to know what damage each of these risks has caused.

In the collapse of Drexel Burnham Lambert in 1990 the issue of credit risk was both simple and writ large. Simply, Drexel did not have cash – banks would not release securities they held to provide the cash and thus Drexel could not get cash. The firm had massive wealth in junk bonds but no one was willing to lend it long-term funds. The Bank of England, as honest broker, cleared Drexel's obligations in London; in New York the Federal Reserve Bank prepared to play the same role in the Ginnie Mae securities markets, for simple, securitised, mortgages. The Ginnie Mae mortgage market in the US was protected from Drexel by an emergency operation that in the end led to another investment bank agreeing to purchase Drexel's entire mortgage portfolio and thus eliminated Drexel's poor credit as a risk factor in the Ginnie Mae market.

Without intervention the failure of Drexel may have blocked the entire international payments mechanism. Yet Drexel was fairly simple. If one looked at the books of the major players in 2007, for example, there wasn't a chance that the authorities could have played such a facilitative role as the matters had become so much more complicated. Credit was the only issue involved with Drexel. Other institutions were unwilling to release securities because they were afraid that Drexel would not pay for them. No one had any doubt about what these securities were really worth. Yet the complexity of the new financial markets made it difficult thereafter for even experts to work out what securities are worth. Nowhere was this problem more acute than in the market for mortgage obligations. This is an example of how credit risk can be a problem.

Most mortgage loans made in the US become securitised. Buyers collect pools of mortgages and issue securities against these pools. The buyers of the securities receive a stream of principal and interest payments from the pool, made up of all the homeowners' monthly payments, combined together. There is a risk to the buyer of a mortgage security. The risk is that a homeowner may pay off the mortgage prematurely – usually through refinancing. Borrowers normally have a right to repay mortgages at any time without penalty. In fact, in most states, the right is guaranteed by law, In effect almost all mortgage borrowers have an option, and that option is one of the biggest sources of risk in the financial system. The risk is enlarged when lending is extended to those that cannot pay the mortgage, and this is rolled into the pool, and the mortgagees default. This is basically what happened in 2007 when there was both refinancing and default.

Financial engineers also treat mortgage payments as mathematical equations. A mortgage payment is the sum of a principal repayment and an interest payment, and one of the first steps in the design of the contemporary mortgage security was to split the principal from the interest payment on some tranches. Interest payments went to investors who purchased 'interest only' securities – principal payments went to investors who purchased 'principal only' securities. Other refinements of the basic mortgage security soon followed. 'Inverse floaters' for example are mortgage securities that pay investors more when interest rates go down and less when interest rates go up. They are pegged to a variety of indices. Residuals are all the cash flows that are left over when more desirable securities have been created.

All of these securities and their multiple permutations are mathematically designed to balance each other and add up to the sum of the payments from a given pool of mortgages. Some buyers of mortgage securities relied on the mathematical relationships between these securities to design elaborately balanced investment portfolios that would capture high returns with very low risk. Others used the same securities to make massive, highly leveraged bets on the direction of interest rates. Unfortunately, the instruments themselves were so complex that even experts had trouble telling the difference between a safe, low-risk strategy and a highly speculative plunge. By the mid-1990s it turned out that the mathematical relationships between securities were no more than an untested and ultimately invalid hypothesis. By 2007 when both safe and toxic packages of varying combinations were being offered it was impossible to tell what was what.

Markets in risk had developed because some parties needed to get rid of risk, and others were willing to take risk in order to make a profit. At first, only a few big banks and investment banks had the technology to take financial risks and trade for profit. They made a lot of money. Soon competitors rushed in to take a piece of the action. In order to keep ahead of their competitors the risk takers had to develop ever more complex and subtle trading strategies. As soon as competitors found out about it they imitated and sold it cheaply. Thus a cycle of innovation was started in derivative products that became ever more complex. Even by the 1990s the plain so-called vanilla products were no longer profitable. The real money could only be made in new, usually complicated feats of financial engineering. The banks endeavoured to keep these feats secret from the competition and usually compensated the financial wizards who developed and traded the new risk management products with a percentage of the money they made. No one was really sure what risks were being taken anymore. The environment was rife for abuse. Difficulties at both Bankers Trust and AIG occurred during the 1990s and more after 2007.

Importantly this sort of risk extended to companies too. In the 1990s both Metallgessellschaft Refining and Marketing and General Electric Company's Kidder Peabody both suffered large losses on hedge fund contracts that not only they and their Boards did not understand, especially when they tried to liquidate the positions, but additionally neither had any idea of what their traders had been doing in their name. This 'gambling' culture extended well into the 2000s and resulted in the demise of several household names. At the same time, in order to make sure bets could be won, many financial houses who were technically regulated managed to leave 'back doors' to their trading rooms open and free from regulation in order to ensure that winning and profitable positions could be exploited. The problem was, of course, that these back doors also allowed rogue traders to be concealed too.

Though operational risks were shocking, even well-managed institutions faced dangerous threats from sudden changes in law and the interpretation of laws. Traders may have deceived their managers or the competitive dynamic of the market may carry some institutions beyond the pale of safe and sound practice but all finance depends on legally enforceable contracts. The foundations of the whole system would crumble if courts ruled these contracts illegal. In 1990 that occurred for the first time when Hammersmith and Fulham Council was generating 25 per cent of all the interest rate swaps in the UK. Banks were delighted to get the business and the local authority spread the business through as many as 50 banks to execute its transactions. They weren't the only local authority to do this, others followed suit. However, most thought this was too risky as the downside, a rise in interest rates, looked likely. The rise took place and to cut the story short the House of Lords eventually ruled the swaps *ultra vires*. Swaps became difficult to pin down legally. The US Government Accounting Office noted that many derivative contracts could be ruled illegal. In other countries a case could be made that some of the new financial contracts violated laws against gambling and fraud. However, lobbying action by the industry was slowly and steadily winning victories and eliminating legal barriers to the enforceability of its contacts – allowing the problems of 2007 to occur.

Financial reports had once been very useful to people who wanted to understand whether or not a particular institution was financially healthy. Now the old financial reports were not very useful. They had been designed to cope with a whole different environment. Regulators worried about a lack of transparency in the system, this resonates today a decade or so later. Not only was it difficult for them to figure out what was happening inside the banks and other institutions they regulated, clearly in many cases the CEOs of the biggest institutions had no idea what real risks they were taking.

Every day traders and banks trade more than $1 trillion across the currency markets. To give an idea of the scale of this daily trading rate, this is the size of the UK's national debt. It is the approximately half the GDP of each of Britain, Italy and France and a little less than half of Germany's. These are huge sums. When control is lost of these sums, as it was in 2007, then the problems that followed are understandable. Whether it is right that the traders and markets should have such an impact on social matters, and the high interest rates used to defend currencies, and their effect in turn on the general population, is a point that continues to be debated. It used to be the case that these matters were separated.

As noted in Chapter 2, the key issue behind the financial crisis of 2007 onwards was the repeal of the US Banking Act (1933) in 1990, and banking deregulation in the UK by the then UK Chancellor of the Exchequer over the period 1997–1999. The context of this repeal is important. The US Banking Act (1933) was a law that established the Federal Deposit Insurance Corporation (FDIC) in the US and introduced banking reforms, some of which were designed to control speculation. It is most commonly known as the Glass–Steagall Act, after its legislative sponsors. Some provisions of the Act, such as Regulation Q, which allowed the Federal Reserve to regulate interest rates in savings accounts, were repealed earlier in 1980. Provisions that prohibit a bank holding company from owning other financial companies were repealed on 12 November 1999, by the Gramm–Leach–Bliley Act. The banking industry had been seeking the repeal of Glass–Steagall since the 1980s. In 1987 the Congressional Research Service (1987) prepared a report which explored the cases for and against preserving Glass–Seagall.

The repeal of the act caused a jump from 10 per cent to more than 30 per cent in terms of the sub-prime products held by the banks. This correlation is not necessarily the sole cause of recent problems as there are several other significant events that impacted the sub-prime market during that time. These include the adoption of mark-to-market accounting, implementation of the Basel Accords, the rise of adjustable rate mortgages and so on. Boyd (2011) confirms the radical effect of the Glass–Steagall Act repeal on the business methods of Salomon Brothers. Greenspan (2011) described this overall 'problem' as 'The Flaw'.

On 21 January 2010, US President Obama proposed bank regulations similar to some parts of Glass–Steagall in limiting certain of banks' trading and investment capabilities. The proposal was dubbed 'The Volcker Rule', for Paul Volcker, who has been an outspoken advocate for the reimplementation of many aspects of Glass–Steagall and who appeared with President Obama at the press conference in support of the proposed regulations. Richardson and Cooley (2011) describe how the subsequent Dodd–Frank Act came about in an attempt to both reinstate the Glass–Steagall Act and re-regulate Wall Street.

In mainland Europe, notably in France, Germany and Italy, an increasing number of think-tanks, such as the Canadian European Economic Council (2010), were calling for the adoption of stricter bank regulation through new national and EU-wide legislations based on the Glass–Steagall Act. In 2010 the legislation was enacted.

In August 2011 the UK unveiled the Vickers Report (2011) suggesting the division between retail and investment banking. The timetable for implementation is nearly a decade hence, but the relevant bill was included in the 2012 UK Queen's Speech, 9 May 2012. Two days after the Vickers unveiling, UBS lost £1.3bn to a rogue trader and it was noted that the bank had not learnt the context lessons of the last few years and that the bank's risk processes and compliance procedures were inadequate. The day after the Queen's Speech in 2012, JP Morgan admitted losing over £1bn (later £2.8bn) in London with a consequent devastating impact on their share price.

The second key issue to the 2007 onwards problem is described by Patterson (2010b). He describes how the markets had become dominated by 'The Quants' – cerebral and highly qualified mathematicians drafted in to the investment houses to develop sophisticated algorithms to make money. The links between their equations and the difficulties in the products these created and derived, particularly in the housing market, were another reason for market collapse. Khandani and Lo (2008) describe the systemic risks that were being run by 'The Quants' and the contribution they made to the difficulties of 2007. Khandani and Lo (2008, p54) graphically illustrate the effect this had on company values and why 'Hardening' the investment and 'softer' side of a business is more important now than it has ever been.

The economic crisis of 2007 onwards was perpetrated by a series of events linked to the sale of sub-prime mortgages in the US and, as importantly, the bundling of the notes covering these mortgages in derivative products.

This allied to a failed market in what are termed Credit Default Swaps (CDS) and caused the difficulties at Bear Stearns, Lehman Brothers and AIG – thereby triggering the need for the massive bank bail-out and the subsequent recession. In 2011/2012 it was unclear if the bail-out of Greece would trigger a massive CDS-driven collapse as these 'insurance' vehicles are themselves triggered by debt default. *The Times* (2011b) carried a leader that Europe had, soon, to decide whether to back the euro or abandon it. The background was more complicated, and remains so, than immediately obvious.

Much of the reaction to these events came through in 'real time' and hence the Internet played a large part in both the timeliness and availability of information. The blogs that became required reading were those of Randall (2007 onwards), Peston (2007 onwards) and Cable (2007 onwards).

In terms of understanding what happened, and why, to the economy and risk management then a number of authors are important. Augar (2009) explains the forces that went unchecked, Cable (2009) gave probably the most understandable and wide-ranging description of the events, what they meant and who was responsible, Soros (2009) gave us his Reflexivity Theory to explain why it happened, why he was able to forecast it, how he made money from it, and what should be done in the future. Not all have realised the importance of the Glass–Steagall Act and the relevance of the 'The Quants'.

Allen (2008) discussed the impact of regulation. This reminded of the symbiotic nature of the relationship between the regulator and the banks. In good times there tends to be light regulation, at others, for example, as this book is written, more regulation is called for. Hutton (2009) explained why Turner (2009) was right to try and regulate the banks further. The debate around regulation will to and fro because it also becomes a pawn in location arguments. However, it is likely that the banks will be taxed and regulated more in all parts of the world. That the debacle damaged the West more than the East is a lesson to be learned – and it would be safe to say that the City of London and New York will remain targets of organised bear raids in the future. Note that there is less enthusiasm in the East for more regulation, where there has often been little appetite to sign up to the Basel Accords, for example. This may become a competitive disadvantage for the West.

For nearly half a century, a type, and since revised, of the Black and Scholes (1973) model has dominated derivative, hedging and option trading. This model's underlying tenets were partly called into question by the derivative trading catalyst to the 2007 onwards financial crisis. The model depended on the 'rational' man scenario; and also the use of normal distributions. Soros (2009) discounted the first and Taleb (2007) both of these approaches.

All of these works suggest that the organisations involved need a different type of structure today in order to protect themselves from the threats of tomorrow. None of them have been specific about what may be required in detail. All of them imply that some form of response to Obstructive Marketing may be a good idea.

The recent crises in the banking industry and elsewhere have demonstrated that there have been shortcomings in the description, measurement and management of risk. A well-defined and holistic approach to risk was written in the 1970s (Rowe, 1977) and is still relevant today – see Chapter 5. It deals with the description and measurement of risks plus consequences. This is a good starting point to compare the winners and losers in the recent crisis as described by Augar (2009), Cable (2009) and others, and more recent organisational approaches to risk, such as those seen in the NHS. The models suggested by Wood (2000) and Gordon (1996) can also be reviewed against a strong disciplinary background. Knight and Pretty's (2000), and Pretty's (2008) work confirms the risk in some corporate activities. This chapter suggests there is some commonality between Rowe (1977) and Soros (2009) and that there have been, indeed, some shortcomings in the management of risk. Following suggestions from Smith and Fischbacher (2009), and building on the work of Rowe (1977), a new model of risk description and measurement might help organisations manage the subject more successfully. By so doing they would become better protected against Obstructive Marketing. Young (2011a) (2011b) confirms the requirement for a new approach to risk in a two-part analysis of the failure of risk management for the BCI. Parker (2012) and Goodwin (2012) have both described how their organisations (UBS and Goodwin plc.) remain deficient in the description, measurement and management of risk. Sjuve (2010) has described well-managed risk in the National Australian Banking Group.

Goodger (2011a; 2011b) and Gall (2010) view the world as volatile, uncertain, complex and ambiguous. They state there is no clear predictive design mechanism(s) for understanding emergence within the complex adaptive information ecosystem that is today's world. They suggest a need for a predictive dynamic risk framework. They also complain that most are unable to comprehend or explain risk in logical terms. Goodger and Atkinson (2011) see the biggest risk to society as a lack of an integrated approach to the virtual and physical worlds. As stated elsewhere there is little research into this subject.

Davis (2012) explained how the risks businesses and banks run are still not properly managed some four years after the banking crisis.

A sovereign wealth fund is a state-owned investment fund composed of financial assets such as stocks, bonds, property, precious metals or other financial instruments. Sovereign wealth funds invest globally. Most sovereign wealth funds are funded by foreign exchange assets.

Some sovereign wealth funds may be held by a central bank, which accumulates the funds in the course of its management of a nation's banking system. This type of fund is usually of major economic and fiscal importance. Other sovereign wealth funds are simply the state savings that are invested by various entities for the purposes of investment return, and that may not have a significant role in fiscal management.

The accumulated funds may have their origin in, or may represent, foreign currency deposits, gold, Special Drawing Rights (SDRs) and IMF reserve positions held by central banks and monetary authorities, along with other national assets such as pension investments, oil funds, or other industrial and financial holdings. These are assets of the sovereign nations that are typically held in domestic and different reserve currencies (such as the dollar, euro, pound and yen). Such investment management entities may be set up as official investment companies, state pension funds or sovereign oil funds, among others.

There have been attempts to distinguish funds held by sovereign entities from foreign exchange reserves held by central banks. Sovereign wealth funds can be characterised as 'maximising long-term return', with foreign exchange reserves serving short-term 'currency stabilisation', and liquidity management. Many central banks in recent years possess reserves massively in excess of needs for liquidity or foreign exchange management. Moreover it is widely believed most have diversified hugely into assets other than short-term, highly liquid monetary ones, though almost no data is publicly available to back up this assertion. Some central banks have even begun buying equities, or derivatives of differing ilk (even if fairly safe ones, like overnight interest rate swaps).

Some countries may have more than one sovereign wealth fund (see also the list of largest sovereign wealth funds as shown in Table 7.1).

Table 7.1   Sovereign wealth funds – the top 40

Rank	Country	Funds	Assets (US$Billion)	Origin
1	China	CADF/CIC/NSSF/SAFE	1,189.4	Non-commodity
2	United Arab Emirates	ADIA/ADIC/EIA/ICD/ IPIC/MDC/RIA	816.6	Oil
3	Norway	GPF	715.9	Oil
4	Saudi Arabia	PIF/SAMA	538.1	Oil
5	Singapore	GIC/TH	405	Non-commodity
6	Hong Kong	HKMA	298.7	Non-commodity
7	Kuwait	KIA	296	Oil
8	Russia	RNWF	175.5	Oil
9	Qatar	QIA	115	Oil
10	United States	APF/NMSIOT/ PWMTF/PSF/ATF/ NDLF	93.4	Oil and Gas/Non-commodity/Minerals/ Public lands
11	Australia	AFF/WAFF	83.3	Non-commodity
12	Libya	LIA	65	Oil
13	Kazakhstan	KNF	61.8	Oil
14	Algeria	RRF	56.7	Oil
15	South Korea	KIC	56.6	Non-commodity
16	Iran	NDFI	42	Oil
17	Malaysia	KN	39.1	Non-commodity
18	Azerbaijan	SOF	32.7	Oil
19	Brunei	BIA	30	Oil
20	France	SIF	25.5	Non-commodity
21	Chile	SESF/PRF	20.9	Copper/Non-commodity
22	Ireland	NPRF	19.4	Non-commodity
23	New Zealand	NZSF	16.6	Non-commodity
24	Canada	AHSTF	16.4	Oil
25	Brazil	SFB	11.3	Non-commodity
26	East Timor	TLPF	11.1	Gas/Oil
27	Bahrain	MHC	9.1	Oil
28	Oman	OIF/SGRF	8.2	Gas/Oil
29	Peru	FSF	7.1	Non-commodity
30	Botswana	PF	6.9	Diamonds/Minerals
31	Mexico	ORSFM	6	Oil
32	Angola	FSA	5	Oil
33	Trinidad and Tobago	HSF	2.9	Oil
34	Italy	ISF	1.4	Non-commodity
35	Nigeria	NSIA	1	Oil
36	Palestinian territories	PIF	0.8	Non-commodity
36	Venezuela	FEM	0.8	Oil
37	Vietnam	SCIC	0.5	Non-commodity
38	Kiribati	RERF	0.4	Phosphates

Rank	Country	Funds	Assets (US$Billion)	Origin
38	Gabon	GSWF	0.4	Oil
39	Indonesia	GIU	0.3	Non-commodity
39	Mauritania	NFHR	0.3	Gas/Oil
39	Panama	FAP	0.3	Non-commodity
40	Equatorial Guinea	FFG	0.08	Oil

Think tanks such as the World Pensions Council (WPC) have argued that the extended investment horizon of sovereign wealth funds allows them to act as long-term investors in less liquid assets such as unlisted companies, commodities, real estate and infrastructure assets, a trend likely to develop further as banks and insurance companies decrease their exposure to these asset classes in the context of the Basel 2 and Solvency 2 regulatory constraints.

What Obstructive Marketing impact do they have?

There are several reasons why the growth of sovereign wealth funds is attracting close attention:

- as this asset pool continues to expand in size and importance, so does its potential impact on various asset markets;

- some countries worry that foreign investment by sovereign wealth funds raises national security concerns because the purpose of the investment might be to secure control of strategically important industries for political rather than financial gain. These concerns have led the EU to reconsider whether to allow its members to use 'golden shares' to block certain foreign acquisitions. This strategy has largely been excluded as a viable option by the EU, for fear it would give rise to a resurgence in international protectionism. In the US, these concerns are addressed by the Exon–Florio Amendment to the Omnibus Trade and Competitiveness Act of 1988, Pub. L. No. 100–418, § 5021, 102 Stat. 1107, 1426 (codified as amended at 50 U.S.C. app. § 2170 (2000)), as administered by the Committee on Foreign Investment in the United States (CFIUS);

- their inadequate transparency is a concern for investors and regulators. For example, size and source of funds, investment goals, internal checks and balances, disclosure of relationships and holdings in private equity funds. Many of these concerns have been addressed by the IMF and its Santiago Principles, which set out common standards regarding transparency, independence and governance;

- sovereign wealth funds are not nearly as homogeneous as central banks or public pension funds;

- the governments of sovereign wealth fund's commit to follow certain rules:
  - accumulation rule (what portion of revenue can be spent/saved);
  - withdraw rule (when the government can withdraw from the fund);
  - investment (where revenue can be invested in foreign or domestic assets).

Sovereign wealth funds are estimated to manage close to $5 trillion of assets, twice as much as the hedge fund industry. According to popular belief, these funds can invest for the long term without the baggage of liabilities and short-term constraints that impede other institutional investors. Research organised by the Edhec-Risk Institute and Deutsche Bank has suggested otherwise, and a survey conducted in 2011 confirms this view.

A paper published in 2010 put forward a model to optimise the investment and risk management practices of sovereign wealth funds, drawing on the liability-driven investing paradigm developed in the pension fund industry. The model suggests the investment strategy of a sovereign wealth fund should involve dynamic allocation to three main building blocks: a performance-seeking portfolio using optimal diversification to reap the highest possible risk-adjusted rewards; a liability-hedging portfolio protecting the fund against risks undermining its ability to perform its specific mission (for example, protect the real value of savings for future generations); and a portfolio hedging the fluctuations in the endowment stream that aims to reduce the fund's dependence on the main sources of wealth of the country.

The third block is a distinguishing feature of sovereign investment. Like the previous block, it is customised to the specificities of each fund, but in general, assets that benefit from rising oil prices would be natural candidates for inclusion in the endowment-hedging portfolio of foreign reserve funds whose economies are vulnerable to oil price appreciation, while the reverse would be expected for oil funds.

These academic findings contradict the widespread view of sovereign wealth funds as relatively free agents, so the Edhec-Risk Institute asked sovereign investment practitioners about their perceived constraints and liabilities and the theoretical and practical appeal of dynamic asset-liability management. Conducted over 2011, the survey generated 27 responses from senior executives and investment officers working for 24 sovereign investment vehicles and central banks around the world.

A large majority (89 per cent) of the respondents agree that sovereign wealth funds are subject to implicit short-term constraints such as maximum drawdown and minimum performance due to peer comparison, loss aversion or sponsor risk. Just as many respondents (92 per cent) think implicit liabilities, such as the future use of the wealth, should be taken into account.

Responses also offer a strong rebuttal of the purported irrelevance of asset-liability management for sovereign investors. Seventy per cent of the respondents agree that extending the liability-driven investing paradigm to sovereign wealth management provides a better understanding of optimal investment policy and risk management practices; the remaining 30 per cent neither agree nor disagree. The majority of respondents (63 per cent in agreement vs. 22 per cent in disagreement) also recognise the need to hedge fluctuations in endowment flows.

Finally, a majority (55 per cent in agreement vs 23 per cent) endorse the particular approach put forward by the Edhec-Risk Institute. The concerns of the minority point to the need for further applied research and education aimed at illustrating how the approach can be tailored to a particular fund's policy and its specific governance model.

With respect to policy, it is important to underline that the structure of the endowment- and liability-hedging portfolios, as well as the dynamic allocation between the three blocks, would reflect the objectives and the constraints of each individual fund.

These results provide practical vindication of the asset-liability management analysis of sovereign investment, as the majority of sovereign investment managers surveyed lament the lack of genuinely dedicated solutions for asset-liability and risk management, opportunities exist for investment banks, asset managers and consultants to better serve these increasingly important investors.

Jonsson (2007) gives another perspective:

> *Liberal democracy, led by the United States may have emerged triumphant from the struggles of the 20th century. But the rise of the non-democratic powers of Russia, China and the Islamist states utilizing the combined power of control of energy resources and the growth of Sovereign Wealth Funds leaves the liberal democracy's ultimate victory and future dominance in doubt. Overseas investments by Sovereign Wealth Funds have always had the potential to cause alarm in the destination countries. Because they are driven by governments of the totalitarian and Authoritarian Great Powers, they compel countries to take immediate attention.*

> *How powerful Sovereign Wealth Funds decide to invest their vast armoury of cash will play a pivotal role in reshaping financial markets in the next decade. These funds are going to have the ability to buy any global company, to create panic in markets if they move too precipitously, even to dwarf the political clout of international financial institutions. They can no longer be ignored. The Sovereign Wealth Funds are potentially a powerful tool of asymmetric warfare like none witnessed before.*

> *The Leftist/Marxist–Islamist Alliance is using its propaganda machine to convince us that Investment funds run by authoritarian governments sound scary. They are not. So trumpets* The Economist *print edition of July 26, 2007. On the other hand go for a walk in Chelsea, an expensive bit of London, and you may stroll by the Coldstream Guards' barracks, now the property of the government of Qatar; a branch of the venerable Barclays bank, soon to be part-owned by the People's Republic of China; and then buy a picnic at Sainsbury's, Britain's oldest supermarket, which the Anglophile Qataris are trying to buy too. What goes for Chelsea may soon be true for neighbourhoods in open economies all over the world: governments are on a shopping spree.*

> *In considering the role of Sovereign Wealth Funds it is imperative to consider the difference between state vs. private ownership. However, in some cases the difference is blurred because in some cases the state influence, political motives and ideology override the fund ownership as in the case of funds from Islamist countries.*

In much of Europe and emerging markets, it took decades for many economies to be free from the controls of state-owned enterprises (SOEs). Are we now seeing the return of state ownership in the infrastructures and large industries, not by the local governments, but by foreign states?

In any case, there should be more discussions and studies on whether Sovereign Wealth Funds are really returning our Western economies to the former days of state-owned enterprises, but to an even worse case that of foreign state owned entities.

Beware, Wakeup, a foreign state entity – be it either from an Authoritarian Islamist state or Russia or China – they may be the new owner of your newspaper, radio station, electric utility, and even your most sensitive supplier of war material. The rapid growth of Sovereign Wealth Funds poses risks beyond that of national security. There are worries over competence within some funds; concerns that their scale and ability to affect asset prices could lead to market volatility; and suspicion that they could help countries preserve a favorable currency regime. If decisions are swayed by political considerations, they could also undermine market discipline that matches rewards to sound corporate governance. The ownership may also have a devastating impact on employment practices and human rights. Big and powerful they are coming to company near you or one you work for.

Although a somewhat strident piece there is some resonance in Jonsson's comments with remarks made earlier in this book. For example, it has been noted how difficult it is to generate growth from an economy so strongly in foreign hands and how, even at Secretary of State board meetings, there is an inability to change the course of the economy in a way that would have been possible a generation ago.

A free and open market and vast sovereign wealth viewing UK assets as relatively risk free may be more of a problem than at first appeared. It is not just a UK problem, but the UK is particularly vulnerable because of the openness of the market there.

8

Obstructive Marketing and Asymmetric Warfare: Asymmetric Obstructive Marketing

In the *Financial Times* on 25 February 2013, Zbigniew Brzezinski commented as follows:

> The two centuries since the Congress of Vienna have seen the gradual codification by the 'international community' of the 'rules of the game' for guiding interstate relations, even between unfriendly countries. The basic premise has been the formula 'don't do to me what you don't want me to do to you'. However, technological advances mean that today those rules are being dangerously undermined. The international system, is at risk … today the interstate rules of the game are degrading … scientific advances have also increased the potential scope of acts of war whose perpetrators may not be easily identified … a rogue but technologically sophisticated state can now gain the capacity to launch non-lethal but paralysing cyber attacks on the socioeconomic system and the most important state institutions of a target country.

This article sums up much of what this book is about – at least from the cyber-security perspective. It suggests how a cyber-security attack from a small but sophisticated state can launch attacks on much bigger powers. This is the essence of asymmetry. Similar descriptions of asymmetric attacks on countries and organisations can be given from the casual, competitive, criminal, cultural and capitalist viewpoints. Some of these have already been noted in the case studies.

In *The Economist* of 23 February 2013 two other articles of relevance were carried. The first dealt with the issue of cyber-crime out of China. This summarised the tracing of the hacking attack on *The New York Times*, a comment on which opened this book, to a Chinese Military back to China, and commented on peripheral involvement of Russian intelligence agencies and Eastern European interests. The second dealt with more traditional corporate espionage. This discussed gangs stealing intellectual property in China, sleepers who sit inside a company and wait to steal secrets, PhD sleepers who work quietly for years inside major pharmaceutical companies before walking away with invaluable intellectual property, and a range of other issues and protection mechanisms that this book has either already covered or will cover in a later. Suffice to say this is yet more evidence of the inherent Obstructive Marketing problems abroad and the links to Asymmetric Warfare. Where all these issues interplay with the new rules of warfare we have a new term to bridge the gap: Asymmetric Obstructive Marketing. This combines both the Asymmetric Warfare trends and Obstructive Marketing trends. This chapter now moves on to describe how Asymmetric Obstructive Marketing might develop in the future, its relevance to prevailing military doctrine and its role in Brzezinski's changes in the rule of the game. As noted elsewhere in this book, China should not be looked upon as a singular problem in a historical context.

The Asymmetric Military Balance was explained in Chapter 6.

Organisations, risk doctrine, information infrastructure and value systems need to be structured to cope with the widening spectrum of threats of those who seek to undermine organisational commercial capabilities, democratic freedoms and cultural values.

The more frequent occurrence of what this book has so far called Obstructive Marketing could be further refined into, as noted earlier, Asymmetric Obstructive Marketing, a new term original to this book, as a consequence of the obvious and increasing use of organisations and commerce in warfare. This is a subject for further research.

The key issues regarding Obstructive Marketing have been identified as follows:

- casual threats;

- competitive threats;

- criminal threats;

- cultural threats;

- critical infrastructure threats;

- capital threats.

The key marketing mix issues are:

- product;

- price;

- place;

- people;

- promotion.

In recent years terms such as processes and physical evidence, and more recently a number of Internet-related terms, have been added to the traditional, marketing mix. Here the five original terms will suffice for the purpose of describing a potential campaign.

Looking at these in the form of a matrix, Table 8.1 helps to identify what the key aspects of an Asymmetric Obstructive Marketing campaign might look like. Using the matrix we could create an example of an Asymmetric Obstructive Marketing campaign. For the sake of balance let us assume that the target company is a Chinese manufacturer of motor vehicles launched on a global basis. The company is based in a strong Han Chinese area – but this area is one which has been only recently dominated by Han Chinese and there is much resentment in the local community because of the take-over of land and territory and the favouritism shown to the Han in terms of employment within the car factory. The local community despite its small size is particularly influential in a number of key economic areas and has a strong international and expatriate community that repatriates money and information from a well-placed intelligentsia. A small but determined group of locals decide that enough is enough and launch a secret campaign against the car manufacturer. The following is a summary of how the campaign might develop.

Table 8.1   Asymmetric Obstructive Marketing campaign

	Product	Price	Place	People	Promotion
Casual	Deprecation	Price fixing or underpricing	Damage	Disgruntled employees	Web attacks
Competitive	Reverse engineering, copying	Loss leaders drive product out of the market. Cartels	Market denial through law, agency retention	Sleepers	Adverse press and PR from competitors
Criminal	Counterfeiting	Cartels. Monopolies	Damage or attack. Control of supply lines or routes to market	Infiltration	Extortion, pressure, bad press and PR
Cultural	Denial	Different type of banking, salary and wage payments. Feudal or tribute systems	Routes to market controlled in a different manner	Refusal to work with a product or service on cultural grounds	Culture prevents usual Promotion patterns
Critical infrastructure	Hacking	Online changes	Denial of utilities/breach of security	IT department infiltrated or 'hacked'	Denial of water, sanitation, food and so on
Capital	Capex denied	Finance dictates prices	Product development curtailed	Unsupportive bank. Poor or anti-finance staff. Trading mistakes and so on	Rise in credit risk. Bad news released by bank or financier. Call in of loans at short notice. Changes in facility

Despite the recruitment process favouring the majority some key positions require the skills of the locals. This allows them to infiltrate important areas of the manufacturer to:

Casual

- modify the production process so that the cars are not built to the quality standard;

- amend stock process so the cars are sold too cheaply;

- undertake a campaign of physical damage to the plant;

- encourage complaints about working conditions and pay;

- make internal attacks on the website.

Competitively

- operatives in another country hand-over plans of the car to a competitor enabling a similar car to be built in short order;

- the threat of the new car becomes well-known and competitors determine to modify their own cars, value engineer them and 'dump' product in target markets;

- trade and technical barriers suddenly appear in target markets;

- although agencies are granted to interested parties in other countries to sell the cars it transpires that these are held by family members of competitors. Market penetration is lower than expected;

- competitors' sleepers from the local community both transmit information and modify information in the manufacturer;

- *Top Gear* in the UK and similar car promotion TV programmes 'trash' the car.

Criminal

- in Eastern Europe a virtually identical car is developed laundering both drug and arms sales money in the process;

- in South America the drug cartels get the car banned in return for access to the Chinese middle-class drug market;

- supplies of parts from neighbouring Chinese provinces and neighbouring countries are squeezed by theft and transport 'inefficiencies';

- various criminal fraternities infiltrate the plant and the supply and distribution network;

- dealers face extortion in Europe and North America, bad press follows the TV stories and key press and PR agencies don't support the product.

Cultural

- the local community has a strong spiritual leader who galvanises international support against the Han take-over;

- the use of parallel banking systems channels money back to the community from worldwide sources giving the campaign a strong financial base;

- the community uses a variety of tactics to deny certain routes to market on cultural grounds;

- the community describes the product as offensive to its culture, origins and beliefs and encourages the international community not to handle it in any way;

- similarly the promotion of the vehicle is hit by various cultural challenges across the world.

Critical infrastructure

- hacking modifies product designs to damage production quality and parts;

- unauthorised online changes are made to parts and complete vehicle prices;

- prices vary between different markets;

- electricity and gas supplies are damaged, stopping production lines. Security is regularly breached both physically and virtually;

- the IT department is run by individuals who know more about the system than the management and therefore control the plant;

- water, sanitation and food becomes intermittent, demoralising people.

Capital

- the working and development capital required suddenly becomes difficult to obtain;

- finance is dictating prices which suddenly become higher than the market will bear;

- product development and the life span of the car is thereby curtailed;

- production is intermittent as suppliers are not paid and banking covenants not met;

- to make up the Financial Director (FD) starts trading and loses large amounts of foreign exchange (FOREX);

- the company's credit risk is increased and this becomes known in international circles.

Of course there is a certain amount of licence taken here on a number of subjects, and it is an entirely fictional scenario. However, looking back at the case studies there is nothing in this scenario that has not been covered in those. So the scenario is not unlikely, indeed a number of the scenarios on the case studies are similar.

It is hopefully unnecessary to add that, on a personal level, all the author's dealings with Chinese individuals and businesses have been genuine, open and honest, as they have with Japanese, Korean, American and French individuals and businesses. Personal experiences, however, do not necessarily reflect national policy, imperatives or tensions.

The addition of a relatively small-scale military or terrorist element would complete the campaign. Key executives are kidnapped for ransom or pure terror. Small-scale 'hit and run' attacks are mounted on the facility. Demonstration executions are occasionally carried out. These, too, are familiar and resonate with the opening comments of this chapter.

It is not necessary to carry out such a co-ordinated campaign. The use of small-scale hit and run attacks plus the denial of critical infrastructure has, as this is written in 2013, already been shown to be more than capable of disrupting key installations. The delivery via employees or remotely of the Stuxnet virus has already shown that large-scale infrastructure can be disabled remotely in ways that do not hurt the civilian population but cause political and infrastructure chaos. The fragility of the world in which all seek to operate is suddenly very apparent.

Is this new? In historical terms probably not. It is possible to go back to Confucius, Sun Tsu, Machiavelli, Napoleon and Clausewitz to understand that the ideas are not new, they have developed and have a modern twist, but they are not essentially new. What is new, particularly for the North and West of the world, is that the dominant, safe, democratic, resource rich, market controlling, militarily powerful, information and data secure world it thought it ran is no longer. This is a profound shock to at least two generations: the baby-boomers and their offspring. The parents of the baby-boomers in the West had, with the exception of, or in some cases including, the Second World War, a life that brought steadily increasing growth, prosperity and security in an essentially well-controlled bi-polar world. The two succeeding generations in the North and West are likely to see a decline in growth, prosperity and security in an increasingly poorly controlled and insecure multi-polar world. This is a reality which has yet to be fully faced by Northern and Western politicians. In this respect they play into the hands of the asymmetric counter marketers because they have not developed the tools or understanding to combat this new force. This is not scaremongering – academics have been teaching of the new security realities for a decade, the case studies show what is going on and the scenario described in this chapter has already been launched against one or more Northern and Western companies.

Protecting from this threat is the subject of the next chapter.

9

Protecting Against Obstructive Marketing

There are probably two key areas to concentrate on in regard to protection against Obstructive Marketing. The first of these is at society level and the second at organisation level. It may be that this book has not paid sufficient attention to the issues at society level. In many ways, as noted from the comments made about Secretary of State Board Meetings in the UK, there is a parallel between the escape of critical infrastructures from government control over the last 50 years and any government's ability to control Obstructive Marketing. There is an impotence to control the market and, if we keep the UK as an example, there is nothing of real relevance in the Civil Contingencies Act of 2004 to ensure that as a nation or society at large the population is protected from Obstructive Marketing attacks, just as they are not protected from attacks on critical infrastructure – most of which is also owned by foreigners. The ownership is not necessarily a bad thing but it is surprising how surprised, in turn, politicians still are to find how much of the UK infrastructure and business is no longer a strategic national asset, but someone else's and some other nation's asset.

In an earlier book on critical infrastructures the author recommended that a national force be established to look after critical information infrastructure in the UK. This has now been established under the control of an Army Major General. Here it is worth suggesting that both the National Risk Register and the tasks of MI5 are extended a little more towards ensuring that the country is well-protected against Obstructive Marketing threats. As noted earlier there are some gaps on the National Risk Register. As Goodger (2010) has commented there is an opportunity to develop any protection into a national asset or unique selling point (USP). That would be a reverse irony of significant proportions – to build a national USP out of protecting the nation against Obstructive Marketing. It is certainly something that a number of key academics believe is possible in both the critical information infrastructure and Obstructive Marketing fields.

In order to be effective a PMESTEL approach needs to be taken. This should align itself closely with the spectra identified for these issues in Chapter 4. In the 'Godfearing' model, Obstructive Marketing was only one antithesis depicted. However, this book has, hopefully, demonstrated how intertwined all the theses and antitheses of the model are. So in defending the nation against an Obstructive Marketing attack:

- sustainable organisations are required to manage the balance between globalisation and Obstructive Marketing;

- Christian values (or morals and ethics), in the case of the UK, must both be understood and promoted because they underpin UK society. The nation may be secular but the values that underpin the way of life are still Christian;

- the military need to develop the Asymmetric Military Balance approach described here. The closest to success on this was probably the Malayan campaign of the 1960s. Neither Iraq nor Afghanistan can be seen as successes against the requirements of an Asymmetric Military Balance;

- social cohesion, not division, should be the political watchword;

- the technologies that control both the physical and virtual worlds need some interlocutor. Just as it is difficult for a traditional policeman to understand the computer nerd who keeps the Internet crime under control so it is with balancing the physical and virtual worlds. This is important from an Obstructive Marketing point of view as companies exploit the virtual at the expense of the physical with the consequence of the taxation issues and barren high streets seen in recent years. This is an area that should perhaps have been better explored in this book;

- resource-hungry nations need to face up to the requirements for a balanced earth approach – so that there is enough left for our children's children. Few policies deal with this;

- international law needs fulsome support across the board. More effort needs to be put into this – and again this is an opportunity to maintain what is already an international lead in law, particularly commercial law, for the UK;

- organised crime needs constant attention. The UK's police forces are either extremely highly regarded for their expertise or the butt of an international joke. The UK TV programme *Traffic Cops* is a comedy show in the Netherlands where the similarity between the police and their targets is regularly commented upon, as is the passion for both wrecking and using fast cars. Somewhere the police institutions have to rediscover their purpose to counter criminal organisations who are identifiably brighter than the police;

- IT. In terms of managing IT some progress has been made in the last five years. More is required to secure the nation properly.

Tackling these issues at national level requires strong leadership. It is to be hoped that the political, church, military and intelligence, social, business, legal and police organisations are themselves sufficiently well-led and robust to develop this leadership role appropriately.

This leads on to how organisations themselves can protect themselves from the consequences of Obstructive Marketing and some of the other issues noted in the 'Godfearing' model in Chapter 4. One way of protecting an organisation from Obstructive Marketing is by 'Hardening'. 'Hardening' is a new term in this context and one of the new ideas explored by this book. 'Hardening' encompasses the context model described in Chapter 4, the risk and dependency models described in Chapter 5 and additional models on staff, crises and in general.

The 'Hardened Organisation'

Protection from disruptive and potentially lethal events has become an important subject for organisations, particularly when facing either Asymmetric Warfare or Obstructive Marketing attacks. Over the past 25 years the general approach to protection has developed from the means of disaster or business recovery, through 'business' continuity, to a current emphasis on resilience. Looking further ahead it is logical to assume that beyond the resilient organisation lies the 'Hardened organisation'. This theme is now further explored and looks forward to how a 'Hardened organisation' might develop.

While it is assumed that the term resilience and other related continuity terms are understood, it is important to define 'Hardened' and 'organisation'.

The strategic context for both is the democratic capitalist system. This context could be more closely defined as those organisations in countries/nation-states who might expect to be attacked by either Asymmetric Warfare or Obstructive Marketing techniques. In general these are likely to be the constituent members of the G8/20, OECD or North Atlantic Treaty Organization (NATO) and their national organisations – be they private, public or third sector.

In computing, 'Hardening' is the process of securing a system. This work is necessary to protect systems against hostile environments or attackers. Hardened steel is steel which will not deform or degrade. Hardening in martial arts is the process of strengthening the body to withstand various attacks. Hardened shelters are those which will withstand military attacks. In French the verb 'racornir' means both to 'toughen' and 'harden'. This would be an appropriate word to use.

Organisation is a term that refers to a functional social body that operates, usually, in a defined environment and has a defined boundary. The word 'usually' is stressed because it is increasingly clear that some organisations have 'fuzzy' or poorly defined boundaries – a consequence of either the personnel involved or business process design. This is particularly the case with 'virtual' organisations.

The 'Hardened organisation' can therefore be defined as a public, private or third sector organisation within the context of a democratic and capitalist state which can withstand, and is protected from, Asymmetric Warfare or Obstructive Marketing attacks. The 'Hardened organisation' differs from the resilient organisation in that it is not damaged by an attack and therefore has no need, as the resilient organisation has, to 'bounce back in its original form' from an attack. It is therefore even more robust than the resilient organisation.

The 'Hardened organisation' represents the pinnacle of a 'business (or organisation) continuity' hierarchy comprising:

- recovery;

- continuity;

- resilience;

- hardening.

This hierarchy has evolved over the last 25 years from those early days when it was realised that, for example, the loss of organisational data needed to be recovered in order for an organisation's operations to continue. This process was (and still is) much in evidence in the banking sector. As this process was tamed so others followed suit. Led again by the financial services industry, it further dawned on those responsible for maintaining operations in time and space that all business processes must be planned and controlled so that business could continue in the event of more widespread asset loss or damage. This marked the beginning of business continuity and the pursuit of the resilient business. Gradually it became clear that not just businesses required such strategies and tactics but that the term was appropriate for all organisations regardless of their purpose or sector.

For many organisations it is clear that a 'Hardened' approach is appropriate and achieved by striking an appropriate cost/benefit balance. It would probably be inappropriate on one hand for a high-street sole-trader to harden their business from the outset. But on the other hand there are compelling reasons why many cross-border multi-nationals, banks and international oil companies for example, need to 'Harden' all or part of their business for all of the time.

Figure 9.1 shows the improving and sequential steps of an organisation's ability to withstand attack or disaster (although a 'Hardened organisation' should never, by definition, suffer a disaster).

Figure 9.1   The 'Hardened organisation' and the business continuity hierarchy

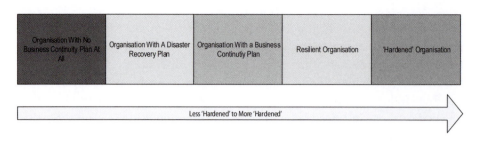

Figure 9.2   The 'Hardened organisation' and the business continuity spectrum

Source: Maitland P. Hyslop, 2013, © Northumbria University.

This hierarchy has at its base those organisations that rely on some form of business or disaster recovery plan to get back on their feet after some damaging event. Statistically, these organisations have a poor chance of survival, less than 25 per cent according to London Resilience (2012). The next stage up consists of those organisations that have a business continuity plan. Yet a business continuity plan does not guarantee safety, as 90 per cent of businesses that lose data are forced to shut down within two years (Business Continuity, 2010). Many of these do have a business continuity plan. The resilient organisations are those that can 'bounce back' after an event. As noted, this group accounts for much less than 10 per cent of all organisations. At the top is the Hardened organisation, the organisation that does not have a problem at all following an event that challenges business continuity.

In an environment where globalisation has been met by Obstructive Marketing and asymmetric challenges, then the 'Hardened organisation' is an appropriate posture in order to withstand and respond to most, if not all, threats to organisations. It is important to stress here that this does not mean just large organisations; increasingly all members of a private, public or third sector supply chain are being required to demonstrate some evidence of Hardening. As Chapter 2 showed, this is led by the Japanese.

Looked at from another perspective, this may not be a hierarchy at all but much more a spectrum. This follows from the views that not all organisations need the same sort of protection. So, rather than the usual description of business continuity in terms of a pyramid, it is much more appropriate to describe is as a spectrum. This spectrum would look as indicated in Figure 9.2.

Just as this thesis now anticipates organisations requiring different approaches to Hardening, so organisations require different positions on the business continuity spectrum.

The importance of this to the organisations, information infrastructure and critical infrastructures is that there is an immediate and clear path beyond business continuity planning and resilience planning to be followed.

Chapter 4 dealt with context and Chapter 5 dealt with risk and dependency so it is now appropriate to add the staff, crisis and general approaches required to help protect organisations from Obstructive Marketing by completing a 'Hardening' process and forming a model to prevent Obstructive Marketing.

The 'Hyperion' Staff model acknowledges the issues for the requirements of 'Hardened' staffing. There are 22 characteristics useful to have in individuals to create a resilient staff. To this must be added organisational values and those organisational attributes that mean the 'people' side of an organisation is as 'Hardened' as possible. Training is always the key ingredient in building both successful and resilient teams. Well-being in the workplace is increasingly seen as a means of not only keeping staff well but also happy. Recent research suggests that keeping staff well and happy leads to more successful operations. These attributes will be brought together in the 'Hyperion' model.

The 'Watson' Crisis model acknowledges the Chapter 4 conclusion that current crisis management is reactive not proactive. The 'Watson' Crisis model builds planning for crises into the organisation from an early stage and recognises the need to involve many in the solution to a crisis. The model also acknowledges that it is often the 'unknowns' that de-rail a crisis management plan. An example of this would be the furore caused by Tony Hayward when, as CEO of BP during the 2010–2011 Mexican Gulf Oil Spill, he was seen yachting in the Solent with friends, with dire PR consequences. Crises always return the affected organisation to somewhere different. The somewhere different needs to be on the organisation's road map. Therefore, any approach to crisis management needs to be proactive in order to ensure the end point is on the road map.

Finally, this chapter brings all of these together into a general 'Racornir' model that can sit beside or within existing business models and contribute to the efficient management of an organisation. If properly implemented, the model can be used as the basis for the management of an organisation.

The 'Hyperion' Staff Model

In Chapter 3 it was noted that most CEOs and senior managers in the top 30 per cent of organisations do not have succession planning, and staff are seen as both an asset and a liability. In the same chapter it was noted that the disgruntled employee is a serious Obstructive Marketing risk to the organisation. Employees also represent a major IT security vulnerability (with mobile phones and personal digital accessories) for organisations. The staff are important, be they C-suite members, management or staff. All this points to the preparation, training, actions and resilience of individuals being a very important element of Hardening an organisation, or making an organisation more resilient. However, as there is a disconnect between this approach and how the top 30 per cent of businesses view their staff a number of issues need to be resolved.

In a general sense it is important to develop at least 'resilient' individuals. The 22 characteristics derived from a variety of studies in Chapter 3 are that resilient individuals:

1.   have a trusted network;

2.   have behavioural limits;

3.   are shown how to do things right;

4.   learn to be independent;

5.   are assisted when sick;

6.   are liked and loved;

7.   are well behaved;

8.   are respectful of self and others;

9.   are confident;

10.   are communicative;

11.   can control when things go wrong;

12.   are opportunistic;

13.   can get help when needed;

14.   are emotionally fit;

15.   have a stable family;

16.   are physically fit;

17.   are socially at ease;

18.   are spiritually aware;

19.   manage personal energy;

20.   understand context;

21.   avoid thinking traps;

22.   have a clear personal place and development.

The US Army recently adopted a programme that recognises some of these characteristics and developed a programme to increase resilience in soldiers with the purpose of 'Hardening' their operational units. This is now a $125 million Comprehensive Soldier Fitness programme, basically resilience for soldiers, which has seen an improvement in retention and fit-for-purpose assessments amongst American soldiers as well as better operational results, a reduction in post-traumatic stress syndrome and an increased resistance to torture. This approach is summarised by permission as follows.

The Five Pillars of Soldier Fitness

EMOTIONAL FITNESS

An emotionally fit person faces life's challenges in a positive, optimistic way by demonstrating self-control, stamina and balance, never too high, never too low, with his or her choices and actions.

Cast me into a dungeon; burn me at the stake, crown me king of kings,
I can 'pursue happiness' as long as my brain lives – but neither gods
nor saints, wise men nor subtle drugs, can insure that I will catch it.
(Heinlein, 1987)

FAMILY FITNESS

Family fitness is built by being part of a family unit that is safe, supportive and loving, and provides the resources needed for all members to live in a healthy and secure environment.

Pray that your loneliness may spur you into finding something to live
for, great enough to die for. (Hammarskjöld, 1964)

PHYSICAL FITNESS

Physical readiness is the ability to meet the physical demands of any combat or duty position, accomplish the mission, and continue to fight/compete/participate and win.

War makes extremely heavy demands on the soldier's strength and
nerves. For this reason, make heavy demands on your men in peacetime
exercises and training. (Rommel, 2011, 1937)

SOCIAL FITNESS

A socially fit person develops and maintains trusted, valued relationships and friendships that are personally fulfilling. They foster good communication, including a comfortable exchange of ideas, views and experiences.

The quality of a person's life is in direct proportion to their commitment to
excellence, regardless of their chosen field of endeavour. (Lombardi, 1965)

SPIRITUAL FITNESS

Spiritual fitness is built by developing and strengthening a set of beliefs, principles or values that sustain a person beyond family, institutional and societal sources of strength.

In war, the morale is to the material as three is to one. (Bonaparte, 1798)

RESILIENCY TRAINING SKILLS OVERVIEW

The programme goes on to give an overview of the resiliency skills that can be used to help set goals:

- *Skill 1: Activating events, thoughts, and consequences*: Identify thoughts about an activating event and the consequences of those thoughts;

- *Skill 2: Avoid thinking traps*: Identify and correct counterproductive patterns in thinking through the use of critical questions;

- *Skill 3: Detect icebergs*: Identify deep beliefs and core values that fuel out-of-proportion emotion and evaluate the accuracy and usefulness of these beliefs;

- *Skill 4: Energy management*: Enhance self-regulation so that you are able to stay calm and concentrated when facing an adversity or challenge;

- *Skill 5: Problem-solving*: Accurately identify what caused the problem and identify solution strategies;

- *Skill 6: Put it in perspective*: Stop catastrophic thinking, reduce anxiety and improve problem-solving by identifying the worst, best and most likely outcomes of a situation;

- *Skill 7: Real-time resilience*: Shut down counterproductive thinking to enable greater concentration on the task at hand;

- *Skill 8: Character strengths*: Identify your top character strengths and those of others and identify ways to use your strengths to increase your effectiveness and strengthen your relationships;

- *Skill 9: Strengths in challenges*: Identify the specific actions that flow from your strengths in challenges and in successes;

- *Skill 10: Assertive communication*: Communicate clearly and with respect. Communicate in a confident, clear, and controlled manner;

- *Skill 11: Active constructive responding and praise*: Respond to others to build strong relationships and offer praise to build mastery and winning streaks;

- *Skill 12: Hunt the positive*: Hunt the positive to counter the negativity bias, to create positive emotion, and to recognise and analyse what is good.

GOAL-SETTING

Goals are a vital aspect of life. They provide purpose and direction, motivation, commitment and clarity about the desired outcome. Unfortunately, most do not engage in a deliberate and systematic process for identifying goals, or have a plan for getting there. Elite performers do it all the time. Research has shown that goals and goal-setting do affect performance. Setting and achieving goals need not be a burden; there is a method and a process to help chart the way.

Properly applied, this process can add clarity and focus to what has typically been a challenging experience for many soldiers, family members and civilians. By incorporating the process of goal-setting with other resilience skills, lifelong practices develop that enable the achievement of goals and top performance. If done right, a goal-setting process will establish mechanisms that highlight 'goals' every day.

Use of the acronym SMART (Specific, Measurable, Achievable, Realistic, Timely) helps in terms of project and personal management.

The programme review helps to verify and validate the 22 characteristics identified in Chapter 4 and also helps to place these elements into an organisational context.

The Wellington Approach

Happiness and well-being, resilience by another name in this context, has also become a taught course at Wellington College, UK and a number of other institutions. This is important for our understanding of 'Hardening' staff because these approaches produce resilient individuals.

The unique Wellington curriculum has been devised for Wellington by Dr Nick Baylis of the University of Cambridge (Baylis, 2012) one of the world's leading specialists in the science of well-being. The approach is founded on the principle of studying lives that go particularly well, and then using that knowledge to develop and apply strategies and skills that promote all-round progress in a person's psychological, physical and social life. Importantly, the curriculum takes a rounded approach to the subject of life development, combining a core of positive psychology with teaching on a range of other key factors such as sleep, nutrition and exercise. Ten of the school's existing teachers are trained to deliver the curriculum, led by Wellington's Ian Morris who has devised the classroom applications in close collaboration with Dr Baylis.

Special programmes in other schools have tended to target 'youngsters at risk', or children rather than teenagers, or specific maladies such as depression rather than life in general, so the great majority of interventions have been remedial, trying to get youngsters from below average up to average. The Wellington curriculum is aimed at helping everyone to make progress, no matter what the individual's starting point.

The lesson themes are structured around a student's relationship with life, including:

- the relationship between mind and body;

- the relationship between their conscious and subconscious;

- the relationships with people around them;

- the relationship with their past, present, future and fantasy lives;

- the relationship with the natural world.

Techniques and activities in the lessons include: learning how to positively channel emotional energy, working in harmony with the sub-conscious mind, overcoming fears and unhelpful inhibitions and using 'imaginative rehearsal' to improve real-life performance.

These projects follow the general ideas of Seligman (2004) who proposes that 'happiness' and 'optimism' can be taught and who, in 2002, presented a closed session to the US Navy on how to resist torture. These approaches have resonance with the US Army approach described above.

Cathy Severson (2010) summarises the 'Science of Happiness' according to Seligman as follows:

> **Maintenance:** This is not part of the happiness continuum, but maintenance is still an important component in living. These are simply the tasks of things that must get done. They do not bring a sense of happiness, but contribute to the overall well-being of an individual. They are necessary to function in the world. The key to happiness is to not spend all of one's time bogged down in maintenance types of activities. Like most activities in the happiness model, one person's poison is another person's dream. Paying bills, cleaning, doing laundry may be maintenance tasks for you, but a real joy for others. Cooking is a great example of a task that fills some with dread, just look at the number of dinners spent at a fast food restaurant. Alternatively, cooking food is almost a spiritual experience for some.
>
> **Pleasure:** Pleasurable happiness is based on momentary bodily senses. The sensory organs are quite literally hooked to the brain to receive a positive emotion from touching, tasting, smelling, seeing, hearing, and bodily movements.
>
> To understand this kind of pleasure, all we have to do is look at the amazing array of foods available in the world today. Nutritional needs can be met with very basic foods, but the desire for pleasure keeps individuals experimenting with new and different ways to tantalise the taste buds. Part of the reason for an overweight society is the pleasure derived from food. This helps explain addictive behaviour connected to the senses. Society is constantly bombarded with images and ideas that encourage pleasure seeking. Some are addicted to shopping, gambling and extreme sports. A casino's bright lights and colour bombarding customers at every turn, with music and alcohol, are all designed to create a pleasurable sense of being.
>
> This is not to say pleasure is wrong or bad. Contrary to our puritanical ancestors, pleasure is an integral part of our being. It feeds the senses, which not only entices our brain, but can sooth the heart and heal the spirit. The harm, and lack of resilience, comes when people fail to experience other forms of happiness.

Engagement: The second form of happiness is engagement. Seligman's ideas of engagement come from the work of Csikszentmihalyi (1998). Flow is defined as the state of gratification entered when completely engaged in a task. Flow contains a sense of *exhilaration* when performing a task that requires complex abilities that leads to a challenging goal. It appears evolution has built the need for *complexity* in the nervous system. Enjoyment is experienced when individuals are *challenged* by a new activity that uses and stretches talents. There is also a level of *risk* that takes individuals out of their comfort zone. Finding engaging activities has also been a key to successful aging. This is also important for organisations – successful organisations are 'in the flow' constantly. Apple Inc. is a good example.

The key to this form of happiness is tapping into the unique activities that individuals find engaging. Not all become engaged in the same activities. Each has their own unique abilities and characteristics that make certain challenges engaging. It is through engaging in a challenging leisure activity that personality is expressed. Gratification and happiness come from the joy of being able to express personalities in interesting activities or hobbies.

If self-actualisation means simply doing what each was supposed to do and is the highest form of expression of an individual and what he/she desires to be, then everyone has moments of self-actualisation. Maslow (1954) identified these moments as peak experiences. A person having a peak experience, as Maslow (1954) described them, is 'more truly himself, closer to the core of his being, more fully human'. While few may attain a state of continuous self-actualisation, everyone can have those moments where they live authentically. Hardened organisations would seek to help their staff achieve in such ways because they produce more resilient individuals.

Meaning: Beyond engaging in a fulfilling activity, there is another level of being to which people find happiness. Seligman refers to this as the level of meaning; when someone connects to a higher purpose of life or calling. Living through purpose means connecting to something larger than the self; this is a level of living that transcends the self or ego.

Covey (2005) tells us that everyone has a longing to:

Live a life of greatness and contribute, to really matter, to really make a difference, to live a life of significance.

Although the latter is not necessarily true these approaches together with a wider understanding of resilience are behind the US Army programmes and the Wellington programme and a number of other recent ideas regarding both 'happiness' and 'resilience'. Many of the ideas can be traced back to Jung and the concept of self-actualisation.

As a common-sense approach all of these would seem to be reasonable characteristics needed in staff for resilient or 'Hardened'organisations, and combining the approaches would help to create a 'Hardened' organisation. Note that not all individuals necessarily wish to or can conform to these ideas, some care is required in generalising that everyone can or should conform to such a model. However, in a Staff model for organisations a measure of these characteristics will be required to provide the right sort of 'attitude' and resilience in staff from the beginning.

The obvious difficulty with such an approach is that these are not the characteristics that are found in Western children these days but are more often found in the offspring of many eastern cultures (Chau, 2010). Having said this Chau did comment that, in the end, a balanced approach was required. Thus finding people with the right approach for organisations, East or West, is and will be a challenge for Human Resource departments. Human Resource departments have never really had to think about looking for individuals like this before; so the approach will require a change of direction from Human Resource departments too.

Additional, as noted, individual resilience skills might include knowing how to grow and harvest food, exercise, use of alternative fuels at home, protecting oneself from things like bird 'flu (by understanding key personal hygiene rules) and having some sort of individual plan to survive food and other shortages. Above all to do all of this within a society or organisation that has a clearly defined set of values and processes and, by and large, lives them.

Resilience skills are slightly different to learning and understanding skills. Learning skills, and the way in which people learn, has been the subject of much debate (Hammond et al., 2001). This debate has centred on the use of visual, aural, and kinetic learning bias. There is some doubt, particularly in children, if there are such distinct learning skills.

However, in sport, there is clearly the need to teach in these three areas. As a kayak coach the author is encouraged by the British Canoe Union (2010) to teach river skills from a visual, aural and kinaesthetic perspective because canoeing and kayaking involves hearing, seeing and feeling in order to be successful.

There are some problems with understanding the context of organisational learning for some. This is an issue that has exercised, amongst others, the UK Government Communications Headquarters (GCHQ) (2012) and CPNI (2010). The key issue is that any form of learning skill is still not appropriate for an intuitive understanding of the Internet, cf. Huxley (1932). It is extremely difficult for most human beings to grasp the context, size and reach of the Internet. This is evident from anecdotal and formal evidence (GCHQ, 2012). This is a very great danger to organisations in terms of how they might wish to run their affairs in the world context described in this book.

Alexander (2010) has noted that Carl Jung may be the most influential thinker in terms of disaster management in the twenty-first century – not only for his psychological approach, clearly important for reasons noted above, but also for his understanding of how symbolism helps humans understand new concepts (for example, the Internet and new contexts). There is insufficient symbolism to describe the new environment. This has been partially overcome by the use of symbols for text mobile messages, 'emoticons' and the shorthand used for the Internet, but there is a large tract of the electronic environment that awaits either a symbol or language to describe it adequately. Such symbolic progress may help the mass of the population understand the electronic environment, particularly the Internet and what comes after it, better.

In the workplace the research in Chapter 3 suggests that there is poor succession planning for senior staff, an ambivalent attitude on behalf of senior management towards the treatment of staff and the workforce is not always treated as an asset to be developed.

These issues may be summarised as follows:

- individuals need to be resilient in order for organisations to be resilient. There are resilient models for children, high reliability organisations the US military and 'happiness' which demonstrate that improvements in individual resilience are possible;

- learning skills need not only to be visual, aural and kinaesthetic, but also aware of a completely different approach required to understand the context of the Internet and the electronic environment;

- attitudes to staff in the workplace, for senior management, management and the workforce, need to encompass the resilient requirements and learning requirements in order that the organisation becomes a proper learning organisation.

If the key themes of a learning organisation are reprised according to Senge (1990) then 'learning organisations' are those organisations where people continually expand their capacity to create the results they truly desire, where new and expansive patterns of thinking are nurtured, where collective aspiration is set free and where people are continually learning to see the whole together. Senge (1990) argues that only those organisations able to adapt quickly and effectively will excel in their field or market. In order to be a learning organisation there must be two conditions present at all times. The first is the ability to design the organisation to match the intended or desired outcomes, and second, the ability to recognise when the initial direction of the organisation is different from the desired outcome and follow the necessary steps to correct this mismatch. Organisations that are able to do this are exemplary. Note that crises always return organisations to somewhere different and, as noted in Chapter 3, the somewhere different has to be on the organisation's road map and consistent with this approach.

Senge (1990) also believed in the theory of systems thinking which has sometimes been referred to as the 'cornerstone' of the learning organisation. Systems thinking focuses on how the individual that is being studied interacts with the other constituents of the system. Rather than focussing on the individuals within an organisation it prefers to look at a larger number of interactions within the organisation and in between organisations as a whole.

In terms of this book then, the general approach of Senge (1990) would be supported in terms of the organisation. However, this book would suggest that although systems thinking is important the individual needs just as much attention. Combining these means the organisation then becomes greater than the sum of its parts.

This leads to a description of personnel development for an organisation that encompasses:

- values;

- personal resilience;

- learning skill development;

- organisational focus and development;

- systems thinking and individual development.

This model has to be proportional to both the context and type of organisation, the risks being run, dependencies and the value and type of value added. As in other parts of this book there is a spectrum into which organisations would fit. The individual skills required of a knowledge-based multi-national company are clearly different to those of the corner shop. The model, as in previous examples, should be able to demonstrate whereabouts on the spectrum the organisation sits.

The general nature of such a model requires a generic name. The model is called the 'Hyperion' Staff model, because Hyperion was the first to understand light and the movement of the earth and moon, and became the God of Watchfulness and Wisdom. Because of the holistic nature of Hyperion's understanding it is an appropriate name for an organisational and personnel model which requires both a holistic approach and a wide understanding of personnel matters.

The model is shown in Figure 9.3.

CONCLUSION

The more resilient staff can be the more 'Hardened' an organisation will be. The changes in the approach to staff are significant. Not only will HR departments be taking more interest in business continuity, as seen in Chapter 3, but they will also need a completely different training programme for staff and the organisation to 'Harden' both.

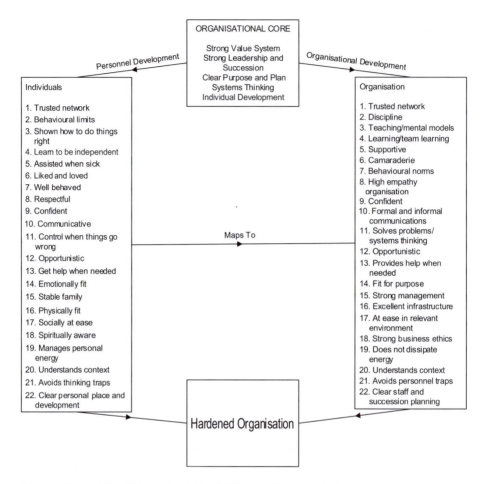

Figure 9.3   The 'Hyperion' Staff 'Hardening' model
Source: Maitland P. Hyslop, 2013, © Northumbria University.

The 'Watson' Crisis model

INTRODUCTION

The failure of the context, risk, dependency and staff models would lead to a crisis. The main objective of crisis management is to help prevent a crisis ever occurring. If a crisis is unavoidable the objective must be to protect the organisation during and after a crisis and return the organisation to somewhere on its development road map, as a crisis always returns an organisation somewhere different. Borodzicz (2005, p81, location 997) states:

Ill structured crises are those which slip through the procedural net; this is why they are often misconceived to be Acts of God, or totally unique abominations. This is not the case.

One of the most damaging aspects of a crisis is the potential for a reduced organisational image and reputation. If handled well, a company can emerge from a crisis with minimal damage and it will be easy to regain the confidence of the target audience. If handled badly, the damage may be irreparable or at least require a lot of money and many years to rectify. As Knight and Pretty (2000) showed, those involved in a crisis can be divided into the 'recoverers' and the 'non-recoverers'. They also demonstrated the importance of managerial competence and a proper crisis management plan.

The conduit that will make or break a company's reputation in time of crisis is the media. Media relations is therefore of extreme importance in a crisis management plan (Watson, 2011; Brassell-Cicchini, 2002).

Another advantage of crisis management planning is that it will enable a business to operate as normally as possible under the circumstances; note a crisis management plan is not necessarily the same thing as a business continuity plan. It will free the management to focus on priorities. Even if the most senior manager is away, the business can still continue to operate.

It must always be remembered, however, that if a crisis hits it will be a dynamic situation and can develop in unexpected ways so vigilance and agility must be applied throughout.

TRADITIONAL CRISIS MANAGEMENT

Traditional crisis management was epitomised by Cockram (2012) but he has recently changed his approach and has been helpful in this context. This is part of the basis for PAS 200, BSI (2012b), which means the industry is still looking at a largely reactive model.

In this traditional model crisis management is based on:

- situational awareness;

- decision-making;

- leadership;

- communications and reputation management;

- plans and procedural development;

- training and exercising.

In this model a crisis is characterised by:

- unpredictability;

- dynamic or volatile progression;

- urgency/pressure;

- accountability;

- uncertainty;

- lack of boundaries;

- media scrutiny;

- complexity.

The crisis is managed by a crisis management team consisting of:

- the gold team of strategic thinkers;

- the silver team of planners and co-ordinators;

- bronze team of the doers.

Information is:

- collected;

- collated;

- analysed;

- distributed.

And the leader is:

- decisive;

- strategic;

- communicator;

- delegator;

- listener;

- respectful;

- self-confident;

- emotionally intelligent.

The issue for the 'Hardened' organisation, as discussed in previous paragraphs, is that it would expect to see most of this covered already and therefore much of what may be put together for a crisis in these terms should already exist on a permanent basis. The following describes what might be different in a 'Hardened' organisation.

PROACTIVE CRISIS MANAGEMENT – THE 'WATSON' MODEL

A permanent crisis management team, not an incident management team which is different, must be identified and appointed. It should include representatives from the main business areas such as marketing communications, development, sales and personnel. An overall manager or team leader should be appointed who may not necessarily be the key spokesperson in the event of a crisis and should certainly not be the CEO.

The crisis management team meets regularly, a minimum of half yearly, to review possible issues, weak points and Black Swans within and without the company that could cause a crisis. These may be the result of legislation or events outside an organisation's control. Ways of avoiding such a crisis should be identified and actioned. In addition 'what if' and creative scenarios should be established in the event of the crisis occurring, and exercised appropriately. Extra time will be needed at the outset in order to create a core crisis management document. This should be reviewed at these meetings and updated, if required.

A comprehensive yet easy to use and easy to update crisis management document should be prepared. It is anticipated that this will include details of:

- the team: including their responsibilities in a crisis with all home and business contact details;

- the target audience: that will need to be focussed upon should a crisis be identified. It is likely to include: existing and potential customers, staff, suppliers and the industry as a whole;

- media handling: details will be set out including responsibilities and procedures;

- scenarios: of typical crises (and some Black Swan thinking should be identified, the corporate response worked out and support material researched and gathered);

- formats: a series of formats should be prepared for use in handling a crisis;

- other information: will include details of general procedures in the event of a crisis; facilities available, location of database and outline of contents, business continuity, disaster recovery and communications planning to follow up a crisis in order to restore confidence.

A database is set up to contain the name, address, email and telephone number of all customers, staff (home details), regular suppliers and industry bodies. A 'wall of influence' is constructed identifying all those above, beside and below the key individuals in the organisation who can help the organisation, internal and external. Social media networks should be used where appropriate.

The facilities required in a crisis must be examined and form part of the plan. In the event of a major crisis, a dedicated communications centre is required. This would be a room which could be turned over at a moment's notice. It would be equipped with computers with Internet connection as well as separate telephone lines that would only be used in the event of a crisis. This would help to ensure that the switchboard remains relatively free and that business areas unaffected by the crisis can continue as normal. Ideally, this would be in a different electric grid and different telephone exchange area than the organisation itself.

Media training is given to all who require it. This may include senior management as well as any other nominated spokespersons.

Clearly, a crisis does not necessarily invoke a business continuity plan and needs to be seen in a different context.

Crises return organisations to a different place. It is important that such a place is where the organisation wants to be. Because of this it is important that organisations have a proactive model, one they control, so that the point of return is positive on the organisation's route map. This is termed the Crisis Positive Restoration Point, a new term original to this book. Further new and original terms associated with this term would be:

- Crisis Negative Restoration Point – the restoration point is not on the organisation's route map and is unhelpful;

- Crisis Neutral Restoration Point – the restoration point may or may not be on the organisation's route map but is not unhelpful.

The adjectives forward, backward and sideways may be added to describe precisely where on the route map spectrum the crisis returns the organisation.

Plans do not usually survive intact their first contact with an event. Therefore the model in Figure 9.4 is an attempt to provide a route to success that can survive first contact with an event.

Figure 9.4   The 'Watson' Positive Crisis Management model

Source: Maitland P. Hyslop, 2011, © Northumbria University.

CONCLUSION

Crises return organisations to a different place. It is important that such a place is where the organisation wants to be. Because of this it is important that organisations have a proactive model, one they control, so that the point of return is on the organisation's route map. Reacting to crises, as any number of examples in this book has demonstrated, does not necessarily return an organisation to where it wants to be. Proactive crisis management 'Hardens' organisations. Crisis management is not the same as incident management.

The 'Racornir' General 'Hardening' model

These models suggest that a new general model can be created, as in Figure 9.5. Such a model would link context, risk, dependency and staff models together and place these in the context of the usual organisational management models. Once these are complete and fully understood then a proactive crisis management plan can be created to complete a general, or 'Racornir', model for a Hardened organisation.

APPLICATION OF THE 'RACORNIR' MODEL

The 'Racornir' model can be applied to any organisational situation, including business continuity. All the 'Northumbria' models that contribute to the 'Racornir' model can be applied to any organisational situation. They are a way of approaching the context, risk, dependency, staff, crisis and general situations in which an organisation may find itself. They include a way of looking at issues in a structured manner which is not specifically replicated elsewhere. As a consequence they represent a new way of looking at an organisation's strategic, operational and tactical planning. They do not replace other models such as those shown diagrammatically at the end of Chapter 2, but they do provide a way of looking at things which does include new ideas and areas often missed by other models.

Although the models can be applied to any organisation they are clearly more relevant to the large and international operation than they are to the corner shop.

A SUGGESTED APPROACH TO OVERCOMING THE 'PERCEPTION' PROBLEM

As identified in Chapter 3, there is a clear perception problem surrounding organisations in the UK in regard specifically to business continuity planning and the Internet.

It could be said that the 'Racornir' model reaches those areas of business continuity planning implicit but not explicit in BS 25999. Explicitly, BS 25999 calls for the premises, processes, people and products (and services) of the organisation to be subject to a business impact analysis and a subsequent remedial business continuity plan. There is relatively poor take-up of this in the UK against the Far East, for example, and even less take-up of testing.

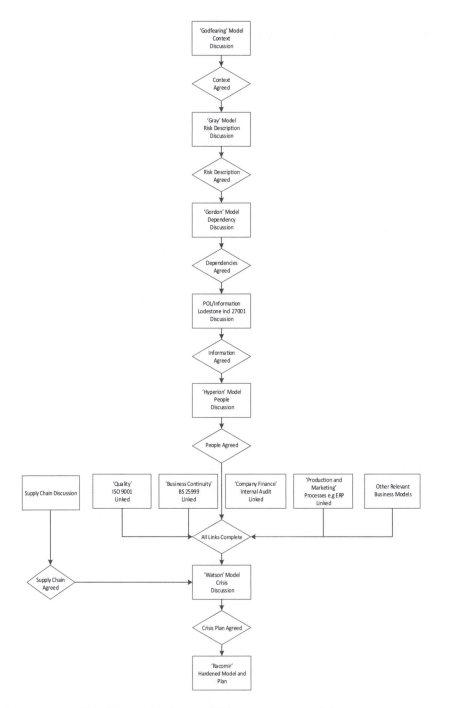

Figure 9.5   The 'Racornir' General Management model

Source: Maitland P. Hyslop, 2012, © Northumbria University.

A key reason for this may be nomenclature and the role of the regulatory authorities. In the UK business continuity planning is seen as an optional spend and even today is not compulsory for all businesses. In many supply chains in the Far East it is compulsory. In this respect it is a competitive requirement, if not an absolute advantage to have a business continuity plan. Business continuity, resilience and 'Hardening' should not be looked at as a 'recovery' but more as preserving and maintaining the gap between market capitalisation and net asset value. It should also be seen as a competitive advantage. If 'Hardening' can be looked at in such a light then it will help the 'perception' problem.

In respect of the Internet the position is a little more complex. The reliance of all organisations on critical information infrastructures has been described in Hyslop (2007b; 2010). Since these publications it has been noted that GCHQ and others have become exercised by the centrality of the Internet to information assurance in business. Much of Chapters 2 and 4 ('Godfearing' model) demonstrated the dependency. The difficulty is that many organisational leaders are ignorant of the 'facts of life' in regard to cyber-warfare in particular, confirmed by IBM (2012). This lack of understanding is so important that just as there are 'Secure Actions for Exporters' used by UK Trade and Industry (UKTI) and others (Hyslop, 2012), there should be 'Secure Actions for Information Assurance in Organisations'.

This requires a public information campaign on the scale of those once used in the 1950s for protection from nuclear war. This is far more important than most other State regulations and information sources. The role of GCHQ and the Ministry of Defence (MOD) in this effort is important, at least as important as dealing with any other threat to the UK, for example, and needs to be taken forward as a joint effort between organisations (British Chamber of Commerce (BCC), Confederation of British Industry (CBI), Voluntary Organisations (VO) and GCHQ/MOD. The key messages must be designed to overcome the ignorance and apathy. While this book is being written, and following discussions with the researcher, the Information Lodestone Concept and Framework (Goodger, 2011b) has been formulated and a company formed to do just this.

Further complications, for which there is no real space to develop fully, might include:

- symbology;

- the battle between Europe and the US regarding control of the Internet;

- further casual, cultural and competitive issues;

- the problems within businesses from legacy systems and the need to bring systems in businesses into some sort of co-ordinated whole;

- the problems with businesses not dealing properly with Pan Organisation Logistics;

- the problems with China-type countries;

- some specific suggestions dealing with travelling abroad.

If what has been learnt of Obstructive Marketing in Chapters 2 and 4 is combined with Trim's (2005) Global Intelligence and Security Environmental Sustainability (GISES) model, then a new model to deal with Obstructive Marketing threats is created that helps both build in security from the beginning but also gives a template against which marketing can be proactively assessed within the context, risk and dependencies identified. This gives a counterbalance to those that threaten activities linked to globalisation. This model could therefore be represented by Figure 9.6.

In this model Black Swans have been added to the 6Cs. Such a model helps to interpret the important context of globalisation. Further, the organisational values, strategy and the models from this book create a core around which strong relationships with key stakeholders such as government, non-government organisations (NGOs) and agencies, the law and intelligence agencies, and the relevant trade associations, chambers and embassies form a defence against the threats of Black Swans and the 6Cs.

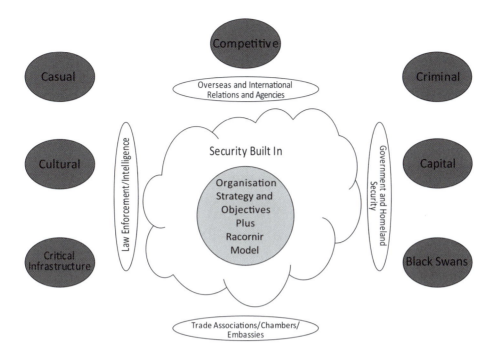

Figure 9.6   How to prevent Obstructive Marketing model

Source: Maitland P. Hyslop, 2012, © Northumbria University.

10

Summary

Chapter 1: Introduction and Definition

- The old bi-polar world of the Cold War was easily understood.
- Recent hacking of US Corporations and physical attacks by Islamic groups in Africa highlight the purpose of this book: Obstructive Marketing.
- Today's landscape is different, it is multi-polar and difficult to understand.
- The rules of war change over time and today the rules are changing apace, and are not just about the military.
- The global financial crisis of 2007/2008 has seen a rebalancing of economic power.
- The world has fragmented from the clear social fabrics that bound the major Western democracies and the Eastern monoliths for decades.
- Not everyone is keen on technology and those that believe that technology challenges the supremacy of God will become an increasing challenge to the technophiles of this world.
- The planet is under threat from pollution, population and the plunder of resources to feed the demand for products.
- Trade is not always conducted legally or in such a simple manner as it used to be.
- Obstructive Marketing is not well understood.
- Obstructive Marketing is 'any process, legal or not, which prevents or restricts the distribution of a product or service, temporarily or permanently, against the wishes of the product manufacturer, service provider of customer.'
- There is now traditional capitalism and state-sponsored capitalism.
- The challenges are the 6Cs: casual, competitive, criminal, cultural, critical infrastructure and capitalism.

- Section 1 deals with the who, what, why, when and how of Obstructive Marketing.
- Chapter 2 deals with the origins of Obstructive Marketing.
- Chapter 3 deals with the principal Obstructive Marketing casual, competitive, criminal, cultural, critical infrastructure and capitalism challenges.
- Section 2 looks at preventing Obstructive Marketing.
- Chapter 4 looks at the modern context in which businesses and organisations have to operate.
- Chapter 5 looks at the description, measurement and management of risk.
- Chapter 6 introduces the concept of Asymmetric Warfare.
- Chapter 7 looks at the capital markets.
- Chapter 8 brings these themes together and introduces new concepts of Asymmetric Military Balance and Asymmetric Obstructive Marketing.
- Chapter 9 looks at how Obstructive Marketing can be prevented.
- Chapter 10 is this summary.
- Chapter 11 looks to the future.

Chapter 2: Obstructive Marketing Origins

- Marketers must be familiar with economics, management science, psychology, sociology and the mathematics of the market place.
- Emphasis on satisfying customer requirements is central to any definition of marketing.
- There are no negatives in marketing definitions.
- Obstructive Marketing is restated.
- Parallels to Sun Tsu, Machiavelli, Newton and Clausewitz are noted.
- Angell's view on the new security paradigm is quoted.
- Competitive pressures as between cultures, from Huntington (1996), are noted.
- The parallel with black holes in astrophysics is developed.
- Marx's view on challenging marketing is quoted.
- As is Mao's view that the US will be hanged for its aggressive policies.
- Islam is not reflective of a capitalist existence is stated.
- Every reason why Obstructive Marketing should exist.
- Thinkers confirm 'intent'.
- Political thought has always dealt with the state, this has changed.

- Rules that have governed society have changed in recent years.
- How casual damage to organisations occurs is introduced.
- Competition and cultural issues are introduced.
- Case study sources are noted.
- The Wharton School approaches are noted. For example, modified vendetta sanctions.
- Review of marketing reveals little written about the downside.
- Internet now a rich source of information. and a conduit of Obstructive Marketing.
- Free market thinkers brooked no Obstructive Marketing interference.
- Crime is introduced as about profit.
- Difficult to control crime.
- Law is difficult to enforce across boundaries.
- Criminal developments are reviewed.
- New type of security force required.
- Organisational continuity and security needs to be proactive.
- Some say American preoccupation with exporting democracy dangerous.
- Others say it has created a stable world.
- Clash of civilisations.
- Islam vs democracy.
- Cold War era to a terrorism era and confusion.
- Obstructive Marketing appears understandable in the new environment.
- Fundamentalism also applies to Christianity.
- Fundamentalist is a term often misused in relation to Islam.
- Fundamentalism has created a fertile backdrop to Obstructive Marketing on both sides.
- Military doctrines ebb and flow and haven't quite come to terms with Obstructive Marketing and Asymmetric Warfare.
- Terrorists understand the path to fear and chaos can be through infrastructure and economic targets.
- Donnelly's (2003) view on security and the partnership required to combat it.
- A problem in the UK is the majority of businesses owned by foreigners. this may be Obstructive Marketing in itself.
- Sovereign wealth funds may also be a problem.
- Organisations need to take steps against Obstructive Marketing.
- UK threat assessments miss key Obstructive Marketing issues.

- US threat assessments understand key Obstructive Marketing issues.
- Elsewhere there is little focus except on US foreign policy.
- Organisational continuity and security is currently reactive.
- Critical infrastructures are now both physical (things) and virtual (also processes).
- Critical infrastructures have escaped from society's control.
- Critical infrastructures are bound by telecommunications and information.
- Critical infrastructures are a major battleground in an Asymmetric War or Obstructive Marketing campaign.
- Critical infrastructure can be defended by governance and business effectiveness. not just geography and physical security.
- Private sector manages security in different ways to governments.
- Asymmetric attacks can damage and be targeted at critical infrastructures.
- Critical infrastructures need to be resilient.
- These days the 'system' has little give to cater for unexpected events.
- Telecommunications and information seem particularly vulnerable.
- Anti-terrorism legislation victimises those it seeks to protect.
- Risk analysis tools would help to reduce this victimisation.
- Critical infrastructure protection could benefit from a risk analysis approach.
- Repeal of the US Banking Act of 1933 in 1990 critical to financial problem in 2007.

Chapter 3: Obstructive Marketing Challenges

- Case studies to categorise and comment on different types of challenge posed by Obstructive Marketing.
- Linked-In survey of the top 30 per cent of organisations.
- Interviews with the top 1 per cent of organisations.
- Case studies from public sources and the Executive Club of Chicago.
- Casual, competitive, cultural and criminal threats initially, critical infrastructure and capital added later.
- 20 per cent of organisations attacked during periods of weakness.
- 33 per cent of organisations attacked during periods of strength and complacency.

- 15 per cent of attacks occurred during entry to new markets.
- 16 per cent of attacks occurred during periods of innovation.
- 20 per cent of attacks occurred during change.
- Obstructive Marketing is clearly a critical challenge to companies and organisations.
- Organisations are not proactive in continuity and security plans. This is because they have reactive plans where they have plans at all.
- Organisations do not appreciate the changed global context. They do not appreciate or understand the relevant contexts.
- Organisations do not appreciate the changed risk environment as they do not have proper risk management.
- Organisations do not fully appreciate the dependency environment. This is because they do not review risks appropriately.
- Organisations do not fully appreciate the staff environment in which they operate. They, generally, have no succession plans and have an ambivalent attitude to staff.
- Organisations do not appreciate the crisis environment. This is because they have not properly planned for any continuity, risk, dependency or staff issue that could lead to a crisis eventuality.
- Organisations do not appreciate the general environment. This is because of the foregoing.
- Most are unaware of the true global context in which they operate.
- Most do not pay more heed to risk management and Obstructive Marketing (probably because they feel they don't need them).
- Most will not pay the competitive cost of doing so. (This is the 'it won't happen to me' or the 'why should I pay more than my competitor scenario?')
- Even when offered the opportunity of more closed questions the answers were the same.
- There is a clear disconnect between how organisations believe they are operating and how they actually are operating.
- The interviewees represented a sample of the top 1 per cent of organisations. What they tell us is that they are much more aware of the Obstructive Marketing aspects of organisational operations and activity than the Linked-In survey group. They are, however, aligned with the Linked-In survey group in respect to their attitudes to risk and staff. It is suggested that these individuals, along with the intelligence operatives questioned, are much more likely, because of their very senior positions and intelligence knowledge,

to be aware of Obstructive Marketing threats than some of their Linked-In colleagues.

- There is still a dichotomy between their awareness and what they do.
- Risk and staff have become the main issues. None have a positive crisis management approach.
- The Charted Institute of Marketing survey said that in regard to the adoption of business continuity management the Institute found the number of organisations with specific business continuity plans covering their operations has fallen slightly to 49 per cent, compared to 52 per cent in 2009.
- The Charted Institute of Marketing Survey also stated that in terms of risks the 'softer' side of continuity planning and security was not well covered. Nevertheless there was a dramatic increase from 11 per cent to 22 per cent in the concentration on corporate image/brand and reputation over 2009. Other 'softer' areas were not well-covered. The dependence of organisations on critical infrastructure was highlighted for the first time. No link was made to either cyber-warfare or the fact that the UK is at war. There is ongoing comment on terrorism, but only marginally. The overall advice of both the survey and the National Risk Register (2012) is to adopt a business continuity standard. As previously noted (Chapter 2) this is not sufficient and is reactive. There was no comment on Obstructive Marketing.
- In regard to:
  - proactive continuity and security plans, these were not in evidence. Reactive business continuity and security plans were in place in less than 50 per cent of organisations surveyed;
  - changed global context, there was no mention of changed global context and the National Risk Register (2012) misses most of it;
  - research published by Marsh Inc. (2010) shows that many firms appear to be overconfident in their ability to manage the business continuity and supply chain risks facing their organisations, leaving them highly vulnerable to physical disruption and economic conditions.
- The case studies are concerned with identifying behaviour against organisations in the empirical sense. This secondary research reflects case studies from the 1990s which identified a range of attacks against organisations. The choice of the 1990s is predicated on five points:

- the information is available;
- it is less contentious than more recent cases;
- it avoids potential legal issues;
- it shows that these issues are not new;
- it aligns with the timing of other studies relevant to this book, particularly the Knight and Pretty (2000) study on the threats to shareholder value.

• The general case studies are described.

• These then are practical examples of Obstructive Marketing and Obstructive Marketing attack that can be found from a study of the media, particularly the Internet and the daily newspapers in the 1990s. They have been replicated many times since. They can be grouped as:
    - cultural;
    - competitive;
    - criminal;
    - casual.

• These groupings will already be familiar in this book. with critical infrastructure being added later to form the 5Cs, and capital(ism) in this book to form the 6Cs. These can be perpetrated by a range of different active or passive groups:
    - institutions;
    - special interest groups;
    - companies;
    - individuals.

• The summary results in Tables 3.4 and 3.5 for the cases in the Appendix reflect what common sense might suggest:
    - institutions. Governments, and quasi government organisations, are interested in maintaining cultural and competitive interests;
    - special interest groups. These have a range of agenda. In this example there is probably strong skew towards the casual (anarchic), largely because they are well reported;
    - companies. Companies, as might be expected, are interested in pursuing their own competitive agenda, legally or otherwise;
    - individuals. Get involved on a casual or competitive basis;
    - the overriding interest is competitive.

• Chapter 2 identified Obstructive Marketing as a potential process for attacking organisations. These case studies have ordered events and experiences into an Obstructive Marketing model consisting of casual, competitive, criminal, cultural and critical infrastructure actions against institutes, special interest groups, companies and individuals in regard to people, product, place, price, promotion, information, finance, competition and co-operation. This effectively gives the beginnings of an Obstructive Marketing model against which organisations must guard.

- The Executive Club of Chicago case studies are described.
- These confirm the general findings.
- Overall these case studies identify that Obstructive Marketing both exists and can be ordered.

Chapter 4: Context

- Marketing is not immune to the physical principle that for every action there is an equal and opposite reaction.
- Obstructive Marketing, Fundamentalism and Asymmetric War fighting techniques are all identifiable reactions.
- In economics the action of globalisation has been met by the reaction of Obstructive Marketing.
- In politics the action of exporting democracy has been met by the reaction of Fundamentalism.
- In the military the action of effects-based operations has been met by the reaction of Asymmetric Warfare.
- The action of structuring international law has met with the reaction of lawlessness and religious and different secular laws rather than consensus.
- Actions and reactions appear to have happened within a five to ten-year timeframe.
- To moderate these reactions further dialectic is required.
- Moral and ethical values need to be supported.
- An Asymmetric Military Balance should be achieved.
- A sustainable economy should be pursued.
- There should be a balance of physical and virtual technology.
- There should be an approach to a balanced earth.
- An international legal environment acceptable to all needs development.
- A co-ordinated response to organised crime is required.
- IT is fundamental to the Western way of life.
- This way of life could now be described as the Christian Military Information Complex.
- The dialectic balance in each case is a spectrum.

- Positioning on the spectrum determines the level of response required to counter Obstructive Marketing.
- Context, with the introduction of ISO 22301 (and its companion ISO 22313), now leaps onto the agenda – centre stage – for all within the continuity community.
- This context approach is summarised by the 'Godfearing' model.
- This means, simply put, that such an environment is subject to dynamic change on an increasingly daily basis, it is absolutely vital that we understand 'context' in setting our organisational priorities for risk, resilience, continuity, security, crisis management and so on. The launch of ISO 22301 in 2012 and its companion ISO 22313 in December 2012 place context at the heart of what it means to do business continuity effectively and represents a significant step change from guidance offered in BS 25999 parts 1 and 2. We are now compelled to step outside the confines, structures and frameworks of our organisations and understand the relationship any organisation has with its wider environment or its context. For example in ISO 22313:2012 the guidance offered is unequivocal.
- 'Organisations should evaluate and understand the internal and external factors that are relevant to its purpose and operations.' This means that we need to understand our organisations in relation to the prevailing 'political, legal and regulatory environment whether international, national, regional or local'.
- Familiarity with our supply chains has been a theme for some years now, likewise drivers and trends, but the inclusion of 'all interested parties outside the organisation' is significant and will ensure we think much more about and engage with whoever is within, or on the edges of, our spheres of organisational influence.
- The real approach to business continuity should be via a spectrum not a pyramid.
- A simple spectrum scorecard is required because the people who actually do this work in organisations need simple and quick models to represent context.
- 'Godfearing' is a thought provoking accident of a term which may make some feel uncomfortable. This is a hoped-for reaction.
- Timing is important and it seems the antitheses appear five to ten years after the theses in the model.
- Critical infrastructures are also important.

- Generally any dialectic should lead to the protection of organisation against Obstructive Marketing.
- The export of democracy, Fundamentalism and Christian values may not, at first sight, have much to do with business continuity. However, with both globalisation and effects-based operations it is part of a trio of actions that have an impact on how, for example, US businesses perform internationally.
- Almost all OECD countries subscribe to similar ideas and ideals.
- Single-issue politics have also become more important. These are often aligned with Fundamentalist positions.
- Practically and philosophically a way of life must be defended.
- The counter to Obstructive Marketing, 'Hardening' needs to take a spectral approach.
- Another way of defining the Northern, Western and, increasingly, other societies' way of life is through capitalism.
- The link between government, Christianity (or Christian values) and the success of capitalism is as old as capitalism itself.
- Today the basis of our way of life and our way of doing business must be continually clarified and communicated to ensure it has a resonance with those who appreciate it's tolerance but are faced with being outcast for embracing it within a Fundamentalist context.
- It is ironic, perhaps, that so-called global companies cannot escape the political context of their origins or beliefs.
- The term Asymmetric Military Balance sounds like an oxymoron. It is not. It is a way of describing the state of affairs that needs to prevail in order that the export of democracy and globalisation can flourish within a relevant military doctrine.
- The nature and practice of asymmetry is 'as old as warfare itself'.
- It is important to understand that from the enemy's point of view an asymmetric approach may well neutralise any effects-based strategy.
- Modern Western military strategy is still based on rules of engagement, treaties, values and equipment that were relevant to the first half of the twentieth century.
- The major battle ground of the first half of the twenty first century is largely a virtual battleground. It is between the states and stateless, rather than between states.
- What has changed, however, is a widening of the range or spectrum of threats faced today and this has significant implications for how risk, information infrastructure, continuity professionals and organisations generally might respond.

- Organisations, risk doctrine, information infrastructure and value systems need to be structured to cope with the widening spectrum of threats of those who seek to undermine organisational commercial capabilities, democratic freedoms and cultural values.
- History demonstrates the need to be tuned to uncertainty and the asymmetrical approach however uncomfortable the outcome.
- Companies become targets in a politically motivated asymmetric campaign.
- International law regarding both critical infrastructures and information infrastructures is sparse.
- In the EU, the European Commission has started to make an effort to deal with the problem.
- It is recommended that the OECD takes on the international strategic responsibility for resilience in critical infrastructures and critical information infrastructures.
- Sitting in the background of the context model is organised crime, possibly the biggest threat to organisations and business continuity.
- Organised crime has some parallels with Asymmetric Warfare, and indeed is often used as a proxy in fighting an asymmetric war.
- Some countries will give only lip service to the international treaties that they are signed up to.
- Big businesses, when they get caught up in large-scale frauds or criminal activity – where they are either the victims or the unwitting vehicles through which criminal activity is effected – have a recognisable selfish attitude.
- All this activity is now aided, abetted and largely conducted over the Internet.
- The importance of organised crime to organisations, information infrastructure and critical infrastructures is immense.
- IT threats (that is, threats which do not include physical attack) to organisations and critical infrastructure may be categorised both by the motivation and resourcing of the attacker or other threat agent, and by the means of attack.
- The Internet has become ubiquitous in developed nations, so most IT-borne attacks have been carried out over the Internet.
- Technological development involves increasing complexity.
- Securing computer systems and maintaining their security requires considerable expertise.

- The importance of this to the business continuity profession lies not only in the legacy of methodology from the 'data retrieval' days but also in the need to look forward and create what we might call an American Petroleum Institute/Energy Institute/Institute of Petroleum environment.
- The oil and gas industry has, worldwide, managed to introduce a set of standards that apply to an 'intrinsically safe' electric/electronic environment. This is the challenge for the business continuity profession in terms of IT.
- The North and West of the world can therefore be described as a Christian Military Information Complex (a new term).
- Effects-based operations have their place but their nemesis has been asymmetric war-fighting techniques.
- The best example of overcoming this was probably the British Malayan campaign of the 1960s.
- In the modern era it is important to learn from this and similar examples in order to strike an appropriate balance between effects-based operations and its asymmetric counter so that a form of balance is attained.
- This new approach is termed the 'Asymmetric Military Balance'.
- In the economic context the globalisation ambitions of the North and West must take account of those Obstructive Marketing initiatives they will face in their efforts to advance.
- Underpinning all efforts is IT. This provides the means of delivery for political, economic, social, technical and military thought, campaigns, products and services. In this context the protection of information technology security, and more importantly information security, is the most important single task facing the business continuity professional.
- Countering the organised crime threat is also important.
- So it is the task of business continuity professionals in the North and West, to protect this Christian Military Information Complex. The 'Godfearing' model demonstrates that this is, perhaps, rather more complex a task than has traditionally been accepted by the business continuity community. This is heartening as it gives the profession both an opportunity to develop and an ongoing challenge.
- It is proposed that to counter the antitheses and Obstructive Marketing elements to these three key aspects of North and Western development, and their pervasive and insidious companions, is of relevance to organisations and the business continuity profession.

Chapter 5: Risk and Dependency

- Obstructive Marketing and the response to it are also to do with risk and dependency.
- Recent crises have identified shortcomings in the description, measurement and management of risk.
- A new model of risk description and measurement might help organisations manage the subject of risk more successfully and become less vulnerable to Obstructive Marketing.
- Today's world is a complex adaptive information ecosystem and there is need for a predictive dynamic risk framework according to some.
- There is a lack of an integrated approach to the physical and virtual worlds.
- A dependency model brings together all parts of the organisation into a model that shows how to minimise risk and be successful.
- Not all support dependency modelling because some believe judgement, competitiveness and cost and effort may be adversely affected.
- Risk is often so little understood that it was often misapplied, resulting in the erroneous use of risk concepts.
- The array of risk covers a wide spectrum of human experiences.
- Perceived threats to perceived needs are real.
- There is descriptive uncertainty and measurement uncertainty.
- It is important to note that many decisions arise from uncertainty in man's behaviour as well as from natural processes.
- Processes involving natural phenomena are those that are based on natural laws, or random processes.
- Understanding laws reduces uncertainty and does lead to a potential ability for man to control the environment.
- Statistical processes do involve random behaviour.
- There are limits to descriptive and measurement uncertainty.
- These concepts are important because the increasing concern is with the control of risks at the societal level.
- Risk involves unwanted consequence or loss and an uncertainty in that consequence that can be expressed in the form of probability of occurrence.
- Risk is therefore the potential for the realisation of unwanted, negative consequences of an event.
- Risk assessment involves risk estimation and risk evaluation.

- Risk estimation may be thought of as the identification of consequences of a decision.
- Risk evaluation is the acceptability of risk.
- Additionally, risk identification involves the reduction of descriptive uncertainty, risk estimation involves the reduction of measurement uncertainty and risk evaluation involves risk-aversive action.
- Risk is a function of the probability of the consequence and the value of the consequence to the risk taker.
- The role of the risk evaluator is to ameliorate risk inequities often by regulation. this implies an acceptability of some risk.
- Risks are controlled by reducing the probability of a causative event or by minimising the exposure pathway.
- Regulatory bodies are either permissive, restrictive or both.
- Regulation tends to oscillate depending on the risk climate.
- 'Squawks' tend to be single issues that skew risk judgments, taken advantage of by 'counter marketers'.
- Risk evaluation requires a referent level, an understanding of the level of risk, compare the two and take aversive action.
- Systemic control of risk requires a plan.
- Key problems in risk assessment are: who evaluates, why and what bias is introduced, what is meant by value and utility, can consequence values be assigned, and how do cultural, situational and dynamic considerations affect consequence and what factors affect the assignment of value?
- In real life there are always winner and losers, Lehman were losers and National Australia Bank Group winners.
- Risk scorecards look at the risk to organisations from different perspectives.
- Some organisations, for example, the UK's National Health Service, often completely misinterpret risk.
- Risk likelihood and impact are often expressed as a 5 x 5 matrix where a score of 1 is virtually no risk and one of 25 very high risk.
- Others, such as Soros comment on the need for financial institutions to depend on confidence and trust to do business, He challenges the rational man concept.
- Soros' Reflexivity Theory is a two-way connection between the participants' thinking and the situation in which they participate.

- Pretty has identified the links between catastrophes, reputation and shareholder value.
- The foregoing demonstrates that risk is still not well managed.
- Smith and Fischbacher (2009) contend that there has been a state of evolution in risk management and challenges over the last decade.
- They, and the author, note Black Swans and the borderless nature of risk, and the issue of resilience in temporal and spatial and virtual domains.
- The landscapes in which organisations operate are themselves often fractured and pitted.
- Management itself may erode organisational capability.
- 'Spaces of destruction' may appear as a consequence.
- The need for some flexibility within a 'Hardening' context becomes apparent.
- MBAs will need to encompass these issues, and they do not at the moment.
- Risk needs to be looked at as a function of context, description, measurement, critical information resilience, critical infrastructure resilience, spaces of vulnerability, spaces of destruction, giving rise to a new risk model: The 'Gray' risk model.
- In this model risk could be said to be a function of: description and measurement certainty plus financial and reputational exposure plus a view on virtual form and physical form and vulnerability (known and unknown) to cultural, criminal, casual and competitive threats and a potential for destruction (known and unknown) by cultural, criminal, casual and competitive threats.
- $R = f (D + M + F + R + P + 5CV(K) + p5CV(NK) + 5CD(K) + p5CD(NK))$
  - R = Risk;
  - f = Function;
  - D = Description: A range of values from complex (10) to simple (1). For example: The NHS is a highly complex organisation, the corner shop a very simple organisation;
  - M = Measurement: A range of values from complex (10) to simple (1);
  - F = Financial Risk: interpreted from either exposure or annual report, with high risk (10) or low risk (1);
  - R = Reputation Risk: interpreted from size and/or quality, with high risk (10) and low risk (1);

- – V = Virtual: A range of values from highly virtual (10) to not virtual (1);
- – P = Physical: A range of values from highly physical (10) to not physical (10). (Note: physical is not the same as virtual);
- – p = Probability;
- – 5CV = 5C Vulnerability: vulnerability to cultural, criminal, casual, competitive and critical infrastructure threats expressed as known and a probability of unknown. These risks can be interpreted from various sources;
- – 5CD = 5C Destruction: exposure to cultural, criminal, casual, competitive and critical infrastructure threats expressed as known and a probability of unknown. These risks can be interpreted from various sources;
- – K = Known;
- – NK = Unknown.
- The expression should enable organisations such as:
  - – the country;
  - – the banks;
  - – the globalised company;
  - – the public sector;
  - – national companies;
  - – local companies;
  - – the international charity;
  - – the business continuity profession;

  to be looked at in context, described and measured from a slightly different but holistic perspective. Such a perspective should be proportional to their overall position in a 'Godfearing' context, and their 'Gray' risk index. High contextual visibility and a high-risk index would warrant some protection against Obstructive Marketing.
- Dependency modelling initially developed by Professor John Gordon.
- Modelling supported by software.
- The resultant 'Gordon' model is a tool for analysing risk to any system.
- The model deals with risk by use of a Bayesian engine and Monte Carlo simulations.
- The dependencies in the model all relate to organisational objectives of some description.

- Dependency models can be constructed to deal with almost any organisation, any organisational situation and Obstructive Marketing.
- Measuring and managing risk by dependency modelling works.
- It is not common even amongst banks and other high-risk organisations.
- The dependency modelling tool is to risk as a spreadsheet is to a business plan.
- Lack of such a model leaves an organisation exposed to Obstructive Marketing.
- This chapter has developed two models, one for context and one for risk and dependency.

Chapter 6: Asymmetric Warfare

- The concept of Asymmetric Warfare has been around for millennia. It is the basis of the David and Goliath story.
- There are three disturbing issues:
  - there has been much commentary on the issue in Western military circles over the last two generations but no real consensus;
  - not a lot has necessarily changed in military circles in that time;
  - the world has changed in the meantime from a bi-polar world to a multi-polar world.
- Definitions of war and the rules of law.
- Three perspectives of Asymmetric Warfare from 1997, 2003 and 2011.
- View has not changed much over time, but not much come of it.
- Donnelly (2003) quoted, corporate sector important in countering the asymmetric threat.
- Total war is the complete mobilisation of resources and population.
- Regional and civil wars have been a feature of world order since the inception of warfare, and grow out of regional grievances and conflicts.
- Fear is that these can now more easily escalate.
- An insurgency is an armed rebellion against a constituted authority.
- Asymmetric Warfare is war between belligerents whose relative military power differs significantly.
- The law of war is a body of law concerning acceptable justifications to engage in war.
- The Senior Workshop on International Rules Governing Military Operations (SWIRMO) of 10 October 2012 Kuala Lumpur Malaysia said the nature of combat and conflicts changes constantly, and the aim of the workshop was to adapt the rules accordingly.

- Main point is that over time the rules of war have changed.
- Economic warfare is now dominant.
- Which is where Obstructive Marketing comes in.
- Old rules not recognised by stateless or illegitimate insurgencies.
- Marwick (1968) describes war as it used to be known: putting a nation to the test, he viewed it as potentially positive.
- Today military doctrines are more removed from society.
- RMA three approaches: changes in nation-state, evolution of weapons and technology, not yet occurred.
- Renewed interest after Gulf War in RMA, Asymmetric Warfare a counter to RMA.
- Effects-based operations are 'a process for obtaining a desired strategic outcome or effect on the enemy through the synergistic and cumulative application of the full range of military and nonmilitary capabilities at all levels of conflict'.
- Staten and Rathmell et al. both forecast in 1997 the demise of these two sets of thinking, RMA and effects-based operations, and predicted the rise of Asymmetric Warfare.
- Asymmetric Warfare is a military counterpart to Obstructive Marketing.
- May even be justified in calling a combined approach Asymmetric Obstructive Marketing.
- The Hague Convention is recalled to demonstrate how far reporting and current rules of war have drifted from the 'civilised' norms and rules of warfare.
- In trade there are also rules, for example Incoterms. These are often undermined these days too.
- Chace (2011) develops the asymmetric theme and believes that current strait-jacketed thinking prevents a full understanding of the term.
- Donnelly's (2003) view of the need for a new security environment based on a corporate–government partnership is recalled.
- Jonsson's (2007) view on sovereign wealth funds is introduced.
- UK threats are described.
- US threats are described.
- General threats elsewhere are summarised.
- The term 'Asymmetric Military Balance' is introduced.
- Practice of asymmetry is as old as warfare itself.
- What appears best, most effective and most efficient is often not the case for in strategy, contends Luttwak (1987), actual or possible

conflict between thinking human beings, whether it is played out in political, economic, social, technological or military contexts, is dominated by a paradoxical logic based on the coming together and even the reversal of opposites.

- Modern warfare rules are out of date.
- 'Asymmetric Military Balance' is effected by Asymmetric Warfare, effects-based operations, globalisation with hearts and minds reconstruction against Obstructive Marketing and Asymmetric Warfare.
- Organisations, risk doctrine, information infrastructure and value systems need to be structured to cope with the widening spectrum of threats.
- The more frequent occurrence of what this book has so far called Obstructive Marketing could be further refined into, as noted earlier, Asymmetric Obstructive Marketing, a new term original to this book, as a consequence of the obvious and increasing use of organisations and commerce in warfare.
- The certainty that existed during the Cold War has not been replaced by the hegemony of a single world superpower but has been replaced by uncertainty combined with an evolving group of developing nations and power foci all of whom have slightly different interests.
- Clausewitz (1962) commented that war is the extension of politics (policy) by other means. War has become much more complex.
- Since 2007 the economic crisis has resulted in a rebalancing of the world's economies in favour of the developing countries.
- Socially, there is not only uncertainty about the nation-state but increasing challengers to the existing social status quo.
- The Arab Spring, the UK riots and the African revolutions were managed by social media and the mobile phone, and in part driven by another Black Swan, food shortages.
- Technology is now dominated by the digital and data age.
- IBM (2012) note that only 16 per cent of CEOs fully use the digital tools available to them.
- Environmentally the world has reached a point where if everyone consumed at a European level, three earths would be needed for the resources required, five if it was at US levels.
- Legally, there is the continuing attempt by the US to extend the territorial reach of its laws, the lack of law on the Internet, and the dismissal of laws other than religious ones by fanatical Islamicists amongst others.

- In this milieu it is suggested by this book that organisations need to take a different look at the way they manage themselves in order to be operationally successful.
- In a general sense the economic case and the global drivers prevalent over the last 20 years or so are likely to be modified by recent events.
- Large and geographically spread organisations tend to suffer more from Obstructive Marketing which is, again as noted, a good proxy for those likely to need some sort of co-ordinated response.

Chapter 7: The Effect of the Capital Markets and Sovereign Wealth Funds

- Stock market prices, these days, react to a company's financial risks, and when firms act to reduce the risk, their cost of capital goes down and their stock prices should improve.
- Corporate executives now have the means to control their financial environment.
- When corporate managers stick to hedging risks that immediately affect their own business, risks that they know and whose effects they fully understand, the outcome is predictable: they stabilise their business, and investors are likely to reward them.
- However, when corporate executives become convinced that they understand the direction in which markets are moving well enough to predict the future, and decide to bet their shareholders' capital and their employee's jobs on their view of the markets, they step onto uncertain ground.
- The bankers and brokers from whom corporate executives buy the highly leveraged swaps and options used for such bets seldom if ever take such extreme risks themselves.
- Hidden risks: it is important to understand that many of the mechanisms that can cause disruption to organisation pre-date the most recent crisis. Examples are the Malaysian central Bank, stock exchange futures and later derivatives, collapse of Drexel, the US mortgage market pre-2000 as well as pre-2007, banks trading for profit, the extension of these practices to business and organisations.
- The key issue behind the financial crisis of 2007 onwards was the repeal of the US Banking Act (1933), the Glass–Steagall Act, in 1990.
- The repeal of the act caused a jump from 10 per cent to more than 30 per cent in terms of the sub-prime products held by the banks.

- On 21 January 2010, US President Obama proposed bank regulations similar to some parts of Glass–Steagall in limiting certain of banks' trading and investment capabilities.
- Elsewhere tougher legislation was being encouraged.
- In August 2011 the UK unveiled the Vickers Report (2011) suggesting the division between retail and investment banking.
- The second key issue to the 2007 onwards problem is described by Patterson (2010b). He describes how the markets had become dominated by 'The Quants'. cerebral and highly qualified mathematicians drafted in to the investment houses to develop sophisticated algorithms to make money.
- The economic crisis of 2007 onwards was perpetrated by a series of events linked to the sale of sub-prime mortgages in the US and, as importantly, the bundling of the notes covering these mortgages in derivative products.
- Much of the reaction to these events came through in 'real time' and hence the Internet played a large part in both the timeliness and availability of information.
- Soros (2009) gave us his Reflexivity Theory to explain why it happened, why he was able to forecast it, how he made money from it, and what should be done in the future. Not all have realised the importance of the Glass–Steagall Act and the relevance of the 'The Quants'.
- The crisis reminded of the symbiotic nature of the relationship between the regulator and the banks.
- The debacle damaged the West more than the East is a lesson to be learned.
- For nearly half a century a type, and since revised, of the Black and Scholes (1973) model has dominated derivative, hedging and option trading.
- All of these works suggest that the organisations involved need a different type of structure today in order to protect themselves from these type of Obstructive Marketing threats.
- The recent crises in the banking industry and elsewhere have demonstrated that there have been shortcomings in the description, measurement and management of risk.
- Following the recommendations of Chapter 5 would be helpful in this regard.
- Goodger (2011a; 2011b) and Gall (2010) view the world as volatile, uncertain, complex and ambiguous.

- Goodger and Atkinson (2011) see the biggest risk to society as a lack of an integrated approach to the virtual and physical worlds.
- Davis (2012) explained how the risks businesses and banks run are still not properly managed some four years after the banking crisis.
- A sovereign wealth fund is a state-owned investment fund composed of financial assets such as stocks, bonds, property, precious metals or other financial instruments.
- Some sovereign wealth funds may be held by a central bank, which accumulates the funds in the course of its management of a nation's banking system. This type of fund is usually of major economic and fiscal importance.
- Sovereign wealth funds can be characterised as maximising long-term return, with foreign exchange reserves serving short-term 'currency stabilisation', and liquidity management.
- The assets of 40 sovereign wealth funds are listed.
- Think tanks such as the WPC have argued that the extended investment horizon of sovereign wealth funds allows them to act as long-term investors in less liquid assets such as unlisted companies, commodities, real estate and infrastructure assets, a trend likely to develop further as banks and insurance companies decrease their exposure to these asset classes in the context of the Basel 2 and Solvency 2 regulatory constraints.
- Here are some concerns regarding Obstructive Marketing.
- Some countries worry that foreign investment by sovereign wealth funds raises national security concerns because the purpose of the investment might be to secure control of strategically important industries for political rather than financial gain. These concerns have led the EU to reconsider whether to allow its members to use 'golden shares' to block certain foreign acquisitions.
- Their inadequate transparency is a concern for investors and regulators: for example, size and source of funds, investment goals, internal checks and balances, disclosure of relationships, and holdings in private equity funds.
- Academic findings contradict the widespread view of sovereign wealth funds as relatively free agents.
- Responses also offer a strong rebuttal of the purported irrelevance of asset-liability management for sovereign investors.
- Jonsson (2007) regards sovereign wealth funds as a challenge to democracy's ultimate victory.

- A free and open market and vast sovereign wealth viewing UK assets as relatively risk free may be more of a problem than at first appeared. It is not just a UK problem but the UK is particularly vulnerable because of the openness of the market there.

Chapter 8: Obstructive Marketing and Asymmetric Warfare: Asymmetric Obstructive Marketing

- A *Financial Times* article by Brzezinski (2013) suggests how a cyber-security attack from a small but sophisticated state can launch attacks on much bigger powers. This is the essence of asymmetry.
- In *The Economist* of 23 February 2013 two other articles of relevance were carried.
- The first dealt with the issue of cyber-crime out of China.
- The second dealt with more traditional corporate espionage.
- Combines both the Asymmetric Warfare trends and Obstructive Marketing trends.
- This chapter now moves on to describe how 'Asymmetric Obstructive Marketing' might develop in the future, it's relevance to prevailing military doctrine and its role in Brzezinski's changes in the rule of the game.
- As noted elsewhere in this book China should not be looked upon as a singular problem in a historical context – a century or so ago it was the US and the UK doing the same thing.
- Any asymmetric war necessarily involves organisations.
- What is perhaps new for the West is that the rules that have governed warfare over the centuries are no longer as firm, or as Western focussed, as they were.
- The asymmetric model has further developed through the use of the Internet and mobile phone as means of communication, a weapon and a target.
- The military doctrine required is akin to a see-saw, not too much force to launch the other side off the see-saw ('Asymmetric See-Saw Theory', a new term and original to this book), but enough of a combination of both effects-based operations, appropriate asymmetric techniques and hearts and minds/reconstruction to tip the balance in favour of the North and West while being ready to re-establish equilibrium in any event.
- The more frequent occurrence of what this book has so far called Obstructive Marketing could be further refined into, as noted

earlier, Asymmetric Obstructive Marketing, a new term original to this book, as a consequence of the obvious and increasing use of organisations and commerce in warfare.

- Using the Obstructive Marketing key issues and matching them to the traditional marketing mix allows a matrix of what an Obstructive Marketing campaign might look like to be created.
- This is used to create an Obstructive Marketing campaign scenario which using the casual, competitive, criminal, cultural, critical infrastructure and capital issues shows how an organisation might be derailed.
- It is not necessary to carry out such a co-ordinated campaign. The use of the small-scale hit and run attacks plus the denial of critical infrastructure has, as this is written in 2013, already been shown to be more than capable of disrupting key installations.
- Is this new? In historical terms probably not. It is possible to go back to Confucius, Sun Tsu, Machiavelli, Napoleon and von Clausewitz to understand that the ideas are not new, they have developed and have a modern twist, but they are not essentially new.
- What is new, particularly for the North and West of the world, is that the dominant, safe, democratic, resource rich, market controlling, militarily powerful, information and data secure world it thought it ran is no longer. This is a profound shock.
- This is a reality which has yet to be fully faced by North and Western politicians. In this respect they play into the hands of the 'asymmetric counter marketers' because they have not developed the tools or understanding to combat this new force.

Chapter 9: Protecting Against Obstructive Marketing

- There are probably two key areas to concentrate on in regard to protection against Obstructive Marketing. The first of these is at society level and the second at organisation level.
- There is a parallel between the escape of critical infrastructures from government control over the last 50 years and any government's ability to control Obstructive Marketing.
- It is worth suggesting that both the National Risk Register and the tasks of MI5 are extended a little more towards ensuring that the country is well-protected against Obstructive Marketing threats.
- However, to build a national USP out of protecting the nation against Obstructive Marketing is certainly something that a number of key academics believe is possible.

- So in defending the nation against an Obstructive Marketing attack:
  - sustainable organisations are required to manage the balance between globalisation and Obstructive Marketing;
  - Christian values (or morals and ethics), in the case of the UK, must both be understood and promoted because they underpin UK society. The nation may be secular but the values that underpin the way of life are still Christian;
  - the military need to develop the 'Asymmetric Military Balance' approach described here. The closest to success on this was probably the Malayan campaign of the 1960s. Neither Iraq nor Afghanistan can be seen as successes against the requirements of an 'Asymmetric Military Balance';
  - social cohesion, not division, should be the political watchword;
  - the technologies that control both the physical and virtual worlds need some interlocutor. Just as it is difficult for a traditional policeman to understand the computer nerd who keeps the Internet crime under control, so it is with balancing the physical and virtual worlds. This is important from an Obstructive Marketing point of view as companies exploit the virtual at the expense of the physical with the consequence of the taxation issues and barren high streets seen in recent years. This is an area that should perhaps have been better explored in this book;
  - resource-hungry nations need to face up to the requirements for a balanced earth approach – so that there is enough left for our children's children. Few policies deal with this;
  - international law needs fulsome support across the board. More effort needs to be put into this – and again this is an opportunity to maintain what is already an international lead in law, particularly commercial law, for the UK;
  - organised crime needs constant attention. The UK's police forces are either extremely highly regarded for their expertise or the butt of an international joke. The UK TV programme 'Traffic Cops' is a comedy show in the Netherlands where the similarity between the police and their targets is regularly commented upon, as is the passion for both wrecking and using fast cars. Somewhere the police institutions have to rediscover their purpose to counter criminal organisations that are identifiably brighter than the police;
  - IT. In terms of managing IT some progress has been made in the last five years. More is required to secure the nation properly.

- One way of protecting an organisation from Obstructive Marketing is by 'Hardening'.
- 'Hardening' encompasses the Context model described in Chapter 4, the Risk and Dependency models described in Chapter 5 and additional models on staff, crises and in general.
- These models are the 'Hyperion' Staff model, the 'Watson' Crisis model, and the 'Racornir' General Management model.
- Beyond the resilient organisation lies the 'Hardened organisation'.
- For many organisations it is clear that a 'Hardened' approach is appropriate and achieved by striking an appropriate cost/benefit balance.
- In an environment where globalisation has been met by Obstructive Marketing and asymmetric challenges, then the 'Hardened organisation' is an appropriate posture in order to withstand and respond to most, if not all, threats to organisations.
- Rather than the usual description of business continuity in terms of a pyramid, it is much more appropriate to describe is as a spectrum.
- Organisations require different positions on the business continuity spectrum.
- The 'Hyperion' Staff model acknowledges the issues for the requirements of 'Hardened' staffing. There are 22 characteristics useful to have in individuals to create a resilient staff.
- The 'Watson' Crisis model acknowledges the Chapter 4 conclusion that current crisis management is reactive not proactive. The 'Watson' Crisis model builds planning for crises into the organisation from an early stage and recognises the need to involve many in the solution to a crisis. The model also acknowledges that it is often the 'unknowns' that de-rail a crisis management plan.
- Proactive crisis management 'Hardens' organisations.
- The general 'Racornir' model can sit beside or within existing business models and contribute to the efficient management of an organisation. If properly implemented, the model can be used as the basis for the management of an organisation.
- These models are a way of approaching the context, risk, dependency, staff, crisis and general situations in which an organisation may find itself.
- They help 'Harden' an organisation against Obstructive Marketing.
- As identified in Chapter 3, Research, there is a clear perception problem surrounding organisations in the UK in regard specifically to business continuity planning and the Internet.

- Business continuity, resilience and 'Hardening' should not be looked at as a 'recovery' but more as preserving and maintaining the gap between market capitalisation and net asset value. It should also be seen as a competitive advantage. If Hardening can be looked at in such a light then it will help the 'perception' problem.

- While this book is being written, and following discussions with the author, the Information Lodestone Concept and Framework is being developed to help overcome the information assurance and Internet-related perception issues.

- There are many opponents seeking to minimise the impact of globalisation and using various Obstructive Marketing means to do so. In order to operate in such an environment it is suggested that some organisations need to be 'Hardened'. In order to become 'Hardened' then the organisation needs to understand the context of Obstructive Marketing.

- If what has been learnt of Obstructive Marketing in Chapters 2 and 4 is combined with Trim's GISES model (Trim, 2005) then a new model to deal with Obstructive Marketing threats is created that helps both build in security from the beginning but also gives a template against which marketing can be proactively assessed within the context, risk and dependencies identified.

11

The Future

Gazing into the future is not necessarily a recommended or rewarding pastime, especially for a writer. Astrologers and politicians have a hard enough time convincing their audiences let alone an author writing about the Obstructive Marketing aspects of business. However, this book has looked at some issues concerning Obstructive Marketing and there are some straightforward things about the future that are common sense and will help us all make sense of the world in which we live. If the future gazing is put into the context of the 6Cs discussed in this book this will help give a forward look some structure. This said looking into the future is a very personal reflection and thus this chapter is much more a personal statement than the rest of this book.

Potential casual damage to the organisation has changed. It is far more likely these days that there will be some unintended consequences from trading, from bringing your own device (BYOD) to work, from losing client data or leaving back-doors open (deliberately or otherwise) on computers than it is for a benzene soaked rag to be dropped into a water-bottling line. It is far more likely that the finance director, unknown to the CEO, will make some sort of mistake on the markets that will cost him or her and the staff of the company their jobs than the company will lose out to petty theft. It is far more likely that someone will damage a piece of critical infrastructure, that there will be brown-outs caused by insufficient electrical power, than it is for someone to shoot the CEO. Intellectual property theft, casual or otherwise, will remain a major concern. Casual damage to an organisation, or as part of the Obstructive Marketing mix, will not be unknown. It will not, however, be as it has been.

Competitive pressures will be as strong in the future as they have been in the past. They will also be different. In terms of competition the major change will be the split of the world between the North and West and the South and East. This has been generally evident since 2007 but there are important differences in approaches to be understood. The North and West has, to a certain extent, lost its way competitively. It is bound by rules and regulations which are regarded as luxuries by the South and East. This means jobs are expensive because they come with so many add-ons, it means that production and service is expensive because lifestyles and societal choices have to be met, it means that the great experiment of, for example, European social democracy is in peril because in the end it will just be too expensive. This is not only killing the golden goose but it is shooting economies in the foot, to mix metaphors.

Dinosaur trade unions do not understand that it will be meaningless to protect unemployed workers. Eastern European workers, for example, may benefit the UK economy in terms of productivity and work rates, but the country is done no favours by maintaining an underclass that refuses to work and consumes benefits. This remains a problem waiting to destroy the economy further. Social justice is important but quantity, as Stalin said, has a quality all of its own – and there is little protection against the quantity of Chinese, Indians, Russians and Africans wanting to have a share of the North and West's economic pie by working harder and cheaper.

At a national level there are problems too, particularly in the open economies. In the UK the Government's growth tsar, Michael Heseltine, has not understood that, unlike the 1950s, most of UK business is no longer owned by the British. So this means that not only is the manufacturing portion of the economy too small to make a major difference to overall growth, but also national stimuli becomes irrelevant when 80 per cent of businesses (by GDP) are owned by foreign organisations. At a national level the competitive edge has been lost by a laissez-faire attitude to manufacturing and ownership. This is not a position that the Chinese or Germans suffer from in the same way. They have other pressures. France, which had both a France Fort and Franc Fort policy, has suffered from raids on an overvalued currency and the cost of too much protection of its businesses. Clearly, there is a competitive balance to be struck. For some, maybe the UK and maybe the US, the balance has gone too far one way; Germany still seems to have got it right and for China it remains to be seen.

This is nothing new. There have been shifts in economic power since time immemorial. What is done about it is important. The North and West do not seem to have a plan in place. So the prediction is that competitively things will get relatively, if not absolutely, worse from a competitive point of view for the North and West and relatively, and probably absolutely, better for the South and East.

The growing problem with crime is it's attraction over a law-abiding life style. This is of course a gross generalisation but is supposed to be a challenging statement. When savers in Cyprus have their savings stolen by a treasury in support of a bail-out of their government; when Chinese, Chechens, Russians and the people of Wendover in the UK are forcibly evicted or disadvantaged from their properties in support of development projects without adequate compensation; when rich corporations and individuals pay less tax than the poor; when banks grow rich but taxpayers pay for their misdemeanours; when drug barons lead lavish lifestyles and little is done to control them or their proceeds; when the police and the press are seen as corrupt; when elected politicians seem both corrupt and powerless; when all these things are compounded by involvement with wars with no legal basis – then there is a question mark over the moral compass of society, it's leadership and the rule of law. These are not trivial things, they are the bedrock of a successful society and are ignored at great danger.

Human trafficking is a horrendous crime and the export of women to the Arab, European, American and Asian worlds by crime lords abhorrent. However, when you meet a 20-year-old woman who was bought out of a market and poverty in Yemen by a successful Nigerian Islamic businessman to become the third wife in a successful family – looked after by the other senior wives and treated well by her husband in true Islamic fashion – then life suddenly becomes a little blurred at the edges. The woman is certainly a victim of crime but also of great good fortune and a better lifestyle than she could ever have hoped for before being traded out of the Horn of Africa to a slave market in Yemen to live comfortably in Maiduguri in Northern Nigeria. Traditional law and values, in this case, usurping crime. This is a rare event, but it obviously happens. It is an unusual counterpoint to a terrible trade.

In terms of crime the challenge is the same as it is for law, and the terrorism and freedom fighter argument. Who is to say what works best where – except, and this is the key issue, that civilisation has always been bound by a set of fair laws when it has worked effectively. The Internet may remain an interesting exception, but unlikely. The fall in physical and violent crime in the North and West is paralleled by a rise in Internet crime. The surface altruistic and open appeal of the Internet conceals a deeper criminal and lawless environment and malaise. This challenges society in many ways – one current one is the lack of various societal taxes paid by large Internet traders and the impact of such traders on traditional shopping areas (worldwide). This in turn promotes tax evasion, illegal Internet trade and crime in depressed shopping areas. We all avoid, change or cynically manipulate at our peril.

Unless there is a return to a combined effort by the North and West in favour of the rule of fair law in the physical and virtual world, then covertly, and increasingly overtly, crime will rise. In the South and East there has always been a less clear distinction between what the North and West might call right and wrong, but in the South and East the rise of economic power will challenge the North and West's traditional perception of law and order and right and wrong. The North and West's increasing proclivity to go for single-issue politics, the lowest common denominator rather than the highest common factor, is to be deplored in this respect.

Geographically the drug routes out of South America to Africa to Europe, the drug routes out of the Middle East and Asia to Europe and the US will continue. Increasingly the South and East will consume more recreational drugs. Human trafficking out of Europe, East Europe and poor states in general will continue, as will the associated sex trades. The proceeds of drug laundering now reaches levels of 20 per cent of the economy in developed countries and 100 per cent in some undeveloped ones – which rather begs the question of what is the point of money-laundering questionnaires from lawyers and bankers on transactions for ordinary people when clearly the criminals are managing to deal with proceeds quite effectively. Profiling and research is much more effective than meaningless forms. The same applies to security at airports (except the latter could be seen as an employment scheme). There will be little change in this over the short to medium term.

Piracy, which restarted in Malaysia, spread to the Horn of Africa and is now a worldwide problem, will continue as ships and their cargoes are seen as easy pickings by criminal lords, warlords and poor people in places where life is cheap. In the future it is unlikely that any of this will change because politicians will continue to take the easy options, where they are not bankrolled by the criminal fraternity. Organised crime, as seen in the chapter on context, is a backdrop for everything and a challenge for every marketer.

Culturally, it could be said that the world is in a very interesting if potentially difficult position. The Christian North and West has lost its cultural way in a set of devalued institutions and societal mores plus a wave of immigration that has brought challenges to the cultural *status quo ante*. The Islamic Centre, although at war by proxy with the North and West, has also lost its way in a schism between Sunni and Shia and between the practical and Fundamentalist. A semi-renaissance of orthodoxy in Russia and elsewhere seems to have stalled for the moment. Shintoism has some revival in Japan. Hinduism is under threat in an increasingly secular India and China continues to run roughshod over many separate cultural identities within its borders. Having challenged white on black apartheid in Africa for a century, black Africa now practices black on black apartheid in several states.

Energy demands will be a key Obstructive Marketing issue in the future. Business will, is already, being disadvantaged by unreliable power in parts of Europe and the US. The reliance on systems control and data acquisition (SCADA) systems linked to the Internet means that power grids can be brought down by casual, rogue or criminal forces. If you are a foundry working in the UK midlands and the power goes off in the middle of a process it costs thousands of pounds to restart. The reliance of Europe on Russian gas is a growth depressant. The enervating effect of the major shale gas finds in the US has already had a positive impact on the economy. In China, with a new power station coming on stream every few weeks, usually coal powered, the problems will be different. Costs will rise and resources may become scarce, logistics will become a problem. The effect of high prices on international oil availability will be mixed; a high oil price driven by overall shortage and China will have the effect of powering more discoveries so oil will be available but expensive. This will all add cost, not reduce it, within the economy. Energy will have an effect on everyone's competitive position and continue to be a cost pressure.

Food supply worldwide will become a problem. Poor harvests, drought and floods have all had a worldwide impact on food resources. From a position of record grain reserves some five to ten years ago the cupboard is now bare. This means that prices for food for the North and West and the poor will rise. Food price rises were the 'hidden' catalyst for the Arab Spring. Food habits in the South and East will and are changing. This means greater competition for the foods previously sourced for the North and West from the South and East; it means less food for export from the traditional food producing giants, it means less farmland in the South and East as land is moved into industrial and resource production, it means pressure on wildlife in Africa as more people in the South and East can afford 'traditional' medicines. Food supply problems could, in the worst case scenario, lead to another world war. Extrapolating the events of the Arab Spring does not make this as far-fetched as it might initially sound. The example of the decline of the Roman Empire as it struggled to feed its population as a result of climate change and border clashes is a salutary history lesson.

Health will be a critical issue around the world as the population gets bigger and drugs do not work well any longer. This issue is crystallised by tuberculosis. The drug resistant strains emanating from Eastern Europe and the Far East will eventually take hold in the general population of the North and West and will trigger a rise in a disease not feared for nearly a century. This will be accompanied by the return of other diseases once thought virtually extinct. The reason will again be the lack of efficacy in drug treatment and the mutation of disease plus the cost of administering the drugs will eventually become prohibitive.

Law and order – the good news is that in 2013, China's President Xi Jingping and new premier, Li Keqiang, have both made commitments to the rule of law. This is to be expected as most states go through this process as they approach political and economic maturity. The problem of law and order is in the poor, the rogue and the ill-defined states and the stateless. Here there is increasing disregard for the rule of law and the applicability of international law. Perversely, the country that has most to do with the application and rule of law, the US, is not helping this situation because of its increasing use of its own laws, rather than international law, to extend extra-territorial reach and the international campaign against terror.

Over and above this the Internet is a basically lawless environment. The sanctity of Northern and Western law in relation to trading agreements is likely to come under increasing pressure. So the prediction here is that everything, except perhaps China, is likely to get worse before it gets better. The sanctity of Northern and Western law in trade will be challenged, international banking law and processes will be challenged by the South and East, international law will continue to be run roughshod over by both the US and it's state and stateless enemies and the Internet will remain an essentially lawless environment for the meantime.

Manufacturing's move to the South and East from the North and West will slow as costs in the South and East rise. However, the overall amount of manufacturing in the South and East will continue to rise. Manufacturing will continue to develop at the higher value end in the North and West and the South and East will continue to challenge the intellectual lead and property of the North and West.

National icons and the protection of cultural heritage will be challenged by development and a lack of proportion, understanding and respect for history, Whether it is the Taliban and the Buddha's in Afghanistan or the creation of car parks in the UK, there will continue to be problems with both the relevance and cost of protecting national icons and heritage sites. Despite The Hague and Geneva Conventions and a raft of other international agreements in addition, there is scant respect for the protection of cultural heritage. The looting of museums in Iraq and Libya post their relevant conflicts is testament to this. This is not a geographical split issue – it is a truly international concern as all parts of the world pay, at best, lip service to these issues.

Transport, particularly the Boeing 747 and large tankers/cargo carriers, have transformed the world. Transport is vulnerable to attack, as are the people who use it. In an increasingly asymmetric world it is likely that modes of transport and those that use them will be frequent targets of extremists of one sort or another. There will be no short-term switch to alternative means of transport – except a continued trend away from the bicycle towards the car in Asia and Africa.

In 1983 the author wrote a thesis emphasising the problems with water distribution in the Middle East. The basic hypothesis was that it was water not oil that was causing many of the political difficulties in the Middle East. Water and food have continued to be a problem in the Middle East. This is now so worldwide. 'Boiling points' or places where water is a catalyst for conflict can be mapped all over the world. This will get worse and will be a problem for businesses, organisations and politicians.

As with water, waste water is a worldwide problem. The problem can be unexpected. For example, if the Gulf desalinates salt water for drinking water what is the consequence, as the salt is returned to the sea in the form of brine, of an increased salinity of the Gulf on littoral populations. The Chinese premier has recently acknowledged the problems caused by both sewage and water contamination in China. Often it is not that the treatment plants are not available to treat the water, it is often because they are but that it is cheaper to pump waste water into the sea or water courses rather than treat it.

Whether it is Nepalis infecting drinking water in Haiti with cholera, or the dysentery caused by unclean water in Nigeria, or the river dolphins killed in India or China by polluted rivers, or unlicensed dumping of chemicals in rivers in the UK, the contamination of clean water is an equal problem to the disposal of waste water itself.

Capital will have an impact at the top end too. Bankers' bonuses will be a thing of the past as the great Northern and Western banks come under pressure from not only new competitors in the South and the East but also from new ways of handling capital. Money is treated differently in China, Russia and India. These different ways of dealing with capital are certainly no less valid to companies and organisations in these nations than the traditional capital markets of the North and West. They are different and the balance of capital will shift towards these different ways. Sovereign wealth funds will also have an impact. Despite their generally benign behaviours to date this is certainly not a guarantee of future equanimity. They will be used for political purposes sooner or later, even if there is a belief that this has not happened so far. Nations themselves may come under threat in the North and West as both trends towards federation and separation parallel each other. The North and West have become used to cheap consumer goods from China and cheap food from around the world. Both these will change as more countries in the South and East consume more. Because the new South and East states are becoming richer they will consume more of the food traditionally bought by the North and West.

Critical infrastructures will remain just that, critical. They will be both targets, and in the case of IT, conduits for both Asymmetric Warfare and Obstructive Marketing. There remains an international requirement to handle them correctly as they have progressively escaped from the hands of nation-states and as they become increasingly global in nature. There will be many difficulties in this area because the international structures are just not there to handle them and there does not seem to be any overwhelming desire to put them there. One of the reasons for this is that the largely altruistic and benign approach to putting international structures together after the two world wars has been replaced by a very selfish national attitude. There is not the appetite or concerted approach demonstrated by the West and the Soviet bloc after the Second World War to participate in international treaties on a large-scale basis.

Government services are coming under strain in the West and will continue to do so as the financial resources required to run social democrat programmes starts to dry up as cash is taken by ageing populations and tax takes reduce in response to competition from the South and East, from globalisation, and from the Internet. In the South and East governments will have different problems: how to have an effective legal system, controlling growth, encouraging social justice on the back of tax returns which will be insufficient because there is no traditional understanding of the payment for, or the reasons for the payment of, tax.

Capital may well continue to be tight in the North and West for some time as the consequences of the 2007 crash continue to be felt across all countries in Europe and North America. Capital will become looser in Russia, China and much of the rest of the South and East as large cash balances are generated in response to trade surpluses. This will enhance the power of the sovereign wealth funds who will continue to have a major influence on the development of the world economy. Hopefully, but not necessarily, for the good of all.

Appendix: Additional Obstructive Marketing Case Studies

This Appendix is a list of the:

- major cases in support of Chapter 3 – practical examples of Obstructive Marketing;

- other cases in support of Chapter 3.

Practical Examples of Obstructive Marketing: Main Reference Cases in Support

CASE NO. 1

Company   Jardine Matheson.
Source   Naylor, R.T. (1994), *Hot Money and the Politics of Debt*, Black Rose Books, New York.[1]
Date   1980s.
Relevance to Obstructive Marketing   Another company and financiers prevent Jardines from developing by taking retributive action.
Synopsis   Jardine Matheson, 'Noble House' of Hong Kong, whose 1980s headquarters move from Hong Kong to Bermuda was preceded by events which can be described as a Vendetta Sanction. In this case Chinese-backed financiers successfully 'blew a hole' in Jardine's earnings and balance sheet.
Comment   Retributive action is often taken against companies when the law is unable to take any action, or where the company is effectively beyond the law. This raises interesting issues of policing companies in a global economy. Vendetta sanctions can be political: for example, the stated KGB influence on Nestlé resulting in Case no. 68 below.[2]

CASE NO. 2

Company   US Aerospace vs Japan.
Source   Fialka, J.J. (1997), *War By Other Means*, Norton, New York.
Date   1980s.
Relevance to Obstructive Marketing   Blocking and retaliatory measure to both gain technology and prevent deployment of advanced competing technology – by one country's consortium against another's.
Synopsis   The US tried to enlist the support of the Japanese in a joint venture to develop and sell a new type of short take-off and landing aircraft. Instead of co-operation it got stonewalling and a classic data mining operation, in the guise of assistance, against it. The aerospace business in the US goes on, but it goes on very slowly with Japan, at least as far as TW-68 aircraft technology is concerned. The company concerned, LHTEC, hired a major 'sogoshosha', a type of trading company unique to Japan, C. Itoh and Co. Ltd, to try and sell Japan on the merits of the associated T-800 engine. But the effort has been stymied by recent news that a Japanese consortium of Japanese aerospace companies is developing a very similar engine of their own, and the money earmarked seems to have disappeared from Japan's future budget plans.[3]
Comment   This is blocking tactic extremely common practice in Far East countries. They are to be admired for the way in which this is achieved.

CASE NO. 3

Company   Mitsubishi vs Spero: Intellectual Property.
Source   Fialka, J.J. (1997), *War By Other Means*, Norton, New York.
Date   1980s.
Relevance to Obstructive Marketing   Blocking measure similar to previous case with variant of using bullying tactic – by a big company against a small one.
Synopsis   A trivial (to some) dispute between the giant Mitsubishi Corporation of Japan and Spero Inc. of the US, over the rights to a microwave lamp. It became a *cause celebre* between the US and Japan – but was eventually settled out of court. Spero and others had invented a high-powered microwave lamp – tried to market it in Japan, especially to Mitsubishi, where they made little headway against that country's non-tariff trade barriers and patent laws. A typical

case of David vs Goliath – with David (Spero) almost winning until his shareholders buckled under the pressure and agreed an out of court settlement.[4]

Comment   A remarkable case of a major player, the US, surrendering leading technology to a major competitor. Raises, amongst other points, the question of the relevance of the nation-state in corporate life – a thread running parallel to the study of Obstructive Marketing.

CASE NO. 4

Company   Bull vs Texas Instruments.
Source   Fialka, J.J. (1997), *War By Other Means*, Norton, New York.
Date   1980s.
Relevance to Obstructive Marketing   Acquisition of competing technology, self-inflicted wound. One company accuses another of theft then gets blamed itself.
Synopsis   Bull accuses Texas of a stealing technology – but unwittingly reveals that it had stolen technology from Texas in the first place.[5]
Comment   A case, along with IBM vs Hitachi (q.v.) and Microsoft vs Netscape (q.v.), which demonstrates just how nasty the technical wars between the world's leading computer players can be.

CASE NO. 5

Company   Public Database Mining.
Source   Fialka, J.J. (1997), *War By Other Means*, Norton, New York.
Date   1980s.
Relevance to Obstructive Marketing   Use of intelligence techniques to mine public US databases for competitive advantage.
Synopsis   Ex-intelligence officer uses techniques learned in his 'trade' to mine public databases to the advantage of French and Israeli clients.
Comment   The US Freedom of Information Act has allowed those with the skills and talents to generate income and trade by successfully mining the data available. Such data allows competitors to identify key trends in targeted companies such as rates and overheads. Quality Strategies Inc. is a Virginia company that makes a living in doing this for the telecommunications industry.[6] It is unlikely that the French and Israeli Governments will follow suit with their own Freedom of Information Acts!

CASE NO. 6

Company   Not Revealed.
Source   Fialka, J.J. (1997), *War By Other Means*, Norton, New York.
Date   1990s.
Relevance to Obstructive Marketing   Systematic research into competitor –
             passive.
Synopsis   Wolf Co. wants information about a competitor – Sheep Co. – but
             Wolf Co. does not want to be seen mounting an investigation. The
             consultant begins with a database search. To fill in the blanks after that,
             she sometimes calls Sheep Co. directly and asks lower-level employees
             specific questions about prices and products, blending sensitive
             questions into what might sound like a harmless market survey.
Related Cases   Various.
Comment   This is really an extension of the market research department
             – with a vengeance. The seriousness with which companies will
             pursue competition and their own marketing goals must not be
             underestimated.

CASE NO. 7

Company   Exxon.
Source   Fialka, J.J. (1997), *War By Other Means*, Norton, New York.
Date   1990.
Relevance to Obstructive Marketing   Information brokerage – active.
Synopsis   A Swiss broker named Michael Szrajber tried to bribe an Exxon
             employee in order to identify contract bids. Other oil companies
             were also targeted – and the proceeds sold to, amongst others,
             Japanese trading houses.[7]
Comment   This type of activity is close to industrial espionage. However, in
             many countries – particularly in the Far East, India and Middle East
             – it is not looked upon in necessarily the same light as it might be
             in the US or certain parts of Europe where such corruption would
             involve, as it did in this case, eventual imprisonment.

CASE NO. 8

Company   De Beers (Cartels).
Source   Naylor, R.T. (1994), *Hot Money and the Politics of Debt*, Black Rose
             Books, New York.

Date   1980.

Relevance to Obstructive Marketing   A cartel retaliates against a country wishing
            to market a product of its own, in this case diamonds, independently
            of the cartel.

Synopsis   In 1980 Zaire dropped out of the De Beers cartel. While Zaire had a
            small market share there was a fear that such a move would spread
            throughout the cartel. The cartel responded by dumping. Prices
            collapsed. Zaire rejoined the cartel.[8]

Comment   This case demonstrates that the process can work both ways! Any
            process 'legal or not' can also apply to monopolies keeping their
            markets in line.

CASE NO. 9

Company   Firestone Inc.

Source   Coughlin, P. (Ed.) (1989), *Industrialization in Kenya: In Search of a
            Strategy*, Heinemann, Kenya.

Date   1982–1992.

Relevance to Obstructive Marketing   Government interference with free market
            sale of tyres.

Synopsis   No-objection certificates were part of the elaborate import licensing
            system that tried to protect domestic industries in Kenya. These
            were instituted to facilitate the task of banning the importation of
            products that competed with those of local firms. One of the first to
            get one was Firestone Inc. – which then used the system to prevent
            competitors entering the market. Subsequently, 1992, the company
            was prevented from repatriating profits. In the end this rather
            circular arrangement benefited virtually no one: government,
            company or consumer.[9]

Comment   Coughlin is the main reference for a series of events concerning
            Firestone's attempts to run a business free of government
            interference in Kenya. As with monopolies this is often a double-
            edged sword. The company wants one thing and the government
            another. It is yet another issue if a free market should prevail in
            such circumstances at all. In any event the Kenyan Government's
            attempts to control the manner in which Firestone sold tyres in
            Kenya fulfils the definition of Obstructive Marketing – and is
            therefore relevant.

CASE NO. 10

Company   Various.
Source   Rider, B.A.K. (Ed.) (1991), 'Economic Crime – Due Diligence', *9th Symposium on Economic Crime*, Jesus College, Cambridge.
Date   1980s.
Relevance to Obstructive Marketing   The influence of economic crime on legitimate business trading – and the danger it poses to legitimate trading in various guises throughout the world.
Synopsis Barry Rider, in this and other related publications, describes the effects of economic crime on various businesses. In broad terms his document is an encouragement to 'look before you leap' into markets. It demonstrates the dangers posed to legitimate trading in various guises throughout the world.[10]
Comment   Despite the frequency of reference to economic crime Obstructive Marketing is not entirely concerned with crime. However, when legitimate activities are prevented it is of course the case that crime is high on the list of possible reasons why. Barry Rider is a world leader in his field – and has identified many flaws in the international legal system which can make legitimate trade difficult.

CASE NO. 11

Company   Goodyear.
Source   Tolchin, M.J and Tolchin, S.J. (1992), *Selling Our Security*, Knopf, New York.
Date   1986.
Relevance to Obstructive Marketing   Corporate raiding.
Synopsis Sir James Goldsmith launches a corporate raid on Goodyear Inc. This nets him close to $100 million. It leaves a formerly strong employer and producer of tyres in virtual ruins: forced to fire 4,000 people, farm out its R&D, 'hollow-out' many of its key operations, and sell its aerospace division.[11]
Comment   In a capitalist society it is a moot point that such activities could constitute 'unhelpful' activity. Some would argue that Goodyear needed the whipping, and is now better for it – particularly some shareholders. Nevertheless the company was prevented from marketing products by a particular activity – and this clearly constitutes an Obstructive Marketing event.

CASE NO. 12

Company   Fairchild Semiconductors.

Source   Tolchin, M. and Tolchin, S.J. (1992), *Selling Our Security*, Knopf, New York.

Date   1987.

Relevance to Obstructive Marketing   Hester Prynne Sanction – where a company is labelled as a transgressor of some sort of law or agreement or code.

Synopsis   CEO of Micron described Foreign Direct Investment, particularly the Fujitsu bid for Fairchild, as sometimes search and destroy missions that enabled foreign competitors to dominate an industry. Led to the Exon–Florio amendment of 1987 enabling foreign investors to be labelled security risks. A 'legal' Hester Prynne Sanction.[12]

Comment   The US and Britain are the largest receivers, and investors, of Foreign Direct Investment in the world – generally in each other. Both have taken different views of the subject – Britain hopeful that it would rebuild a damaged manufacturing infrastructure – the US concerned about losing such. Particularly in the US, some bizarre, as the Tolchins' relate, Obstructive Marketing methods were invoked to try and control it – particularly in the 1980s.

CASE NO. 13

Company   Norton – BTR – Compagnie St Gobain.

Source   Tolchin, M. and Tolchin, S.J. (1992), *Selling Our Security*, Knopf, New York.

Date   1990.

Relevance to Obstructive Marketing   'Illegal' use of legislation to prevent an unfavourable take-over by one company in favour of another.

Synopsis   Double-edged use of legislation to stop a take-over. Norton successfully defended a bid by BTR using the previously noted Exon–Florio amendment – but then ignored it to secure a much better deal from Compagnie de Saint Gobain.[13]

Comment   This is not obviously an Obstructive Marketing case. However, the end result was to deprive BTR of a capability to market its products.

CASE NO. 14

Company   Japanese Kereitsus.
Source   Tolchin, M. and Tolchin, S.J. (1992), *Selling Our Security*, Knopf,
            New York.
Date   Late twentieth century.
Relevance to Obstructive Marketing   Japanese trading structure blocks foreign
            companies' attempts to market goods and services.
Synopsis Japanese Kereitsus protect their companies from unwanted
            leveraged buy-outs (LBOs) through a finely honed system of
            interlocking directorates and stable shareholdings; and Kereitsus
            are defined by such relationships often referred to as akin to a
            spider's web. This cozy arrangement leaves managers free to
            conduct their business without fear of raiders, and cushioned
            against some of the predatory dangers of the marketplace. They
            have also been, until very recently, an effective barrier to foreign
            penetration of the Japanese market.[14]
Comment   Until the cracks appeared in the system following the recent
            trouble in the Japanese economy, this was the epitome of the
            opposition to free market capitalism. Few companies legitimately
            cracked the Japanese market.

CASE NO. 15

Company   EU Regional Strategy.
Source   Tolchin, M. and Tolchin, S.J. (1992), *Selling Our Security*, Knopf,
            New York.
Date   1988.
Relevance to Obstructive Marketing   The non-tariff barriers of the EU prevent US
            companies from selling goods and services in the EU.
Synopsis The EU was born of economically strong nations. To maintain
            the strength, regional policy has placed a number of non-tariff
            trade barriers in the way of true free trade. Instruments having
            to pass German TUV tests (*Technischer Überwachungs-Verein*,
            Technical Inspection Associations, are German organisations
            that work to validate the safety of products of all kinds to
            protect people and the environment against hazards), straight
            bananas, and different homologation requirements for cars are
            all examples of this.

Comment   Whether in Japan, Europe or India, non-tariff trade barriers add to the cost of doing business (often they also add to safety too). However, they are equally often used to protect industry. Used in such a manner, non-tariff trade barriers are counter.

CASE NO. 16

Company   Russian Central Bank.

Source   *Risk Management in Eastern Europe and Russia*, Conference, Royal Institute of International Affairs, London, 27 February 1995.

Date   1994.

Relevance to Obstructive Marketing   Russian Central Bank creating a situation of 'delaying effective commercial adjustment' – and thereby holding up both business and trade.

Synopsis   Following a situation where the 'nomenklatura's' principal attributes – a paramilitary hierarchy, hostility towards outsiders and a propensity for illegal behaviour – established its similarity with the criminal societies of the old Russian underworld. The similarity was no coincidence. The organisational model which the Bolsheviks found so attractive in the Russian criminal bands 70 years earlier was internalised in the modern Communist party structure. 'When the wall came down, therefore, neither camp was as uniform or as consistent as the stereotypes of the previous 45 years had led us to believe. In this respect, of course, within a European setting the irony was that as one end of Europe reacted strongly against belonging to a supranational organisation, the other end of Europe was moving closer to a Federal European State' (conference quote under the Chatham House Rule). In this environment central bank funds are identified and allocated, 'in a manner that reflects the recipient's bargaining and political power, not on economic or financial considerations'. This delays effective commercial adjustment.[15]

Comment   Effectively this approach means there is no Western-style capitalist prudence, of any description, within the former Eastern Bloc. (Larry Taepke, VP Bank One, would argue that there is increasingly little in the West too, with too much money floating around – but this is a different issue effectively concerned with startups and growth, not settlement.) The result is that payment for goods and services has often been difficult to effect legally. As the whole idea is to make a legal profit out of selling goods and services this fits the Obstructive Marketing picture well.

CASE NO. 17

Company   Various.

Source   *Organised Crime in Russia*, Conference, Royal Institute of International Affairs, London, 6 March 1995.

Date   1995.

Relevance to Obstructive Marketing   Counterfeiting products.

Synopsis   'Counterfeiters simply copy the most successful name brand products, investing nothing in R&D, marketing or advertising and next to nothing in quality control. American businesses lose over $16 billion to counterfeiters per annum. The intangible loss is more difficult to measure when the manufacturer's reputation and value of its brand is damaged by poor quality fakes.'[16]

Comment   Counterfeiting is a direct threat to legitimate business. It therefore fits the definition of Obstructive Marketing.

CASE NO.S 18–29

Company   See synopsis.

Source   http://www.ufcw770.org/boycotts.htm (accessed: 20 October 1999).

Date   2 May 1998.

Relevance to Obstructive Marketing   Pressure group boycott trying to prevent sale of goods/services.

Synopsis   'The following is a list of businesses UFCW Local 770 asks all members and their families not to patronise. These are companies who refuse to allow employees to organise. Support the right of collective bargaining. Do not patronise:
             • 32nd Street Market (case no. 18)
             • Bristol Farms (case no. 19)
             • Jons Markets (case no. 20)
             • K-Mart Super Centres (case no. 21)
             • Whole Foods (case no. 22)
             • Smart and Final Stores (case no. 23)
             • Superior/Frontier (case no. 24)
             • Target Stores (case no. 25)
             • Treisierras Markets (case no. 26)
             • Top Valu/Valu Plus (case no. 27)
             • Trader Joe's (case no. 28)
             • Wal-Mart/Sam's Club (case no. 29).'[17,18]

Comment   This is a clear attempt to stop businesses operating.

CASE NO. 30

Company   HealthTech International – US.
Source   *The Economist.*
Date   29 November 1997.
Relevance to Obstructive Marketing   Illegal stock market manipulation of shares to company detriment.
Synopsis   Allegedly, organised crime combined with fraudulent company officers and stockbrokers to manipulate company stock price.[19]
Comment   This is a widespread issue: 'In Italy and Japan gangsters have long known how to speculate to accumulate. Risks are low (stock market manipulation is difficult to prove) and the rewards high.'[20]

CASE NO. 31

Company   The Body Shop, 'Body Shop Response to Criticism'.
Source   http://www.bodyshop.co.uk (accessed: 2 May 1998).
Date   1993 to date.
Relevance to Obstructive Marketing   Philosophy and management defamation.
Synopsis   Defamation of company, CEO, CFO and products in the journal *Business Ethics* led to widespread scepticism of company philosophy and management which had been built on 'green' and 'ethical' products. Despite detailed rebuttal of the charges much damage to the company was done. Whether accurate or not the charges certainly prevented Body Shop from trading effectively thereafter.[21]
Comment   This is one of the most interesting areas of Obstructive Marketing as there are a number of motives behind each defamation case: running from the disgruntled employee through to the KGB trap.

CASE NO. 32

Company   TRW and the US Government have been widely reported.
Source   *The Wall Street Journal.*
Date   1997.
Relevance to Obstructive Marketing   Competitive Espionage.
Synopsis   A TRW Inc. research scientist pleaded guilty in Federal Court here to passing classified nuclear weapons information to China more than a decade ago.[22]

Comment   As with the following example, Avery Dennison, an archetypal case of competitive espionage designed to gain product and market advantage for a competitor.

CASE NO. 33

Company   Avery Dennison.
Source   *The Wall Street Journal.*
Date   1998.
Relevance to Obstructive Marketing   Plain competitive espionage.
Synopsis   Avery Dennison employee confesses to being spy for competitor.[23]
Comment   A clear example of Obstructive Marketing, particularly the means employed by some Far Eastern enterprises (see also TRW, q.v.).

CASE NO. 34

Company   All European drug companies.
Source   BioTech '99.
Date   1999.
Relevance to Obstructive Marketing   Selling, by third parties, of drugs acquired in a low-price market into a higher-price market in competition with the manufacturer (parallel trade).
Synopsis   Drug prices in Europe are regulated by nations – not the EC. There are high-price drug countries, for example, UK, Netherlands and Germany and low-price drug countries, for example, Greece, Spain and Portugal. There is wide-ranging trade in buying drugs in a low-price country and selling them in a high-price country. This damages a drug company's ability to recoup the money spent on R&D in countries which have good patent protection (the high-price countries) because of actions associated with countries which have low patent protection (the low-price countries). Examples are Zovirax that is $3 in Spain and $5 in the UK, and Amoxil that is $2 in Greece and $7 in the UK. Test cases have not been helpful to the industry. EU law works against the big company that has expended the R&D effort.[24]
Comment   This issue could kill drug companies. There is more and more pressure to come to the lowest common denominator on price – and this will destroy R&D in many companies.

CASE NO. 35

Company   Shell Oil Company.
Source   *Financial Times*, Internet, various.
Date   1997–1999.
Relevance to Obstructive Marketing   Social action preventing a company
              following a policy.
Synopsis   Shell Oil, a company that had established itself in the 1970s and
              1980s as environmentally conscious ran into serious problems in
              two areas in the 1990s with the Brent Spar disposal problem and
              the Nigeria pollution problem. Both issues led to demonstrations,
              sabotage, a boycott of products and eventual changes in policy
              by the company – despite the fact that its original actions were
              probably both environmentally and economically sound.[25]
Comment   These activities fulfil the definition of Obstructive Marketing because
              they are preventative. It may be argued that overall the end result is
              of benefit to a company that deals with the issues sensitively.

CASE NO. 36

Company   British Airways and Virgin Airways.
Source   *Financial Times*, Internet, various.
Date   1980s and 1990s.
Relevance to Obstructive Marketing   Attempted use of virtual monopoly to
              squash rival.
Synopsis   When Virgin Airways challenged British Airways' effective
              monopoly of certain transatlantic routes a wide range of actions
              ensued: cheap tickets were offered to use the other carrier,
              calling passengers and canceling their flight forcing them to the
              alternative, sending limousines to pick passengers up, accessing
              booking systems, delaying aircraft, 'dumpster diving'.[26]
Comment   This case has become a *cause celebre* of the true David and Goliath
              kind. As a case study it encompasses most of what Obstructive
              Marketing is about.

CASE NO.S 37–43

Company   Various oil companies.
Source   9th Symposium on Microprocessor Based Protection Systems,
              Zagreb, Croatia.

Date   7 December 1995.

Relevance to Obstructive Marketing   This is a case of 'human error' in equipment
design, fabrication and maintenance having a severe effect on
companies' abilities to market their product – but from a less
obvious angle. These remain cases of Obstructive Marketing.

Synopsis   The following incidents were a result of serious 'human error'
during 1995 at various oil facilities around the US:

- Chevron's Pascagoula MS refinery fire (May 1995) (case no. 37);
- Chevron's El Paso refinery explosion (June 1995) (case no. 38);
- Chevron contaminated AvGas problem (Summer 1995) (case no. 39): re-engined North California's Light Aircraft Fleet at cost of $100 million plus;
- Shell Chemical's Belpre OH fire (June1995) (case no. 40): plant out of service for one year. Thermoplastic elastomer supply to international markets strained;
- Texaco's Pembroke Refinery explosion and fire (July 1995) (case no. 41): 10 per cent of UK refining capacity. Both gasoline and crude futures displaced 3 per cent in two days;
- Exxon Chemical's Baton Rouge explosion (August 1995) (case no. 42): plant capacity reduced 80 per cent to 1 per cent of total US production;
- Shell Chemical's Norco LA plant fire (August 1995) (case no. 43): US now has critical shortage of ethylene.

Causes:

- equipment and design failures – 41 per cent;
- operator and maintenance errors 41 per cent;
- inadequate or improper procedures – 11 per cent;
- inadequate or improper inspection – 5 per cent;
- miscellaneous causes – 2 per cent.[27]

Comment   In general these accidents could have been prevented by microprocessor control mechanisms. This series of disasters emphasises,
again, both the very human element and internal nature of
Obstructive Marketing.

CASE NO. 44

Company   Johnson & Johnson.

Source   Internet (see note).

Date   1982.

Relevance to Obstructive Marketing   Looks like Obstructive Marketing but isn't.

Synopsis   Seven people died of cyanide poisoning between 29 September and 1 October 1982 – all after having taken contaminated Tylenol (an analgesic akin to Aspirin). This was not, however, an act perpetrated against the company – but a random poisoning.[28]

Comment   Although these cases certainly damaged the companies distributing the product it is not the case that the company was the target. It is generally agreed that all deaths were the result of products being used to poison individuals, rather than to target companies.

Further Representative Cases Supporting Chapter 3 in General

CASE NO. 45: COCA COLA BOYCOTT BY ARAB COUNTRIES, 1970S

Arab Government boycott of a company for association with Israel and the US Government.[29]

CASE NO. 46: OIL EMBARGO AGAINST RHODESIA, 1965

British Government's boycott (of oil in particular) of Rhodesia for its unilateral declaration of independence. Sanction busting became widespread and therefore sanctions were ineffective.[30]

CASE NO. 47: SANCTIONS AGAINST SOUTH AFRICA, 1980S

Various sanctions to supposedly assist a change in government – merely damaged local employment prospects and multinational corporations (MNCs) in South Africa.[31]

CASE NO. 48: MATRIX CHURCHILL, 1989

A case which seems to be classic in terms of Obstructive Marketing – but not. The whole thing was a cover for various military operations, not commercial ones.[32]

CASE NO. 49: FRENCH LAWS FOR VIDEO IMPORTATION, 1982 ONWARDS

No law against foreign video machine importation – but each had to be inspected. There was only one inspector. Few foreign video machines were sold![33]

CASE NO. 50: BOSNIAN SANCTIONS, 1990S

Sanctions in support of a 'peacekeeping' operation. Somewhat different from the South African model. Stopped trade. An example of sanctions not relevant to Obstructive Marketing.[34]

CASE NO. 51: EU MARKET REGULATION AND COMPETITION POLICY, 1990S

EU market regulation can be seen to be a significant marketing barrier in itself, particularly when looked at from the USA.[35]

CASE NO. 52: WORLD BANK, 1980S AND 1990S

The bank and the IMF have often been accused of lending policies and development policies that increase third world debt and restrict market development.[36,37]

CASE NO. 53: EBRD, 1990S

The debate has raged since formation as to whether or not this bank is helping reconstruction and development – and therefore market development.[38]

CASE NO. 54: MUSLIM RESTRICTIONS – ALCOHOL/DRESS/TV, 1980S AND 1990S

Muslim beliefs restrict the marketing of many Western goods. These restrictions can be circumvented, often, with thought. A better understanding can be gained by reading about the traditions, and the reasons for them.[39]

CASE NO. 55: GLASS BOTTLE/ALUFOIL WAR GERMANY/DENMARK, 1986–1990

This was a prototype corporate war between the glass bottle manufacturers and the alufoil/paper package producers with both sides slinging as much mud as possible at each other.[40]

CASE NO. 56: DIOXIN MILK DEBATE, 1988, 1999

The dioxin in milk debate started because it became possible to measure dioxins – no one is still completely aware of how much dioxin contamination is damaging. There is no doubt dioxins are damaging – but how much causes what damage?[41]

CASE NO. 57: ANIMAL RIGHTS CAMPAIGNS AGAINST FUR FARMS, 1990S

Violent attacks against farms producing fur. Fulfill definition. Only question is why did American mink return to their farm and British mink not?[42]

CASE NO. 58: ANIMAL RIGHTS CAMPAIGNS AGAINST PHARMACEUTICAL COMPANIES, 1990S

PR and physical attacks on pharmaceutical companies, usually for using animals in experiments. Again fulfills the definition.[43]

CASE NO. 59: PERRIER WATER HYDROCARBON CONTAMINATION, FEBRUARY 1990

Perrier withdrew large quantities of water from European shelves following what was at the time thought to be employee product contamination by a benzene rag. Lately it has been thought that benzene contamination may be a more generic problem. Nevertheless the immediate cause was employee contamination.[44]

CASE NO. 60: ESSO/EXXON VALDEZ, 1989

For ten years, Esso, to the detriment of its market and shareholders, has been fighting legal battles consequent to the oil spillage in Prince William Sound, Alaska, and related contamination.[45]

CASE NO. 61: FAR EAST PIRACY AND PRODUCT COPYING, 1990S

Product piracy is damaging worldwide – hindering company development, new R&D, killing jobs in the old and new worlds with equal disdain. Software piracy is particularly rampant.[46]

CASE NO. 62: SHOOTING THE BOSS, 1980S AND 1990S

The ultimate Obstructive Marketing ruse! Often a means to an end in the US – you can't get the staff these days![47]

CASE NO. 63: ADVANCE FEE SCAMS, 1986 TO DATE

The International Chambers of Commerce/International Maritime Bureau has identified a large number of companies adversely affected by advance fee scams – particularly by Nigerians. Victims find it difficult to grow and difficult to operate.[48]

CASE NO. 64: SWISS DIRECTORY FRAUD, 1992 TO DATE

A fraud perpetrated on companies. They subscribe to a non-existent directory – if they are lucky they lose their subscription, if stupid they lose all the money in their bank account.[49]

CASE NO. 65: DEFENSIVE AGENCIES (DUBAI), 1994

This is where a company takes on, either for itself or a partner firm, agencies in a product of which the company already sells a variant itself. This deprives the principal of a market – as the 'agent' has absolutely no intention of selling the principal's goods at the expense of his own favoured line.[50]

CASE NO. 66: AGENCY MONOPOLIES (INDIA), 1995

A variant of the previous case. This time Company A sells pipes, but takes on agencies for steel which it does nothing with. Company B sells steel, but takes on agencies for pipes which it does nothing with. Company A and B carve up the pipe and steel market between them.[51]

CASE NO. 67: MACRO VIRUS ATTACKS, 1996 ONWARDS

Computer virus which temporarily/permanently prevents companies operating effectively: random, not necessarily targeted.[52]

CASE NO. 68: NESTLÉ. HESTER PRYNNE SANCTION, 1980S ONWARDS

Retaliation for allegedly limiting breast feeding in Africa by promotion of baby powder. Anyone who has worked in Africa knows what errant nonsense this is – the women are undernourished, often not enough own milk, and it is dirty water, not milk powder, that kills babies.[53]

CASE NO. 69: FRANCIS CABOT LOWELL, 1811

Stole plans of the Cartwright Loom from the UK, allowing the US to build a textile industry, depriving the UK of a market.[54]

CASE NO. 70: ROMAN CATHOLICISM AND CONTRACEPTION, 1960S TO DATE

This is an issue that helps clarify what legal Obstructive Marketing is about. Religious belief limits the ability of pharmaceutical companies in Catholic countries to market the birth control pill – as such a pill is clearly at odds with papal teaching.[55]

CASE NO. 71: COCA-COLA AS A CONTRACEPTIVE, 1960S TO DATE

Coca-Cola sales in some tropical areas (particularly the Caribbean islands) are out of line with local populations. Although this might be due to smuggling it has been found to be directly attributable to the use of Coca-Cola as a vaginal douche and contraceptive. The consequences of any change in the formula have limited product development in certain territories.[56]

CASE NO. 72: MCDONALD'S AND INDIA (USE OF LAMB RATHER THAN BEEF)

Ever since Ray Kroc took over McDonald's the recipes have been simple and basically based on beef. This makes it difficult in India, where cows are holy, bulls and bullocks rare, and beef very infrequently eaten. It limits the marketing possibilities unless fundamental change is introduced.[57]

CASE NO. 73: IRAN CONTROL GALLEY MAKERS FOR BOEING 747S, 1997

Boeing, a US company, relies on Iranian-owned companies to supply key parts of Boeing 747s. At the time no diplomatic relations existed between Iran and US – and spares for 747s in Iranian hands have been impounded. A different sort of Obstructive Marketing – a way round it![58]

CASE NO. 74: MEDTRONIC'S CHINESE PRODUCT LIABILITY SUIT

When a top Chinese General's pacemaker stopped working a few years ago the company recommended the insertion of a new wire. The procedure, standard in the West, worked. Medtronic, however, were taken to court under a product liability suit. The company prevailed but were left more bruised and battered than the General by the experience. Key was the ability to use 'smear campaigns' as evidence.[59]

CASE NO. 75: MERCOSUR MID-1990

Tariffs that damaged US companies in South America.[60]

CASE NO. 76: WAL-MART'S CESSATION OF TOBACCO SALES IN 1980S – RESULT OF CONSUMER PRESSURE

A successful Obstructive Marketing campaign.[61]

CASE NO. 77: NIKE'S USE OF CHILD LABOUR IN THE FAR EAST

A company admired for its policies and marketing finding itself the butt of boycotts and trenchant humour in 'Doonesbury' (a widely syndicated satirical cartoon strip).[62]

CASE NO. 78: SHELL OIL AND KEN SARO-WIWA, 1997

Among other events, the hanging of Ken Saro-Wiwa orchestrated boycott of Shell's products.[63]

CASE NO. 79: OCTVAR BOTNAR AND THE UK NISSAN FRANCHISE, 1991

Botnar built a personal empire out of the UK (and elsewhere) Nissan franchise – but held up the Nissan's company's UK expansion after the Tyneside factory was built. Eventually Botnar lost his franchise after an IR(S) investigation – and Nissan went on to increase UK market share.[64]

CASE NO. 80: MICROSOFT AND SUN MICROSYSTEMS RE JAVA, 1997 ONWARDS

Java is a cross-platform computer language developed by Sun – which could challenge the ascendancy of Microsoft. Microsoft allegedly tried to control use and distribution, and therefore Sun's market.[65]

CASE NO. 81: HOFFMAN LA ROCHE, 1990S

Pressure group targeted for inappropriate tests on animals.[66]

CASE NO. 82: OILPUMP (PSEUDONYM), SOUTH AFRICA, 1995

Oilpump's ability to market product, and market reputation, was being hampered by theft of petrol and substitution by water. Initially instrumentation was blamed. An early morning visit identified the problem. Perpetrators were a strong political group. Tact was required in resolving the issue.[67]

CASE NO. 83: FERRANTI, 1994

Hostile take-over battle with International Signal and Control Inc.led to the collapse of the business. A spectacular failure of due diligence.[68]

CASE NO. 84: COCA-COLA: FANTA BABES 1969

Coca-Cola was accused, much like Nestlé, of killing babies in Africa. This time, in particular, in Zambia where baby deaths were often recorded as a 'Fanta' death. The real problem was dirty water.[69]

CASE NO. 85: BOOTS (CHEMISTS), 1990S

Targeted by pressure group for pollution and animal testing.[70]

CASE NO. 86: WAL-MART, 1990S

Boycotted for putting small retailers out of business in Middle America. Once the Wal-Mart store arrives out of town, the town centres die. The consumers, however, seem to enjoy the discounted prices.[71]

CASE NO. 87: JOHNSON & JOHNSON, 1990S

Targeted and boycotted for animal testing.[72]

CASE NO. 88: ROCHE – 1988/1989

Accused, and boycotted, for selling non-essential/inappropriate drugs.[73]

CASE NO. 89: PEPSI CO., 1990S

Subsidiaries accused of animal testing. Difficulties over the marketing standards of Kentucky Fried Chicken in India. Both led to boycotts.[74]

CASE NO. 90: PHILIP MORRIS, 1980S AND 1990S

Targeted for killing large numbers of people through tobacco sales. Boycotts and civil action. Eventually led to the 1998/1999 US tobacco settlements – which has not pleased the campaigners. People remain able to make a choice as to whether they smoke or not.[75]

CASE NO. 91: RJR/NABISCO

A classic corporate raid. As in all corporate raids the result is often philosophically debatable – but it is the raw edge of capitalism and archetypal of a certain type of Obstructive Marketing.[76]

CASE NO. 92: GUINNESS, 1987

One of the classic Obstructive Marketing campaigns – even more so because of the enormous obfuscation that still surrounds it.[77]

CASE NO. 93: PFIZER, 1990S

Targeted and boycotted for testing on animals.[78]

CASE NO. 94: EASTMAN KODAK, 1990S

Targeted and boycotted for pollution-related issues.[79]

CASE NO. 95: BP, 1990S

Targeted and boycotted for a range of animal rights, environmental and human rights issues.[80]

CASE NO. 96: UNILEVER, 1990S

Principally targeted and boycotted for polluting the UK's River Mersey.[81]

CASE NO. 97: PROCTER & GAMBLE, 1990S

Targeted and boycotted for animal usage and pollution. Eventually led to change in the company – so Obstructive Marketing campaign can be deemed to have been successful.[82]

CASE NO. 98: RECKITT & COLEMAN, 1990S

Targeted and boycotted for animal abuse, pollution and environmental destruction.[83]

CASE NO. 99: COLGATE, 1990S

Targeted and boycotted for animal abuse, pollution and environmental destruction.[84]

CASE NO. 100: SMITH KLINE BEECHAM, 1990S

Targeted and boycotted for animal abuse and environmental issues.[85]

CASE NO. 101: ENID BLYTON, 1980S AND 1990S

A UK children's author inaccurately accused of sexism and racism. This stopped the sale of her books for nearly 20 years. Her personal life appears to have been neither sexist or racist.[86]

CASE NO. 102: INSTITUTE OF SCIENTIFIC INFORMATION – 'DATA RAPE'

Targeting and acquisition of information on particular companies for competitors.[87]

CASE NO. 103: JAPANESE INFORMATION CENTRE OF SCIENCE AND TECHNOLOGY

Acquires information on foreign competitors.[88]

CASE NO. 104: SOVIET ACADEMY OF SCIENCES

Acquired, systematically, information on potential competitors.[89]

CASE NO. 105: CHINESE GOVERNMENT

Currently acquires information, systematically, on foreign competitors.[90]

CASE NO. 106: CENTRE FOR RESEARCH PLANNING IN PHILADELPHIA[91]

Using databases to identify 'black' (secret and dangerous) military projects in foreign countries, often by tracking the publications of academics.

CASE NO. 107: SHELL

Penetrated by industrial spies selling information to the competition.[92]

CASE NO. 108: BP

Penetrated by industrial spies selling information to the competition.[93]

CASE NO. 109: MARATHON

Penetrated by industrial spies selling information to the competition.[94]

CASE NO. 110: MOBIL

Penetrated by industrial spies selling information to the competition.[95]

CASE NO. 111: STATOIL

Penetrated by industrial spies selling information to the competition.[96]

CASE NO. 112: ITOCHU CORPORATION

Bought information on significant competitors.[97]

CASE NO. 113: MARUBENI CORPORATION

Bought information on significant competitors.[98]

CASE NO. 114: THYSSEN

Bought information on significant competitors.[99]

CASE NO. 115: MANNESMANN

Bought information on significant competitors.[100]

CASE NO. 116: PROCTER AND GAMBLE AS 'PAGANIST' COMPANY, 1999

These allegations have been rumbling for years. Recently cost over $300 million to settle suits, particularly with regard to Amway.[101]

CASE NO. 117: TOSHIBA'S SALE OF SUBMARINE TECHNOLOGY TO SOVIET UNION

Also involved in the cartel to stop production of the US designed dual-deck video recorder.[102]

CASE NO. 118: CHINA

China's prime intelligence agency, the 'Guojia Anquan Bu', has flooded the US with spies. About half the illegal technology transfer cases being investigated on the West Coast involve the Chinese.[103]

CASE NO. 119: NIGERIA

The ability of successive military and civilian governments to control, to the obstruction of foreign and indigenous companies, trade is a history lesson in financial management of a very self-focused nature.[104]

CASE NO. 120: INDIAN HAWALLAH SYSTEM

Along with other country networks, the Chinese in particular, Indian communities often move money outside the official banking system. This sort of activity distorts the regular banking and other markets – to the detriment of legal institutions and companies.[105]

CASE NO. 121: LEVI JEANS

Levi Jeans has suffered on two counts; firstly, the use of cheap labour, and its so-called 'country code' and, secondly, from counterfeiting in all markets.[106]

CASE NO. 122: BAYER, 1997

Suffered a local political and social attack in Taiwan – bringing multi-million dollar investments and jobs into question.[107]

CASE NO. 123: LAKER AIRWAYS, 1982

Was put out of business by aggressive price reductions from its larger competitors. This protected the high-profit transatlantic routes of the major US and UK carriers for about a decade.[108]

CASE NO. 124: BURROUGHS WELLCOME

Sudafed Poisonings 1993. Burroughs suffered when its products were stuffed with poison by outsiders, causing consumer deaths.[109]

CASE NO. 125: EXCEDRIN POISONINGS 1988

Similar to the Burroughs example, this time damaging Bristol Myers Squibb.[110]

CASE NO. 126: GERMANY'S CURRENT, 1995 ONWARDS, NON-TARIFF TRADE BARRIERS

On electronics and instrumentation equipment preventing an open market by demanding higher safety margins for products sold in Germany over other EU markets.[111]

CASE NO. 127: WESTLAND, 1991

Company executives' travel plans targeted during critical development phase, potentially damaging company plans.[112]

CASE NO. 128: OMNI, 1991

Company's executives' travel plans targeted during take-over, potentially damaging company plans.[113]

CASE NO. 129: ESSELTE, 1991

Company executives' travel plans targeted during take-over, potentially damaging company plans.[114]

CASE NO. 130: ROLLS ROYCE, 1971

This is a double-edged story. Tells of how a great company was brought to its knees by over-engineering and a misunderstanding of how the world aero-engine market was changing – the engineers did not understand the market, and there were no marketers in the company at the time. The company was, against all market principles, allowed to go bankrupt and was then rebuilt with government money to become the major threat to American dominance in the aero-engine market by the year 1999.[115]

CASE NO. 131: HUDSON FOODS, 1998

Hudson Foods' beef became contaminated with *E.Coli 0157*. It had to be recalled. The relevant group company was closed and sold.[116]

CASE NO. 132: COCA-COLA, 1999

The combination of a drop in quality standards and contamination at a number of plants on the Belgium/France border brought about a drop in actual volume growth and a significant drop in rate of growth of Coca-Cola in Europe as at end June 1999. This may have been deliberate. Events were blamed for poor performance of Coca-Cola Inc. in second quarter 1999.[117]

CASE NO. 133: REUTERS/BLOOMBERG

The competition between two rival financial information providers reached a crescendo with industrial espionage allegations against Analytics, a Reuter subsidiary, by Bloomberg.[118]

CASE NO. 134: MCDONALD'S

British farmers, fed up with the ban on British Beef following the BSE outbreak, force McDonald's to start buying again by preventing delivery, nationwide, of McDonald's buns. A tactic often used by the French – but generally unheard of in the UK until this event.[119]

CASE NO. 135: DELTA

Accused by rival Continental of trying to steal key executives after failed merger talks.[120]

CASE NO. 136: ASSI DOMAN

Jekyll and Hyde experience in Russian paper plants. Co-operation in St Petersburg but a campaign, and Mafia threats, in Karelia. Classic Russian Obstructive Marketing campaign.[121]

CASES NO.S 137–151 INCL. DELIBERATELY OMITTED

Chapter 3 – 'Executive Club Of Chicago' – Supporting Cases in the Public Domain

CASE NO. 152

Company   Ameritech.
Source   Public Television Advertising.
Date   April/May 1999.
Relevance to Obstructive Marketing   Company – Competitive.
Synopsis   Hostile take-over bid by SBC of Texas produces a string of arguments from both sides describing how bad or good the deal will be for shareholders.[122]
Comment   Ameritech's base stockholders want to remain independent and deploy many 'patriotic' type messages to try and preserve its position; the board has agreed to the take-over, they put out alternative scenarios; the board's view is backed by the bidder who also puts out positive scenarios. Each trying to influence the other – mostly to the immediate detriment of Ameritech's position as a performer and a company.

CASE NO. 153

Company   Amoco.
Source   Personal Communication.
Date   1999.
Relevance to Obstructive Marketing   Company – Competitive.
Synopsis   The received wisdom of the middle management of the Amoco Corporation was that the senior management sold them out to BP in return for large personal fortunes (this would seem to be broadly correct). This was followed by the 'wholesale' slaughter of Amoco executives in preference for BP employees. (This is not necessarily the case – but an interesting perception.)[123]
Comment   The take-over of Amoco by BP has been acknowledged as a personal coup for Sir John Browne, Chairman of BP. He has acknowledged that the personal incentives paid to the Amoco senior executives was instrumental in helping to gain control of the company. Such acknowledgement has extended to the ex-Amoco executives as well.

CASE NO. 154

Company   Andersen Consulting.
Source   *Financial Times.*
Date   1998.
Relevance to Obstructive Marketing   Company – Competitive.
Synopsis   A case of the 'child', Andersen Consulting, outgrowing the 'parent',
             Andersen, and a split resulting – perhaps to the benefit of the child
             but not to the benefit of the 'parent'.[124]
Comment   This is a response to a prolonged Bull Run. How successful the split
             will be in a downturn, if there is one, will be interesting to follow.

CASE NO. 155

Company   Baker & McKenzie.
Source   Personal communication.
Date   1999.
Relevance to Obstructive Marketing   Individual – Competitive.
Synopsis   Baker & McKenzie, the largest law firm in the USA, effectively closed
             for three days after computer virus Melissa (named apparently for
             Bill Gates's wife) attacks email listings. Coincidentally coincided
             with bombings in Kosovo (see the footnotes on origins of leading
             virus writers and anti-virus writers in Case no.37).[125]
Comment   'Melissa' was the most damaging virus to be publicly acknowledged
             since the Internet and email revolution began.

CASE NO. 156

Company   Caterpillar Inc.
Source   Donald V. Fites, Chairman, Caterpillar Inc.
Date   1999.
Relevance to Obstructive Marketing   Institution – Competitive.
Synopsis   Over a number of years the most difficult barrier for Caterpillar
             to overcome has frequently been the unilateral imposition of
             sanctions by the US Government. A case in point is the notification
             that the Sudan was a 'major threat to the State'. As Fites said,
             Sudan cannot pose a real military, political or economic threat to
             the US. All that happened is that Caterpillar lost a market where it
             had been active, and building, for 20 years, overnight, to Komatsu
             of Japan. At the same time the Italian subsidiary of GE made

some inroads to the market. The only people to lose out were the American workers at Caterpillar.

Comment   There are a number of similar cases to this – and although such political policies tend be found most frequently in the US they can also be found in Europe. They are very infrequently found elsewhere in the world – where such practices are looked upon somewhat bizarrely.[126]

CASE NO. 157

Company   Coca-Cola Corporation.

Source   Coca-Cola and the Internet.

Date   1997.

Relevance to Obstructive Marketing   Special Interest Group – Cultural.

Synopsis   The Nigerian Bottling Corporation had links with the Abacha regime in Nigeria. Local political activists tried, and almost succeeded (if Abacha's death had not intervened), in closing the company.[127]

Comment   This is a big problem overseas, particularly in high political risk areas. It is often difficult to establish a company, or do business, without (see next example) being associated with a particular political regime.

CASE NO. 158

Company   EDS.

Source   Follett, K. (1983), *On the Wings of Eagles*, Signet, London.

Date   1978/1979.

Relevance to Obstructive Marketing   Institution – Cultural.

Synopsis   Iranian coup places EDS employees on wrong side of new political divide – and they are arrested.[128]

Comment   As with the Coca-Cola example, except this time more severe, everything can start to go wrong when a company finds itself on the wrong side of a political change.

CASE NO. 159

Company   GM/VW/Lopez.

Source   Various.

Date   1997.

Relevance to Obstructive Marketing   Company – Cultural.

Synopsis   Industrial espionage plus damage to supply chain by overzealous purchasing executive results in market damage to company. Lopez is credited with much success at VW. VW accused GM of industrial espionage when Lopez moved to GM on enticement. However, it cost GM a fortune to put right the warranty claims resulting from Lopez's cost cutting in the supply chain – and more to rebuild the relationships in the supply chain he had destroyed.[129]

Comment   This case is an object lesson in how cost cutting in the supply chain can, VW, and cannot, GM, work.

CASE NO. 160

Company   IBM.

Source   Managing for Fraud Prevention, Royal Institute of International Affairs, Conference, London, 7 March 1995; Perry, S. (1995), *Survival in The Economic Espionage Wars*, Perry Corporation Inc., Chicago, USA.

Date   1980s.

Relevance to Obstructive Marketing   Theft of privileged information (industrial espionage).

Synopsis   Hitachi launches industrial espionage campaign against IBM. This resulted in the theft of the 27 'Adirondack Workbooks' – known internally as the 'Crown Jewels' – containing secret designs IBM planned would take them into the personal computer era.

Comment   Hitachi agreed with US authorities that this was a deliberate, planned operation against IBM to gain new product information for their benefit, and to IBM's cost. A classic case of Obstructive Marketing. This theme was further developed by the 'The Futures Group' in 1997.

According to a recent survey of US businesses conducted by the National Counterintelligence Center and the US Department of State, 74 US corporations reported more than 400 incidents of suspected foreign targeting against their businesses in 1996, only slightly more than half of these businesses were involved in producing technologies included on the National Critical Technologies List.

Sam Perry comments:

If the full marketing ramifications of intellectual property theft and unrestricted technology transfer are factored in, estimates rise to some $240 billion a year as the cost to US commerce with a growth in the problem of 260 percent since 1985.[130]

CASE NO. 161

Company   KPMG.

Source   *The Wall Street Journal.*

Date   1998.

Relevance to Obstructive Marketing   Company – competitive.

Synopsis   The aborted merger of Big Six accounting firms Ernst & Young and KPMG Peat Marwick. By the time they called the whole thing off in February 1998 the New York-based firms had not only wasted time and effort but had also swapped competitive secrets.[131]

Comment   Traditionally, as a Bull Run closes, there is an outbreak of merger mania. Recently, this has not been the case, although the end of a long Bull Run is heralded to some. Instead, the need to be a certain size to compete on a global basis has driven competitors to merge in order to gain the advantages of becoming a global player – when this fails much competitive and valuable information is left in each other's hands. In this case both players changed parts of their operating strategy in response to what they had learnt from the other.

CASE NO. 162

Company   McDonald's.

Source   Internet (see note).

Date   1996.

Relevance to Obstructive Marketing   Special Interest Group – Casual.

Synopsis   The archetypal Obstructive Marketing campaign by activists. Initially McDonald's was accused of lying about the quality of ingredients and other aspects of food in the chain. McDonald's brought a libel suit in response in London. The case went on for years.[132]

Comment   The suit cost McDonald's millions of pounds and exposed every part of their commercial operation to scrutiny. The company survived – but it was not the same organisation afterwards in many respects. The website spawned many other attacks on multi-national companies and is a key reference point for this study.

CASE NO. 163

Company   McDonnell Douglas.
Source   Fialka, J.J (1997), *War By Other Means*, Norton, New York.
Date   1993.
Relevance to Obstructive Marketing   Institution – Competitive.
Synopsis The beginning of the end of the aerospace industry in Columbus, Ohio, came on a hot day in August 1993 when a dozen Chinese visitors wearing business suits walked into Plant 85.
            The Chinese were offering a $1billion aircraft order in return for the missile building capability of Plant 85 – to be moved lock, stock and barrel to China.[133]
Comment   The order did not materialise but the Plant went East. This has had severe implications for the aircraft industry, the Chinese nuclear deterrent and the US missile industry that only became apparent in 1999.

CASE NO. 164

Company   Microsoft.
Source   Various.
Date   1999.
Relevance to Obstructive Marketing   Institution – Competitive.
Synopsis US Government in response to various allegations from Netscape (q.v.) and Sun (q.v.) brings anti-trust suit against Microsoft. This alleges abuse of a dominant market position. Microsoft asks what was it supposed to do except support its shareholders. Government wins a stalemate largely because of apparently poor performance of Microsoft at court.[134]
Comment   An archetypal Obstructive Marketing event. Damages Microsoft whatever the outcome. Raises whole series of Obstructive Marketing issues which cannot be covered here – including relevance of anti-trusts in the Internet age, relevance of Government and so on.

CASE NO: 165

Company   Motorola Inc.
Source   *Crain's Chicago Business*, May 1999.
Date   1999.
Relevance to Obstructive Marketing   Company – Competitive.

Synopsis   Bad staff work in a joint venture resulting in ineffective product launch – showing that Obstructive Marketing can be the result of delinquent internal processes as well as external ones.

An engineering feat, putting 66 satellites into orbit and giving everyone on earth a potential to talk to each other, compromised by marketing failures – the mobile phones are huge and unwieldy and markets have been incorrectly identified, compounded by massive cost overruns.[135,136]

Comment   This case is important because it shows how a certain amount of complacency in a big company can have serious effects – both internally and externally. It is the Black Hole argument which, like the RB 211 engine at Rolls Royce (q.v.), can become an all consuming engineering passion to the detriment of the overall health of the company – particularly when marketing gets it wrong too.

CASE NO. 166

Company   Nestlé.
Source   Private.
Date   1990/1991/1992.
Relevance to Obstructive Marketing   Special Interest Group – Competitive.
Synopsis   As a big cocoa buyer Nestlé is dependent upon commodity prices. Equally, the sellers are interested in knowing when Nestlé is going to buy. In the early 1990s Nestlé employed an outsourcing firm to act for them in a particular function. This company understood when certain executives were travelling to particular destinations. This allowed them to also understand when Nestlé was going to buy cocoa. This helped cocoa sellers get a good price.[137]
Comment   This is a further example of the inventiveness of persons seeking to either damage, or gain advantage, from a company.

CASE NO. 167

Company   Netscape.
Source   Various.
Date   1998.
Relevance to Obstructive Marketing   Company – Competitive.
Synopsis   Netscape developed a 'web browser'. Allegedly Microsoft copied it and then tried to sell it for nothing, incorporating it into their software.[138]

Comment　This together, with Sun Microsytems Java issue (q.v.), led to the US Government's anti-trust case against Microsoft (concluded with a bi-partisan deal in July 1999) – itself an Obstructive Marketing case study (but which cannot be included here for the sake of space) – and a whole series of potential litigation.

CASE NO. 168

Company　Sara Lee Inc.
Source　*Crain's Chicago Business*, May 1999.
Date　1998/1999.
Relevance to Obstructive Marketing　Company – Casual.
Synopsis　Product contamination preventing effective distribution of a good product, and damaging a company's prospects for growth if not survival.

> *Analysts are punishing the Chicago-based company, whose stock hit a 52-week low last week, for one of the deadliest bacterial outbreaks and largest meat recalls in the US.*[139]

Endnotes

1　Naylor, R.T. (1994), *Hot Money*, Black Rose Books, p228.
2　A former head of KGB revealed in a *Discovery Channel* Cable News Bulletin that the KGB had been instrumental in the 'Nestlé Baby Milk' case – see Case no. 68 – April 1999.
3　Fialka, J.J. (1997), *War By Other Means*, Norton, New York, p41ff.
4　Fialka, J.J. (1997), *War By Other Means*, Norton, New York p53ff.
5　Fialka, J.J. (1997), *War By Other Means*, Norton, New York, p95ff.
6　Personal communication, Ken Archer, Quality Strategies Inc., 6 July 1999.
7　Fialka, J.J. (1997), *War By Other Means*, Norton, New York, p131ff.
8　Naylor, R.T. (1994), *Hot Money*, Black Rose Books, New York, p394.
9　Coughlin, P. (1989), *Industrialization in Kenya: In Search of a Strategy*, Heinemann, Kenya, p24ff.
10　Rider, B.A.K. (1991), 'Economic Crime – Due Diligence', *9th Symposium on Economic Crime*, Jesus College, Cambridge.
11　Tolchin, M. and Tolchin, S.J. (1992), *Selling Our Security*, Knopf, New York, p32ff.
12　Tolchin, M. and Tolchin, S.J. (1992), *Selling Our Security*, Knopf, New York, p46ff.
13　Tolchin, M. and Tolchin, S.J. (1992), *Selling Our Security*, Knopf, New York, p58ff.
14　Tolchin, M. and Tolchin, S.J. (1992), *Selling Our Security*, Knopf, New York, p272ff.
15　Bosworth Davies, R. (1995), 'Money Laundering and the Insurance Business', Titmuss, SainerDechert, *Risk Management In Eastern Europe and FSU Conference*, Royal Institute of International Affairs, London, 27 February 1995.
16　March, S.J. (1995), 'Counterfeit Products in the Russian Federation', Pepper Hamilton and Scheetz, Attorneys, UK, USA, Russia, *Organised Crime in Russia, Conference*, Royal Institute of International Affairs, London, 6 March 1995.

17   This site, http://www.ufcw770.org/boycotts.htm (accessed: 20 October 2009) and others that can be accessed under keyword 'Boycott' demonstrate a whole range of actions by various parties against companies wishing to sell goods and services.

18   For the campaign against Wal-Mart in particular see http://www.harbornet.com/pna/us.html (accessed: 20 October 2009).

19   *Economist, The* (1997b), 'Stick 'em up', 29 November, p31.

20   *Economist, The* (1997b), 'Stick 'em up', 29 November, p31.

21   http://www.bodyshop.co.uk (accessed: 20 October 2009) is a good starting point for further study of this issue. Links to other sites are included.

22   Staff Reporter (1997), 'TRW Scientist Pleads Guilty to Giving China Nuclear Information', *The Wall Street Journal*, 9 December, p1.

23   Starkman, D. (1997), 'Secrets and Lies: The Dual Career of a Corporate Spy', *The Wall Street Journal*, 23 October, p1.

24   Personal Communication. (1999) *BioTech '99*, Taylor Joynson Garrett, Lawyers, Conversation with Maitland P. Hyslop. 19 May.

25   Jackson, T. (1997), 'The Global Company', *Financial Times*, 31 October, gives a good summary of both issues.

26   Tucker, E. (1997), 'Branson to Tell EU of Illegal BA Practices', *Financial Times*, 22 October, p10.

27   Nimmo, I. (1995), Honeywell IAC, 'Abnormal Situation Management', *9th Symposium on Microprocessor Based Protection Systems*, 7 December.

28   See http://snopes.simplenet.com (accessed: 20 October 2009) for more information on the 'Tylenol Murders'.

29   http://www.freenigeria.org/coke.html (accessed: 20 October 2009) deals with the latest in a series of boycotts against Coca-Cola from countries with a complaint against Coca-Cola or the US. The Arab boycott from 1967, with potentially a recent reintroduction, was confirmed with the Coca-Cola Company, Atlanta, Georgia, Corporate Communications, Kerry Traubert, on 28 June 1999. Boycott was effective. Since lifted these markets have grown at more than twice the nearby markets: averaging 15 per cent plus per annum volume growth and maintaining six share point advantage.

30   http://www.iie.com (accessed: 20 October 2009) deals with sanctions in general.

31   http://www.iie.com (accessed: 20 October 2009) deals with South Africa, too.

32   Henderson, P. (1993), *The Unlikely Spy*, Bloomsbury, London.

33   Hyslop, M.P. (1997b), 'Obstructive Marketing', *Journal of Business and Industrial Marketing*, Vol. 12, No. 5, 1997, pp339–343.

34   See http://www.usaengage.org (accessed: 20 October 2009) plus footnote 4.

35   http://www.ljextra.com (accessed: 20 October 2009) gives an idea of how complex it can be to market in the EU.

36   http://news.bbc.co.uk/hi/english/special_report/1998/10/98/Dmf (accessed: 20 October 2009) explains some of the issues.

37   Oxfam (1999), 'IMF Product Recall', Advertisement, *Financial Times*, 27 September 1999, p5.

38   http://snipe.ukc.ac.uk (accessed: 20 October 2009) gives a history of the institution, and the effect it can have on markets.

39   http://www.submission.org (accessed: 20 October 2009) is a good place to start an understanding of Islam.

40   Confirmed via Claes Nermark, Marketing Director, Tetra Pak, Lausanne, Switzerland, in a personal communication 1988.

41   http://www.babymilkaction.org (accessed: 20 October 2009); http://www.greenmarketplace. com (accessed: 20 October 2009); http://www.enviroweb.org (accessed: 20 October 2009); Hyslop, M.P. (1993), 'Improved Profitability via Oil Product Inventory Control', *Petroleum Review*, December – all comment on dioxins. Most recently all major newspapers carried the Belgium dioxin scare, when large amounts of food product were withdrawn from shelves over the weeks 14–28 July 1999 following dioxin contamination.

42   http://www.petra-online.org (accessed: 20 October 2009) lists activities.

43   http://www.petra-online (accessed: 20 October 2009) and http://www.angelfire.com (accessed: 20 October 2009) list the companies.

44 http://www.mindspring.com (accessed: 20 October 2009) explains the benzene position at Perrier from an outsiders point of view.

45 See http://www.thestandard.net (accessed: 20 October 2009) and http://www.greenpeace.com (accessed: 20 October 2009) for later difficulties with regard to a rig disposal in Norway.

46 http://www.notepage.com/nppiracy.htm is a particularly useful guide to what piracy is about.

47 Examples can be seen at http://www.ecnet.com (accessed: 20 October 2009) and http://www.emergency.com (accessed: 20 October 2009).

48 ICC/IMB Special Report (1989), *Nigerian Oil Frauds*, Witherby and Co., London and related IMB publications.

49 This fraud was last seen on 22 June 1999 – a list of all major frauds can be found at http://www.tap.net/~hyslo/fmenu.htm (accessed: 20 October 2009).

50 Personal experience, Dubai and elsewhere.

51 Personal experience, India and elsewhere.

52 Bontchev, V. (1996), 'Possible Macrovirus Attacks and How to Prevent Them', *Virus Bulletin Conference*, September.

53 http://www.action4corpacct.org is one Internet site targeting Nestlé (accessed: 20 October 2009).

54 Fialka, J.J. (1997), *War By Other Means*, Norton, New York.

55 Confirmed with the Roman Catholic Church, Chicago, June 1999.

56 Confirmed with the marketing department of the Coca-Cola Company, Atlanta, Georgia, USA, June 1999.

57 http://www.indiaserver.com (accessed: 20 October 2009) explains some of the issues behind the McDonald's investment in India.

58 Personal communication, continuing, Bernard Murray, Seattle, Washington, USA, January 1998.

59 Smith, C.S. (1997), 'Chinese Discover Product Liability Suits', *The Wall Street Journal*, 13 November 1997, p1.

60 See http://www.usitc.gov (accessed: 20 October 2009).

61 See: http://www.envirolink.com (accessed: 20 October 2009); http://www.user.globalnet.co.uk (accessed: 20 October 2009).

62 See http://www.globalexchange.org/corpacct/nike/nikepledge.html (accessed: 20 October 2009.

63 See http://www.sierraclub.org (accessed: 20 October 2009); http://www.prairienet.org (accessed: 20 October 2009) for background.

64 See http://www.detnews.com/1998/autos (accessed: 20 October 2009).

65 See http://www.sun.com (accessed: 20 October 2009) for more information.

66 See http://www.enviroweb.com (accessed: 20 October 2009).

67 Personal involvement and resolution, 1995. Similar events in the Middle East occurred with JetFuel in 1995 and 1996.

68 See http://www.ferranti.technologies-co.uk (accessed: 20 October 2009); http://www.mhawkes.demon.co.uk/ferranti.html (accessed: 20 October 2009).

69 See http://www.enviroweb.org (accessed: 20 October 2009).

70 See http://www.enviroweb.org (accessed: 20 October 2009).

71 See http://www.enviroweb.org (accessed: 20 October 2009).

72 See http://www.enviroweb.org (accessed: 20 October 2009).

73 See http://www.enviroweb.org (accessed: 20 October 2009).

74 See http://www.enviroweb.org (accessed: 20 October 2009).

75 See http://www.enviroweb.org (accessed: 20 October 2009).

76 Burrough, B. and Helyar, J. (1991), *Barbarians at the Gate: The Fall of RJR Nabisco* Harper and Row, New York.

77 Saunders, J. (1988), *Nightmare*, Arrow Books, London.

78 See http://www.enviroweb.org (accessed: 20 October 2009).

79 See http://www.enviroweb.org (accessed: 20 October 2009).

80 See http://www.enviroweb.org (accessed: 20 October 2009).

81 See http://www.enviroweb.org (accessed: 20 October 2009).
82 See http://www.enviroweb.org (accessed: 20 October 2009). Led to declaration to curb tests: Edgecliffe-Johnson, A. (1999), 'Procter and Gamble to Curb Tests on Animals', *Financial Times*, 1 July 1999, p1.
83 See http://www.enviroweb.org (accessed: 20 October 2009).
84 See http://www.enviroweb.org (accessed: 20 October 2009).
85 See http://www.enviroweb.org (accessed: 20 October 2009).
86 See http://falcon.jmu.edu (accessed: 20 October 2009) and http://ericir.syr.edu – both give background on the Enid Blyton 'Blight and Plight'. Rudd, D. (1995), 'Five Have a Gender-ful Time: Blyton, Sexism and the Infamous Five', *Children's Literature In Education*, Vol. 26, No. 3, p185–196, September 1995, also refers.
87 Fialka, J.J. (1997), *War By Other Means*, Norton, New York, p128–129.
88 Fialka, J.J. (1997), *War By Other Means*, Norton, New York, p128–129.
89 Fialka, J.J. (1997), *War By Other Means*, Norton, New York, p128–129.
90 Fialka, J.J. (1997), *War By Other Means*, Norton, New York, p128–129.
91 Fialka, J.J. (1997), *War By Other Means*, Norton, New York, p128–129.
92 Fialka, J.J. (1997), *War By Other Means*, Norton, New York, p131.
93 Fialka, J.J. (1997), *War By Other Means*, Norton, New York, p131.
94 Fialka, J.J. (1997), *War By Other Means*, Norton, New York, p131.
95 Fialka, J.J. (1997), *War By Other Means*, Norton, New York, p131.
96 Fialka, J.J. (1997), *War By Other Means*, Norton, New York, p131.
97 Fialka, J.J. (1997), *War By Other Means*, Norton, New York, p131.
98 Fialka, J.J. (1997), *War By Other Means*, Norton, New York, p131.
99 Fialka, J.J. (1997), *War By Other Means*, Norton, New York, p131.
100 Fialka, J.J. (1997), *War By Other Means*, Norton, New York, p131.
101 See http://www.omaha.com/OWH/AP/Stroyview/1,2038,69565,00.html (accessed: 20 October 2009) and http://www.mcjonline.com/news/news/3069.htm (accessed: 20 October 2009).
102 Fialka, J.J. (1997), *War By Other Means*, Norton, New York, p54 and Tolchin, M. and Tolchin, S.J. (1992), *Selling Our Security*, Knopf, p170.
103 Fialka, J.J. (1997), *War By Other Means*, Norton, New York, p12.
104 Naylor, R.T. (1994), *Hot Money*, Black Rose Books, New York, pp240–244.
105 Robinson, J. (1995), *The Laundrymen*, Pocket Books, p16.
106 http://www.tibet.org/sft/levi.html (accessed: 20 October 2009) deals with the first and Levi Executives Wendy Juster and Larry Russ attested to the second in personal communication 29 June 1999.
107 http://www.indian-express.com/fe/daily/19971208/34255643.html (accessed: 20 October 2009); Hung, A. (1997), 'Bayer's Taiwan Unit Faces Referendum', *Financial Express (India)*, 8 December 1997, p1.
108 Summary in Bower, T. (1993), *Tiny Rowland: A Rebel Tycoon*, Heinemann, London, pp501–502.
109 See http://snopes.simplenet.com (accessed: 20 October 2009).
110 See http://snopes.simplenet.com (accessed: 20 October 2009).
111 Personal communication, executive of Endress & Hauser Limited, 15 June 1999.
112 Personal communication, Westland plc, 1991.
113 Personal communication, Omni Inc., 1991.
114 Personal communication, Esselte, Sweden, 1991.
115 Gray, R. (1971), *Rolls On The Rocks*, Panther Books Limited, London.
116 See http://www.tabloid.net/97/09/05C1.html for details of the Hudson 20 million pounds of beef infected with E.Coli recall of 5 June 1998 – and subsequent sale of the company. See http://www.safetyalerts.com (accessed: 20 October 2009) for more on E.Coli 0157.
117 Deogan, N. et al. (1999a), 'Anatomy of a Recall', *The Wall Street Journal*, 29 June, p1. 'One of the worst crises in the company's 113 year old history – was Coke contaminated with rat poison?'; Deoghan, N. et al. (1999b), 'Coke Estimates European Volume Plunged 6–7% In Second Quarter', *The Wall Street Journal*, 1 July 1999, p1.

118 Lorenz, A. and Alexander, G. 'Reuters Hits Trouble with Bloomberg', *The Sunday Times* (UK), 8 February 1998, p3; *Financial Times* 31 January 1998/1 February 1998, p1.

119 Leake, J. (1998), 'Rural Rising', *The Sunday Times* (UK), 8 February, p15.

120 MacDonnell, E. and Lublin, J.S. (1998), 'In the Debris of a Failed Merger: Trade Secrets', *The Wall Street Journal*, 10 March, pB1.

121 McIvor, G. (1998), 'Doing Business in Russia', *Financial Times*, 6 March, p31.

122 Public Television Advertising June/July 1999 – *Channel 7 Chicago*.

123 Personal communication, Ray Broz, BP, 15 March 1999.

124 Personal communication, B.W. Winne, Andersen Consulting, 22 April 1999.

125 Personal communication, Jonathan Wilson, Lawyer, Baker and Mckenzie, 22 April 1999.

126 Donald V. Fites at *The Executive Club of Chicago*, 22 April 1999.

127 Confirmed with the marketing department of the Coca-Cola Company, Atlanta, Georgia, USA, 29 June 1999.

128 Follett, K. (1983), *On The Wings Of Eagles*, Signet, London.

129 Personal communication with Executives of GM, Volkswagen, and Breed Technologies and others at the US Society of Automotive Engineers Show, Detroit, 1998 and 1999.

130 Perry, S. (1995), 'Economic Espionage and Corporate Responsibility', http://www.acsp.ulc.edu (acessed:20 October 2009) *CJ International,* March–April 1995.

131 MacDonnell, E. and Lublin, J.S. (1998), 'In the Debris of a Failed Merger: Trade Secrets', *The Wall Street Journal*, 10 March, pB1.

132 See http://www.envirolink.org/mcspotlight (accessed: 20 October 2009) – a classic of its type.

133 Fialka, J.J. (1997), *War By Other Means*, Norton, New York, p29ff.

134 Covered extensively in *The Wall Street Journal, Financial Times* and *The Economist*.

135 Rose, B. (1999), 'Iridium Mess: Fallout for Motorola', *Crain's Chicago Business*, May 1999.

136 *Financial Times*, 16 August 1999 carried the story, repeated in *The Wall Street Journal* of the same day, of the Iridium JV filing for Chapter 11 bankruptcy protection, both on p1.

137 Personal communication, Nestlé UK, 1992.

138 Covered extensively in *The Wall Street Journal, Financial Times* and *The Economist*.

139 Rewick, C.J. (1999), 'Wall Street Sure Doesn't Like Sara Lee' *Crain's Chicago Business*, May 1999, p1.

Bibliography

Aaker, D.A. (2008) *Strategic Market Management*. Wiley India Pvt. Ltd, New Delhi.

Abler, R., Adams, J.S. and Gould, P. (1972) *Spatial Organisation*. Prentice Hall, New York (accessed: 24 October 2012).

Ackoff, R., Magidson, J. and Addison, H.J. (2006) *Idealised Design: How to Dissolve Tomorrow's Crisis … Today*. Pearson Prentice Hall, New York.

Ackoff, R., Addison, H.J., and Bibb, S. (2007) *Management F-laws: How Organisations Really Work*. Triarchy Press, New York.

Addi, L. (1992) 'Islamicist Utopia and Democracy', *American Academy of Political and Social Science*, Vol. 524, No. 1, 120–130.

Aker, B. (1997) Available at www.futuresgroup.com (accessed: 20 October 2010).

Akin, T. (2002) *Hardening Cisco Routers*. O'Reilly, Farnham, UK.

Alamo Group Europe (2012) Chairman interview with Maitland P. Hyslop, 25 January.

Alavi, M. and Carlson, P. (1992) 'A Review of MIS Research and Disciplinary Development', *Journal of Management Information Systems*, Vol. 8, No. 4, 45–62.

Albanese, J.S. (2004) *Organized Crime in Our Times*. Anderson Publishing, Cincinnati, Ohio.

Alexander, D.E. (2000) *Confronting Catastrophe: New Perspectives on Natural Disasters*. Terra Publishing, Harpenden, UK and Oxford University Press, New York.

Alexander, D.E. (2010) Available at http://d-alexander.blogspot.com (accessed: 12 April 2010).

Alexander, K. and Ferran, E. (2011) 'The European Systemic Risk Board and the Hard Edges of Soft Law'. *University of Cambridge Faculty of Law Research Paper No. 36/2011*. 4 November.

Allen, N. (2008) 'The Regulator – Facilitator or Enforcer', *Continuity*, July, pp3–24.

Allen, R.H. (1997) 'Asymmetric Warfare: Is the Army Ready?' Available at www.amsc.belvoir.army.mil/asymmetric_warfare.htm (accessed: 1 October 2009).

Alstom (2011) Country President interview with Maitland P. Hyslop, 22 May.

American Constitution (2007) Available at http://www.gpo.gov/fdsys/pkg/CDOC-110hdoc50/pdf/CDOC-110hdoc50.pdf (accessed: 26 August 2013).

American Declaration of Independence (2007) Available at http://bookstore.gpo.gov/products/sku/027-002-00535-0 (accessed: 26 August 2013).

Anderson, B. (1949) *Economics and the Public Welfare*. D. Van Nostrand Company, New York.

Anderson, R. and Moore T. (2006) 'The Economics of Information Security'. Available at www.cl.cam.ac.uk/~rja14/Papers/econ_science.pdf (accessed: 14 February 2010).

Angell, I. (1995) 'The Impact of Globalization on Today's Business and Why Information System Security Is Strategic', RIIA Conference Managing for Fraud Prevention, RIIA, London, 7 March.

ANSI (2009) ASIS SPC.1-2009. *Organisational Resilience: Security Preparedness and Continuity Management Systems – Requirements with Guidance for Use*. ASIS/American National Standards Institute, Inc., Alexandria, VA.

ANSI (2012) Available at www.ansi.org (accessed: 28 August 2012).

Application of Dynamic Modelling. Published PhD Dissertation, Delft.

Argyris, C. and Schon, D. (1978) *Organisational Learning: A Theory of Action Perspective*. Addison-Wesley, Reading, MA.

Argyris, C. (1999) *On Organisational Learning*. 2nd edition. Blackwell Publishing, Oxford.

Armitage, M. (2012) Personal communication with leading business continuity standard planner and assessor, 27 April 2012.

Augar, P. (2009) *Chasing Alpha: How Reckless Growth and Unchecked Ambition Ruined The City's Golden Decade*. The Bodley Head, London.

Australian Government Attorney General (2006) 'Trusted Information Sharing Network for Critical Infrastructure Protection'. Available at www.tisn.gov.au and www.e.govt.nz/policy/trust-security/niip-report/paper3.html (accessed: 14 February 2010).

Australian Industry Group (2009) 'Pandemic Hardening'. Available at http://pdf.aigroup.asn.au/events/2009/7434_pandemic_flyer.pdf (accessed: 1 October 2009).

Bartels (1988) *The History of Marketing Thought*. Columbus, Publishing Horizons.

Barth, J.R., Brumbaugh, R.D., and Wilcox, J.A. (2000) 'Policy Watch: The Repeal of Glass–Steagall and the Advent of Broad Banking', *Journal of Economic Perspectives*, Vol.14, No.2, April, 191–204.

Barthelemy, B. (1997) *The Sky Is Not The Limit – Breakthrough Leadership*. St. Lucie Press, London.

Barton, A.H. (1970) *Communities in Disaster: A Sociological Analysis of Collective Stress Situations*. Doubleday, New York.

Bateson, G. (1973) *Steps to an Ecology of Mind: Collected Essays in Anthropology, Psychiatry, Evolution, and Epistemology*. University Of Chicago Press, Chicago.

Baudrillard, J. (1983a) *Simulations*. New York, Semiotext(e).

Baylis, N. (2012) Available at www.nickbaylis.com (accessed: 24 October 2012).

BBC (2008) 'Final Goodbye for an Early Web Icon'. Available at www.bbc.co.uk (accessed: 30 October 2011).

BBC (2010a) 'Women Still a Minority in the UK Boardroom'. Available at www.bbc.co.uk/news/business-10648355 (accessed: 30 October 2011).

BBC (2010b) 'German Values'. Available at www.bbc.co.uk (accessed: 9 November 2010).

Beck, U. (1992) *Risk Society: Towards a New Modernity*. Trans. M. Ritter. Sage, London.

Benbasat, I., Goldstein, D.K. and Mead, M. (1987) 'The Case Research Strategy in Studies of Information Systems', *MIS Quarterly*, Vol. 1, No. 3, 369–386.

Bennet, S. (Ed.) (2012) *Innovative Thinking in Risk, Crisis and Disaster Management*. Gower, Farnham, UK.

Bens, I. (2006) *Facilitating to Lead*. Jossey-Bass, New York.

Berlitz (1998) 'Cultural Solutions'. Available at www.berlitz.com (accessed: 20 October 2010).

Bernstein, R. (1983) *Beyond Objectivism and Relativism: Science, Hermeneutics and Praxis*. Oxford, UK, Basil Blackwell.

Bet 365 (2012) Chairman interview with Maitland P. Hyslop, 22 February.

Bhaskar, R. (1975) *A Realist Theory of Science*. Leeds, UK, Leeds Books.

Bhaskar, R. (1989a) *Reclaiming Reality: A Critical Introduction to Contemporary Philosophy*. London, Verso.

Bhaskar, R. (1989b) *The Possibility of Naturalism*. 2nd edition. Hemel Hempstead, UK, Harvester.

Bhaskar, R. (1993) *Dialectic: The Pulse of Freedom*. London, Verso.

Bingham, P.T. (2001) 'Transforming Warfare with Effects-Based Joint Operations', *Aerospace Power Journal*, Spring.

Bird, C. (1940) *Social Psychology*. New York, Appleton-Century.

Birtles, J. (2003) 'BCI – Why It Matters', *1st European Telecommunications Resilience and Recovery Association Conference*, Newcastle, UK, 11–13 June.

Birtles, J. (2005) 'Summary of the Civil Contingencies Act'. Available at http://www.thebci.org/ccact.htm (accessed: 12 April 2010).

Black, F. and Scholes, M. (1973) 'The Pricing of Options and Corporate Liabilities', *Journal of Political Economy*, Vol. 81, No. 3, 637–654.

Blair, D.C. (2010) Senate Select Committee on Intelligence: US Intelligence Community Annual Threat Assessment: Statement for the Record, Office of the Director of National Intelligence, 2 February, 7–8. Available at http://www.dni.gov/testimonies/20100202_testimony.pdf (accessed: 24 October 2012). Hereinafter: *Blair, Annual Threat Assessment*, 2 February, 2010.

Blank S.J. (2003) *Rethinking Asymmetric Threats*. Strategic Studies Institute Monograph, US Army War College, 1 September.

Blank, S.J. (2004) 'Rethinking the Concept of Asymmetric Threats in US Strategy', *Comparative Strategy*, Vol. 23, No. 4–5, October.

Boin, A. and Smith, D (2006) 'Terrorism and Critical Infrastructures: Implications for Public–Private Crisis Management', *Public Money and Management*, 26(5), November, 295ff.

Boin, A., McConnell, A. and t'Hart, P. (2010) *Governing after Crisis*. Cambridge Press, Cambridge.

Bonaparte, N. (1798) Available at www.napoleonguide.com/maxim_war.htm (accessed: 28 August 2012).

Bontchev, V. (1996) 'Possible Macrovirus Attacks and How to Prevent Them', *Virus Bulletin Conference*, September, 97–127.

Bontis, N. and Serenko, A. (2009b) 'Longitudinal Knowledge Strategising in a Long-term Healthcare Organisation', *International Journal of Technology Management*, Vol. 47, No. 1/2/3, 276–297. Available at http://foba.lakeheadu.ca/serenko/papers/IJTM_47_123_Published_Bontis_Serenko.pdf (accessed: 12 April 2010).

Bontis, N. and Serenko, A. (2009a) 'A Causal Model of Human Capital Antecedents and Consequents in the Financial Services Industry', *Journal of Intellectual Capital*, Vol. 10, No. 1, 53–69. Available at http://foba.lakeheadu.ca/serenko/papers/Bontis_Serenko_causal_model.pdf (accessed: 12 April 2010).

Bontis, N., Crossan, M. and Hulland, J. (2002) 'Managing an Organisational Learning System by Aligning Stocks and Flows', *Journal of Management Studies*, Vol. 39, No. 4, 437–469.

Booker, C. and North, R. (2009) *Scared To Death: From BSE to Global Warming*. Continuum, London.

Borodzicz, E.P (2010) 'Risk and Resilience'. Available at www.thebci.org/workshops (accessed: 24 October 2012).

Borodzicz, E.P. (2005) *Risk, Crisis and Security Management*. John Wiley and Sons, London.

Bosworth Davies, R. (1988) *Fraud In The City: Too Good To Be True*. Penguin, London.

Bosworth Davies, R. (1995) 'Money Laundering and the Insurance Business', Titmuss, Sainer, Dechert, *Risk Management in Eastern Europe and FSU Conference*, RIIA, 27 February 1995.

Bower, T. (1993) *Tiny Rowland: A Rebel Tycoon*. Heinemann, London, 501–502.

Boyd, R. (2011) *Fatal Risk*. Wiley, New York.

BP (2007) C-Suite Officer interview with Maitland P. Hyslop, 19 September.

Bragg, R. (2004) *Hardening Windows System*. Emeryville, CA, Osborne McGraw-Hill.

Brassell-Cicchini, L.A. (2002) Available at www.disaster-resource.com/articles/02p_101.shtml (accessed 19 December 2011).

Brierley, P. (2003) 'Business Resilience: A Guide To Protecting Your Business', Aviva, Norwich, UK. Available at www.aviva.co.uk/risksolutions/pdf/business-resilience.pdf (accessed: 1 October 2009).

Briggs, R. and Edwards, C. (2006) *The Business of Resilience*. DEMOS, London.

British Airways (2012) Chief Executive interview with Maitland P. Hyslop, 2 March.

British Army (2010) Former Chief of the General Staff interview with Maitland P. Hyslop, 19 October.

British Canoe Union (2010) Available at http://bcucoaching.org.uk/ (accessed: 28 August 2012).

British Continuity Institute (2012) – see under Steelhenge.

British Standards Institute (2009) 'Paper for Directors on ISO 27001' – see under ISO 27001.

British Standards Institute (2010a) 'BSI 25999 Checklist'. Available at www.bsi.org.uk (accessed: 30 October 2011).

British Standards Institute (2010b) Personal communication, 28 June 2010.

British Standards Institute (2011) PAS 99. Available at www.bsigroup.co.uk/en/Assessment-and-Certification-services/Management-systems/Standards-and-Schemes/PAS-99/ (accessed: 24 October 2012).

British Standards Institute (2012a) *Moving From BS 25999-2 to ISO 22301*. British Standards Institute, London, UK.

British Standards Institute (2012b) PAS 200. Available at http://shop.bsigroup.com/en/ProductDetail/?pid=000000000030252035 (accessed: 12 October 2012).

British Standards Institute (2006) *BS25999-1: 2006 Business Continuity Management Part 1: Code of Practice*. London, British Standards Institute.

Bronfen, E. (2001) 'Fault Lines: Catastrophe and Celebrity Culture', *European Studies*, Vol. 16, 117–139.

Brooklyn College (2007) Available at www.aldridgeshs.eq.edu.au/sose/modrespg/isms/Glossary%20Brooklyn%20College.htm (accessed: 24 October 2012).

Broz, R. (1999). Senior BP Executive interview with Maitland P. Hyslop, 15 March.

Brzezinski, Z. (2013) 'The Cyber Age Demands New Rules of War', *Financial Times*, 24 February. Available at http://www.ft.com/cms/s/0/170b2a62-7c5a-11e2-99f0-00144feabdc0.html (accessed: 31 August 2013).

Buckingham Foods (2011) Senior Executive interview with Maitland P. Hyslop, 28 January.

Bulmer, M. (Ed.) (1982) *Social Research Ethics: An Examination of the Merits of Covert Participant Observation*. London, Macmillan.

Bunge, W.W. (1966) *Theoretical Geography*. Lund Studies in Geography, Gleerup, Lund.

Burgin, S. and Stepney, K. (2011) 'The Future of Engineering', *STEM Conference*, Alstom UK, 13 December 2011 (Steve Burgin is Alstom's UK Country President and Ken Stepney was Head of Group Personnel at JCB).

Burns, J.M. (1978) *Leadership*. New York, Harper and Row Publishers Inc.

Burrough, B. and Helyar, J. (1991) *Barbarians at the Gate: The Fall of RJR Nabisco*. Harper and Row, New York.

Bursk, E.C. and Chapman, J.F. (1964) *Modern Marketing Strategy*. Harvard University Press, Cambridge, Mass.

Burton, E. (2003) Interview with Maitland P. Hyslop, 3 March.

Burton, I., Kates, R.W. and White, G.F. (1978) *The Environment as Hazard*. New York, Oxford University Press.

Business Continuity (2010) Available at www.businesscontinuity.org (accessed: 24 October 2012).

Business Continuity Institute (2003) 'Business Continuity and Crisis Management'. Available at http://www.instam.org/student_info/reading_room/general_mgt_strategy/bci_business_continuity_planning.pdf (accessed: 1 October 2009).

Business Continuity Institute (2009) Available at http://www.brighttalk.com/community/all-community/summits?q=BS+25999 (accessed: 1 October 2009).

Business Continuity Institute (2012) 'Organisational Resilience'. Working Paper, March.

Business Insider (2012) 'Private Equity CEO Shot' Available at: http://www.businessinsider.com/private-equity-ceo-shot-dead-in-office-2012-7 (accessed: 31 August 2013).

Byrnes, E.J. (2010) 'Teaming Enterprise Management and Business Continuity', *Proceedings CPM East 2010*, Jacob K Javits Conference Centre, New York, 3–4 November.

Cabinet Office (2008) *The National Security Strategy of the United Kingdom*. London, Cabinet Office.

Cable, V. (2007) Treasury Spokesman for the Liberal Democrats. Available at http://www.vincentcable.org.uk/ (accessed: 1 October 2009).

Cable, V. (2009) *The Storm: The World Economic Crisis and What It Means*. Atlantic Books, London.

Cairns, A. (2009) quoted in Thomson, D. (2009) 'Unravelling Lehman', Business Turnaround, Inserted in *The Economist*, London, 14 May.

Calder, A. (2005) *IT Governance: A Manager's Guide to Data Security and BS7799/ ISO17799*. London, Kogan Page.

Canadian European Economic Council (2010) 'Orthodoxiefinancière', *Canadian Journal of Economics*, Vol. 30, No. 1, 208–223.

Carlyle, T. (1841) *On Heroes, Hero-Worship, and the Heroic in History*. London, James Fraser.

Carr, Sir P. (2011) Interview with Maitland P. Hyslop, 23 June.

Caterpillar (2012) Senior Executive interview with Maitland P. Hyslop, 18 May.

Cesari, J (2004) *When Islam and Democracy Meet: Muslims in Europe and in the United States*. New York, Palgrave Macmillan.

Chace, J.G. (2011) 'Defining Asymmetric Warfare: A Losing Proposition', *Joint Force Quarterly*, 2nd Quarter, Issue 61, p123.

Channel 7 (1999) Public Television Advertising, Chicago.

Charrier, G.O. (1972) 'COG's Ladder', *Procter and Gamble Newsletter*.

Chartered Institute of Marketing (UK) (1976) Available at www.cim.co.uk (accessed: 12 April 2010).

Chartered Management Institute – see under Woodman.

Chau, A. (2010) *Battle Hymn of the Tiger Mother*. Penguin, New York.

Chirbon, J.T. (1996) *Interviewing in Depth: The Interactive-Relational Approach*. London, Sage.

Chung, T.S. (1995) *Sunzi Speaks: The Art of War*, Trans. Bruya, B. New York, Anchor Books.

Chung, T.S. (Ed.) (1994) *The Wisdom of Confucius*. Random House, New York.

City of London (2012) Available at http://www.london.gov.uk (accessed: 28 August 2012).

Civil Contingencies Act (2004) Available at www.cabinetoffice.gov.uk/uk resilience (accessed 12 April 2010).

Civil Service (2012) Director of Communities, Local Government interview with Maitland P. Hyslop, 31 May.

Clausewitz, C. von (1962) *On War*. London, Amereon Limited.

Clydesdale Bank (2010) Risk Manager interview with Maitland P. Hyslop, 15 February.

CNE (2011) Anonymised leader of NHS in North East of England interview with Maitland P Hyslop, 23 June.

Coca-Cola (1999) Head of Marketing telephone interview with Maitland P. Hyslop, 29 June. See also Deogan, N. (1999) 'Anatomy of a Recall', *The Wall Street Journal*, 29 June, p1.

Cocchiara, R. (2005) 'Transforming Your Company into a Resilient Business', *Proceedings CPM East 2005*, Gaylord Palms Resort, Kissimmee, Florida, USA, 11–14 November.

Cockram, D. (2012) Steelhenge CEO interview with Maitland P. Hyslop, 19 March.

Collins, A.E. (2010) Introduction to Dealing with Disasters Conference, Northumbria University, 23–24 November, speaking to delegates said: 'This partnership between universities and the organisations involved in resilience planning, emergency response and post disaster development is a key feature of the Dealing with Disasters conference series. Building on the success of the Conferences over the last five years, a key aim of this year's programme is to focus on ten years of progress in linking disaster and development and prioritisation for the following ten years.'

Common, R. (2004) 'Organisational Learning in a Political Environment: Improving Policy-making in UK Government', *Policy Studies*, Vol. 25, No. 1, 35–49.

Congressional Research Service (1987) Glass–Steagall Act: Commercial vs. Investment Banking. Congressional Research Service, USA.

Control Risks (2010) Director interview with Maitland P. Hyslop, 30 October.

Cooper, R. (2003) *The Breaking of Nations: Order and Chaos in the Twenty-First Century*. London, Atlantic Books.

Cooperation Ireland (2012) CEO interview with Maitland P. Hyslop, 21 May.

Corbin, M. (2001) 'Reshaping the Military for Asymmetric Warfare', *Center for Defense Information*, 5 October. Available at www.cdi.org/terrorism/asymmetric.cfm (accessed: 1 October 2009).

Corlett, J.A. (1989) 'The Modified Vendetta Sanction', *Journal of Business Ethics*, Vol. 8, 937–942.

Cornish, M. (2008) 'BS25999: Key Issues to Address for Certification', *Business Continuity Journal*, Vol. 3, No. 3, pp25–32.

Coughlin, P. (1989) *Industrialization in Kenya: In Search of a Strategy*. Kenya, Heinemann, p24ff.

Council of Europe Convention on Cybercrime (2004) Available at http://conventions.coe.int/treaty/en/treaties/html/185htm (accessed: 12 April 2010).

Covey, S. (1989) *The Seven Habits of Highly Effective People*. New York, Free Press.

Covey, S. (2005) *The 8th Habit: From Effectiveness to Greatness*. New York, Free Press.

CPNI, UK (2010) Director interview with Maitland P. Hyslop, 16 February.

Craig, L. (2007) *Designing Resilience into Secure Power Systems*. London, Riello UPS.

Creswell, J.W. (2010) *Research Design: Qualitative, Quantitative, and Mixed Methods Approaches*. London, Sage.

Crichton, M. (1997) *Airframe*. New York, Ballantine.

Crichton, M.T., Ramsay, C.G. and Kelly, T. (2008) 'Enhancing Organisational Resilience through Emergency Planning: Learnings from Cross-Sectoral Lessons', *Journal of Contingencies and Crisis Management*, Vol. 16, No. 4, 24–37.

Csikszentmihalyi, M. (1998) *Finding Flow: The Psychology of Engagement with Everyday Life*. New York, Basic Books.

Culp, C.L. (2001) *The Risk Management Process: Business Strategy and Tactics*. New York, Wiley.

Czinkota, M.T. and Ronkainen, I.A. (1995) *International Marketing*. New York, Dryden.

Dana Petroleum (2012) Finance Director interview with Maitland P. Hyslop, 9 March.

Davidson, J.H. (1975) *Offensive Marketing*. London, Pelican.

Davis, E. (2012) 'The Bottom Line', BBC Radio 4, London, 30 May, 20.30 hours.

Davis Langdon and Everest, Mott Green, and Wall (2001) 'Data Centre and CoLocation Cost Model', *Building*, No. 21. Available at www.building.co.uk/story.asp?storycode=1007597# (accessed: 1 October 2009).

Dawood, N.J. (Ed.) (1982) *The Koran*. London, Penguin.

De Beers (2011) Chief Executive interview with Maitland P. Hyslop, 21 November.

Defence Academy (2010) Conversation with Maitland P. Hyslop, 22 July.

Deloitte (2010) Available at www.deloitte.com/view/en_GX/global/industries/technology-media-telecommunications/c4d38a120c9a8210VgnVCM200000bb42f00aRCRD.htm (accessed: 28 August 2012).

Deloitte Touche Tohmatsu (2005) 'Disarming the Value Killers'. Available at www.corp.gov.deloitte.com/binary/com/disarming_the_value_killers.pdf (accessed: 12 April 2010).

Deloittes (2011) Senior partner interview with Maitland P. Hyslop, 10 July.

Deogan, N. (1999a) 'Anatomy of a Recall', *The Wall Street Journal*, 29 June, p1. 'One of the worst crises in the company's 113 year old history – was Coke contaminated with rat poison?'

Deoghan, N. (1999b) 'Coke Estimates European Volume Plunged 6–7% in Second Quarter', *The Wall Street Journal*, 1 July 1999, p1.

Der Derian, J. (2001) *Virtuous War: Mapping the Military-Industrial-Media-Entertainment Network*. Boulder, Westview Press Inc.

Diacon, S. (2011) Conversation and email to Maitland P. Hyslop, 14 June.

Dixon, N.F. (1976) *On the Psychology of Military Incompetence.* London, Futura.

Dixon, N.F. and Dixon, M. (2011) *On the Psychology of Military Incompetence.* London, Pimlico.

Donnelly, C. (2001) 'Balancing Security Requirements', *Law Enforcement and National Security Conference,* Edinburgh, UK, 21 June.

Donnelly, C. (2003) 'Security in the 21st Century – New Challenges and Responses', *1st European Telecommunications Resilience and Recovery Association Conference,* Newcastle-upon-Tyne, UK, 23 June. Available at www.European Telecommunications Resilience and Recovery Association.org (accessed: 1 October 2009).

Dorfer, I. (2004) 'Old and New Security Threats to Europe, Sweden', *Swedish Defence Research Agency.* Available at www.afes-press.de/pdf/Doerfer-Mont -9.pdf (accessed: 12 April 2010).

Doswell, B. (2000) *A Guide to Information Security Management.* Leicester, Perpetuity Press.

Doswell, B. (2001) *A Guide to Business Continuity Management.* Leicester, Perpetuity Press.

Doswell, B. (2003) 'Effective Business Continuity (in a Global Framework)', *1st European Telecommunications Resilience and Recovery Association Conference,* Newcastle, UK, 11–13 June.

Dotlich, D.L. and Cairo, P.G. (2003) *Why CEOs Fail.* New York, Bass.

Drucker, P.F. (1968) *The Practice of Management.* London, Pan.

Drucker, P.F. (2006) *Profession of Management.* New York, Harper.

Drudge Report, The (1999) Available at www.drudge.com (accessed: 20 October 2009).

Dunfee, T.W. (1999) Personal communication, 21 March 1999, repeated 2 February 2008. Thomas Dunfee was Professor of Legal Studies and Business Ethics at Wharton, Pennsylvania. He died on 2 June 2008, but just before he died he confirmed the general direction of both 'Obstructive Marketing' and 'Hardening' – particularly in multi-national companies.

Dunfee, T.W (2008) Personal communication, 2 February.

Dunn, M. and Wigert, I. (2004) *Critical Information Infrastructure Protection.* Zurich. Switzerland, The Swiss Federal Institute of Technology. Available at http://www.isn.ethz.ch/crn (accessed: 1 October 2009).

Durkheim, E. (1964) *The Rules of Sociological Method.* Glencoe, IL, The Free Press.

East of England Ambulance Service (2010) Chief Executive interview with Maitland P. Hyslop, 15 September.

Easterbrook, S. (2005) 'How Theses Get Written', University of Toronto. Available at http://cs.toronto.edu/~sme/presentations/thesiswriting.pdf (accessed: 5 August 2012).

Easterby-Smith, M., Crossan, M. and Nicolini, D. (2000) 'Organisational Learning: Debates Past, Present and Future', *Journal of Management Studies*, Vol. 37, No. 6, 783–796.

Economist, The (1997a) 'Management Consulting, Spouse Trouble'. Available at http://www.economist.com/node/90664?zid=297&ah=3ae0fe266c7447d8a0c 7ade5547d62ca (accessed: 8 December 2012).

Economist, The (1997b) 'Stick 'em up', 29 November, p31.

Economist, The (1999) 'The Net Imperative', 24 June. Available at http://www. economist.com/node/215657 (accessed: 31 August 2013).

Economist, The (2009) 'FSA at Bay', 13 March. Available at www.economist. com/world/britain/displaystory.cfm?story_id=E1_TPPTVVNP (accessed: 14 February 2010).

Economist, The (2012) 'Cyber Crime: A Spook Speaks', 30 June. Available at www.economist.com/node/21557817 (accessed: 24 October 2012).

Economist, The (2013) 'Getting Ugly', 23 February. Available at http://www. economist.com/news/leaders/21572200-if-china-wants-respect-abroad-it-must-rein-its-hackers-getting-ugly (accessed: 31 August 2013).

Edgecliffe-Johnson, A. (1999) 'Procter and Gamble to Curb Tests on Animals', *Financial Times*, 1 July 1999, p1.

Edwards, S.J.A. (2000) *Swarming on the Battlefield: Past, Present and Future*, Rand Monograph MR-1100. Rand Corporation. Available at http://www.rand.org/ pubs/monograph_reports/MR1100 (accessed: 24 October 2012).

Eisenhower, D.D. (1961) 'Military Industrial Complex Speech'. Available at http://coursesa.matrix.msu.edu/~hst306/documents/indust.html (accessed: 24 October 2012).

eJustice Project (2006) Available at www.onenortheast.co.uk/page/business/ ejustice.cfm (accessed: 12 April 2010).

El-Erian, M. (2008) *When Markets Collide*. Columbus, McGraw Hill.

Elliot, R. (2003) 'Multiple Providers, a Threat to Resilience', *1st European Telecommunications Resilience and Recovery Association Conference*, Newcastle, UK, 13 June.

Elliott, D., Swartz, E. and Herbane, B. (2001) *Business Continuity Management*. New York, Routledge.

Envirolink (1999) Available at www.envirolink.org (accessed: 28 August 2012).

et Régulationbancaire: les Leçons du Glass-Steagall Act'. Available at www. canadianeuropean.com/yahoo_site_admin/assets/docs/Bank_Regulation_ and_Financial_Orthodoxy__RAF__Jan_2010.784613.pdf (accessed: 24 October 2012).

European Security Strategy (2012) Available at http://www.eeas.europa.eu/ csdp/about-csdp/european-security-strategy/ (accessed: 3 November 2013).

European Union (2003) *A Secure Europe in a Better World*. Brussels, Belgium: European Institute for Security Studies.

European Union (2011) Directive 2011/61/EU. Available at http://europa.eu/ legislation_summaries/internal_market/single_market_services/financial_ services_transactions_in_securities/mi0083_en.htm (accessed: 27 December 2013).

Evans, J. (1995) *Feminist Theory Today: An Introduction to Second Wave Feminism*. London, Sage.

Fair, C. (1971) *From the Jaws of Victory*. New York, Simon and Schuster.

Fialka, J.J. (1997*) War by Other Means*. New York, Norton.

Financial Services Authority (2006) 'BCM Practice Guide', November. Available at www.fsa.gov.uk/pubs/other/bcm_guide.pdf (accessed: 1 October 2009).

Financial Services Authority (2008) *Data Security in Financial Services*. London, Financial Services Authority.

Financial Times, The (1999) The back pages throughout the year.

Finkelstein, S. (2003) *Why Smart Executives Fail*. London, Portfolio.

Firzli, M.N. (2010) 'Bank Regulation and Financial Orthodoxy: the Lessons from the Glass-Steagall Act' [French], *Revue Analyse Financière*, January, Q1 (34) 49–52.

Fischer, G. and Palen, L. (1999) 'Organisational Learning', Spring Semester, University of Colorado. Available at http://l3d.cs.colorado.edu/courses/ csci7212-99/pdf/organisational-learning.pdf (accessed: 28 August 2012).

Fites, D. (1999) CEO of Caterpillar speaking at the Executive Club of Chicago, 22 April 1999.

Fleetwood, C. (2010) Interview with Maitland P. Hyslop, 10 February.

Flood, R.L. (2009) *Rethinking the Fifth Discipline: Learning within the Unknowable*. London, Routledge. Available at http://books.google.com/books?id=3H65 KbRvdLQC (accessed: 12 April 2010).

Follett, K. (1983) *On the Wings of Eagles*. London, Signet.

Follett, M.P. (1942) *Dynamic Administration*. New York, Routledge.

Foti, R.J. and Hauenstein, N.M.A. (2007) 'Pattern and Variable Approaches in Leadership Emergence and Effectiveness', *Journal of Applied Psychology*, Vol. 92, 347–355.

French, P. (1988) 'On Corporate Punishment', *Journal of Business Ethics*, No. 7, 205–210.

Frenkiel, M. (2012) Personal communication with Maitland P. Hyslop, 13 September.

Friedman, T.L. (1999) *The Lexus and the Olive Tree*. New York, FSG.

Fry, T.C. (1928) *Probability and its Engineering Uses*. New York, D. Van Nostrand Company, Inc.

Fukuyama, F. (1992) *The End of History and the Last Man*. New York, Free Press.

Fukuyama, F. (1996) *Trust*. New York, Free Press.

G7 Financial Action Task Force (2004) Available at http://www.fatf-gafi.org/pages/aboutus/ (accessed: 31 August 2013).

Galeotti, M. (2001) 'The Future of Organised Crime', *Law Enforcement and National Security Conference*, Edinburgh, UK, 21 June.

Gall, N. (2010) 'From Hierarchy to Panarchy: Hybrid Thinking's Resilient Network of Renewal', *Gartner, G002909754*, 22 December.

Galliers, R.J. (1991) 'Choosing Appropriate Information Systems Research Approaches: A Revised Taxonomy', Nissen, H., Klein, K. and Hirschheim, R.A. (Eds), *Information Systems Research: Contemporary Approaches and Emergent Traditions*. Amsterdam, North Holland, 327–345.

GCHQ (2010) Personal communication and discussion regarding society's ability to cope with the speed of Internet and information development. The issue of Consumerism versus Information Assurance Protection versus Corporatism, 6 October.

GCHQ (2010) Personal communication to Maitland P. Hyslop, 21 July.

GCHQ (2011) Personal communication to Maitland P. Hyslop, 17 January.

GCHQ (2012) Personal communication to Maitland P. Hyslop, 2 July.

Gershenoff, A.G. and Foti, R.J. (2003) 'Leader Emergence and Gender Roles in All-Female Groups: A Contextual Examination', *Small Group Research*, Vol. 34, 170–196.

Gharajedaghi, J. (1999) *Systems Thinking: Managing Chaos and Complexity*. Woburn, MA, Butterworth-Heinemann.

Gibb, C.A. (1970) *Leadership (Handbook of Social Psychology)*. Reading, MA, Addison-Wesley, 884–889.

Gibson, E. (2011) Interview with Maitland P. Hyslop, 16 June.

Giddens, A. (1990) *The Consequences of Modernity*. Cambridge, Polity.

Gladwell, M. (2000) *The Tipping Point*. London, Little Brown.

Glaser, B. (1993) *Examples of Grounded Theory: A Reader*. Mill Valley, Sociology Press.

Glaser, B. and Strauss, A. (1967) *The Discovery of Grounded Theory*. Chicago, Aldine.

Goldratt, E.M. (1984) *The Goal*. Great Barrington, The North River Press.

Goodbaby (2011) Senior Executive interview with Maitland P. Hyslop, 4 March.

Goodger, A. (2010) Personal communication, *2nd CIIP Workshop*, Birkbeck College, University of London, UK, 29 March 2010 and 28 April 2010.

Goodger, A. (2011a) 'UK Resilience Blueprint Framework', Working Paper, 4 June.

Goodger, A. (2011b) 'Emergent Engineering Design for a Predictive Dynamic Risk Framework in the Complex Adaptive Information Ecosystem', PhD proposal to Cambridge University, November.

Goodger, A. and Atkinson, S.R. (2011) 'Information Lodestone', Working Paper, July.

Goodwin PLC (2012) Chairman interview with Maitland P. Hyslop, 29 March.

Gordon, J. (2010) Personal communication with Maitland P. Hyslop re Dependency, 15 September.

Gordon, J. (1996) Personal communication about dependency modelling and the use of the Dependency Modelling Tool and its application to various scenarios, 20 June. (Professor John Gordon was Visiting Professor of Mathematics at Hertfordshire University and a Home Office Advisor on Risk.)

Gotowicki, S.H. (1997) 'Middle East Terrorism: New Form of Warfare or Mission Impossible?' *US Army, Military Review*, May–June. Available at http://leav-www.army.mil/fmso/fmsopubs/issues/terror/terror.htm (accessed: 1 October 2009).

Goulding, J.G. (2000) 'Back to the Future with Asymmetric Warfare', *Parameters*, Winter. Available at http://carlisle-www.army.mil/usawc/Parameters/00Winter/goulding.htm (accessed: 1 October 2009).

Graham, S. (2011) *Cities under Siege*. London, Verso.

Grant Electricals (2012) Chairman interview with Maitland P. Hyslop, 13 February.

Gray, R. (1971) *Rolls On The Rocks*. Panther Books Limited.

Greenspan, A. (2011) 'The Flaw'. Available at www.economist.com/node/21518764 (accessed: 19 June 2011).

Griffiths, K. (2012) Interview with Maitland P. Hyslop, 19 June.

Grimshaw, N. (2009) 'Employer Profile: Yorkshire and Clydesdale Banks', 5 May. Available at http://www.employeebenefits.co.uk/item/8806/pg_dtl_art_news/pg_hdr_art/pg_ftr_art (accessed: 14 February 2010).

Grotberg, E. (1998) 'The International Resilience Project', *55th Annual Convention, International Council of Psychologists*, Graz, Austria, July 14–18, 1997 (published 1998).

Guardian, The (2011a) Available at http://www.guardian.co.uk/commentisfree/2011/jan/27/wapping-news-international-1986 (accessed: 24 October 2012).

Guardian, The (2011b) 'A Brief History of the Body Shop'. Available at http://www.guardian.co.uk (accessed 30 October 2011).

Habermas, J. (1984) *Theory of Communicative Action. Vol. 1: Reason and the Rationalization of Society*. Trans. T. McCarthy. Cambridge, UK, Polity.

Habermas, J. (1987) *Theory of Communicative Action. Vol. 2 Lifeworld and System: A Critique of Functionalist Reason*. Trans. T. McCarthy. Cambridge, UK, Polity.

Habermas, J. (1989) *Knowledge and Human Interests*. Originally published 1968. Trans. J.J. Shapiro. Cambridge, UK, Shapiro.

Habermas, J. (1990) *On the Logic of the Social Sciences*. Originally published in 1970. Trans. S.W. Nicholsen and J.A. Stark. Cambridge, UK, Polity.

Hadley Group (2012) Chairman interview with Maitland P. Hyslop, 28 February.

Hague, W. (2012) 'An Open Internet Is The Only Way to Support Security and Prosperity For All'. Available at http://www.fco.gov.uk/en/news/latest-news/?view=Speech&id=818554782 (accessed: 12 October 2012).

Hallows, J.E. (2004) *Information Systems Project Management: How To Deliver Function and Value in Information Technology Projects*. New York, Amacom.

Hammer, M. and Champy, J.A. (1993) *Reengineering the Corporation: A Manifesto for Business Revolution*. New York, Harper Business Books.

Hammerskjold, D. (1964) Available at http://integral-review.org/documents/Stalne,Meaning-makingofHammarskjold,Vol7,No.2.pdf (accessed: 28 August 2012).

Hammond, L.D., Rosso, J., Austin, K. and Orcutt, S. (2001) 'How People Learn, Introduction to Learning Theories'. Available at http://www.stanford.edu/class/ed269/hplintrochapter.pdf (accessed: 9 December 2012).

Hammond, R. and McCullagh, P.S. (1974) *Quantitative Techniques in Geography*. Oxford, Oxford University Press.

Handy, C. (1997) *The Empty Raincoat*. London, Hutchinson.

Hanson, D. (1998) CEO of Rocky Mountain Internet Inc. speaking to *The Wall Street Journal* after the 1998 market drop forced him to postpone a $175 million junk bond issue, 21 August.

Harding, S. (1991) *Whose Science? Whose Knowledge? Thinking from Women's Lives*. Milton Keynes, Open University Press.

Hassell, J. (2004) *Hardening Windows*. Berkeley, CA, Apress.

Hawking, S.W. (1988) *A Brief History of Time: From the Big Bang to Black Holes*. London, Bantam Press.

Hawthorne, N. (1850) *The Scarlet Letter*. Boston, Ticknor, Reed and Fields.

Hayek, F.A. (1944) *The Road to Serfdom*. London, Routledge.

Hayek, F.A. (1960) *The Constitution of Liberty*. Chicago, University of Chicago Press.

Hayek, F.A. (1988) *The Fatal Conceit: The Errors Of Socialism*. Chicago, University of Chicago Press.

Haylock, C.F. and Muscarella, L. (1999) *Net Success*. Holbrook, Adams.

Hazlitt, H. (1946) *Economics in One Lesson*. London, Crown.

Hazlitt, H. (1959) *The Failure of the 'New Economics'*. New York, Foundation for Economic Education.

Heinlein, R.A. (1987) *Starship Troopers*. New York, Ace.

Heisenberg, W. (1927) 'Ueber den anschaulichen Inhalt der quantentheoretischen Kinematik and Mechanik', *Zeitschrift für Physik*, Vol. 43, 172–198.

English translation in Wheeler and Zurek (1983) *Quantum Theory and Measurement*, Princeton, Princeton Univeristy Press, 62–84.

Hemingway, P. and Brereton, N. (2009). 'What is a Systematic Review'. What is...? series, 2nd edition. Hayward Medical Communications, Hayward Group Ltd. Available at http://www.whatisseries.co.uk (accessed: 31 August 2013).

Henderson, P. (1993) *The Unlikely Spy*. London, Bloomsbury.

Her Majesty's Government (2010) *Securing Britain in an Age of Uncertainty: The Strategic Defence and Security Review*. Norwich, UK, TSO.

Herald Tribune, The (2010) 'Elders of Wall St. Favor More Regulation', 17 February.

Heseltine, M. (2012) Personal communication with Maitland P. Hyslop at Staffordshire County Council and later at Birmingham City Council Offices, 4 May.

Hiles, A. (2007) *The Definitive Handbook of Business Continuity*. Chichester, UK, John Wiley.

Hirschheim, R.A., Fitzgerald, G., Mumford, E. and Wood-Harper, A.T. (1985) 'Epistemological Perspectives on Multi-Method Information Systems Research'. Available at http://is2.lse.ac.uk/asp/aspecis/20050138.pdf (accessed: 28 August 2012).

Hoffman, R. (1998) UK Director of Chicago Business, personal communication with Maitland P. Hyslop, 21 August.

Hore, P. (Ed.) (2003) *Patrick Blackett: Sailor, Scientist and Socialist*. London, Frank Cass.

HSBC (2011) *The Future of Business*. London, HSBC.

Hudson Foods. Available at www.tabloid.net/97/09/05C1.html (accessed: 20 October 2009).

Humm, M. (Ed.) (1992) *Feminisms: A Reader*. London, Harvester, Wheatsheaf.

Hung, A. (1997) 'Bayer's Taiwan Unit Faces Referendum', *Financial Express (India)*, 8 December 1997, p1.

Huntington, S. (1996) *The Clash of Civilizations And The Remaking Of World Order*. New York, Simon & Schuster.

Hutton, W. (2009) 'Lord Turner Is Right – Gordon Brown Must Now Cut the City Down To Size', *The Observer*, 30 August, p26.

Huxley, A. (1932) *Brave New World*. London, Chatto and Windus.

Hyslop, M.P. (1993) 'Improved Profitability via Oil Product Inventory Control', *Petroleum Review*, Vol. 47, No. 563, 565–568.

Hyslop, M.P. (1997) 'Obstructive Marketing', *Journal of Business and Industrial Marketing*, Vol. 12, No. 5, 339–343, November.

Hyslop, M.P. (1999) *Obstructive Marketing: Challenges to Globalizing Companies*. MSc Thesis, Huddersfield University Business School/Chartered Institute of Marketing.

Hyslop, M.P. (2003) 'Asymmetric Warfare', *Global Business Continuity Congress 2003*, London, 8–9 October. Available at http://www.iir-conferences.com/site/_docs.cfm?iv=24%20&DirName=cg2126&ConfCode=cg2126 (accessed: 30 September 2009).

Hyslop, M.P. (2006a) 'Business Recovery', *Continuity Professional (USA)*, February. Available at http://www.contingencyplanning.com (accessed: 1 March 2010).

Hyslop, M.P. (2006b) 'Business Continuity', *Continuity Professional (USA)*, March. Available at http://www.contingencyplanning.com (accessed: 1 March 2010).

Hyslop, M.P. (2006c) 'Business Resilience', *Continuity Professional (USA)*, April. Available at http://www.contingencyplanning.com (accessed: 1 March 2010).

Hyslop, M.P. (2007a) 'A Suggested National and International Approach to Resilience in Critical Infrastructure and Critical Information Infrastructure Protection', *The 3rd CAMIS Security Management Conference: Strategizing Resilience and Reducing Vulnerability*, Birkbeck College, London, 5–7 September.

Hyslop, M.P. (2007b) *Critical Information Infrastructure, Resilience and Protection*. Boston, MA, Springer.

Hyslop, M.P. (2008a) 'Hardening the Organisation', *FST Conference 2008*, IOD Hub, London, 2 July.

Hyslop, M.P. (2008b) 'A Model to Protect Against Emerging Threats to Business Continuity', *Financial Times*, 12 October.

Hyslop, M.P. (2008c) 'Beyond Resilience', *Proceedings CPM 2008 East*, Hilton International Resort, Kissimmee, FL, 14–17 November. This discussed 'Hardening the Organisation.'

Hyslop, M.P. (2009a) 'IT Security in an Economic Downturn', *Guidelines for IT Management*, National Computing Centre, No. 323, February.

Hyslop, M.P. (2009b) 'Hardening the Organisation', *4th CAMIS Security Management Conference*, Birkbeck College, University of London, 7 September.

Hyslop, M.P. (2009c) 'The GODFEARING Model', *Dealing With Disasters Conference*, Kathmandhu, Nepal, 11–12 November.

Hyslop, M.P. (2009d) 'Towards the Hardened Organisation', Trim, P. and Caravelli, J. (Eds), *Strategizing Resilience and Reducing Vulnerability*, Hauppage, NY, Nova Science, 150–163.

Hyslop, M.P. (2010) *Critical Information Infrastructure, Resilience and Protection*. Boston, MA, Springer.

Hyslop, M.P. (2012) 'A Suggested Approach to Individual, Corporate, National and International Resilience and Critical Infrastructures and Critical

Information Infrastructures', Defence IQ. Available at www.cdans.org/ Event.aspx?id=598076 (accessed: 5 February 2012).

Hyslop, M.P. and Collins, A.E. (2013) 'Hardened Institutions and Disaster Risk Reduction', *Environmental Hazards*, Vol. 12, Issue 1, 19–31.

Hyslop, M.P. and Royds, J. (2008) 'The GODFEAR Model', *Business Continuity Symposium*, 8 October, Brighton (Keynote Paper). This discussed 'Hardening the Organisation.'

IBM (2000) 'IBM and the Future of Crime'. Available at http://www.ibm.com/ ibm/ideasfromibm/ca/en/cybercrime/jul18/ibm_future_crime.html (accessed: 28 August 2012).

IBM (2009) *The New Voice of the CIO*. Somers, NY, IBM.

IBM (2012) 'CEO Study 2012'. Available at www.ibm.com/ceostudy2012 (accessed: 24 October 2012).

ICC (2011) 'INCO Terms 2010'. Available at http://export.gov/logistics/eg_ main_018118.asp (accessed: 24 October 2012).

ICM (2008) 'Comprehensive Business Continuity Solutions'. Available at http:// www.icm-continuity.co.uk (accessed 1 October 2009).

ICM (2009) 'Where To Start With Business Continuity'. Available at http:// www.icm-continuity.co.uk (accessed 1 October 2009).

Ikenberry, J. (1999) 'Why Export Democracy?: The "Hidden Grand Strategy" of American Foreign Policy', *The Wilson Quarterly*, Vol. 23, No.2 (Spring), 56–65.

Imants, J. (2003) 'Two Basic Mechanisms for Organisational Learning in Schools', *European Journal of Teacher Education*, Vol. 26, No. 3, 293–311.

IMF (2009) 'Comments on the UK Economy'. Available at www.imf.org/ external/np/sec/pn/2009/pn0984.htm (accessed: 14 February 2010).

IMF (2010) 'Comments on the Australian and New Zealand Economy'. Available at www.imf.org/external/pubs/ft/survey/so/2010/CAR012210A. htm (accessed 14 February 2010).

Infosecurity (2012) 'Iran Develops New Cyber Army'. Available at www. infoecurity-magazine.com/view/2061/iadevelops-new-cybearmy (accessed: 23 February 2012).

Institute of Petroleum (2002) Available at www.energyinst.org/home (accessed: 24 October 2012).

International Maritime Bureau (2009) 'Live Piracy Map'. Available at www.icc-ccs.org (accessed 12 April 2010).

ISO 27001/BS7799 (2008) 'Directors' Briefing Paper'. Available at www.ecsc. co.uk (accessed 1 October 2009).

Jackson, T. (1997) 'The Global Company', *Financial Times*, 31 October.

Janis, I.L. (1963) 'Group Identification under Conditions of External Danger'. *British Journal of Medical Psychology*, Vol. 36, 227–238.

JCB (2012) Group Personnel Director interview with Maitland P. Hyslop, 22 May.

Jenkins, S. (2010) 'The West's Dubious Export of Democracy', *The Hindu Times*, 10 April.

JLR (2012) Executive Director interview with Maitland P Hyslop, 24 July.

Jobaggy, Z. (2008) 'Scrutinising Effects-based Operations: On Military Genius, Causality and Friction in War', *AARMS*, Vol. 7, No. 1, 167–174.

Jobbagy, Z. (2003) 'Powered Flight, Strategic Bombing, and Military Coercion: Study on the Origins of Effects-Based Operations', *TNO Report, Clingendael Centre for Strategic Studies*, CCSS-05-006.

Johnson Matthey (2012) Senior Manager interview with Maitland P. Hyslop, 20 April 2012.

Johnson Tiles (2012) Managing Director interview with Maitland P. Hyslop, 15 March.

Johnson, B.B. and Covello, V.T. (Eds) (1987) *The Social and Cultural Construction of Risk: Essays on Risk Perception and Selection*. Dodrecht, D. Reidel.

Johnson, D.W., Johnson, R.T. and Holubec, E.J. (1990) *Circles of Learning*, 3rd edition. Edina, Interaction Book Company.

Jonsson, D.J. (2007) 'Sovereign Wealth Funds: A Potential Tool of Asymmetric Warfare'. Available at www.newmediajournal.us/guest/jonsson/08112007.htm (accessed: 12 April 2010).

Jung, C.G. and Associates (1964) *Man and His Symbols*. Garden City, NY, Doubleday.

Juster, W. and Russ, L. (1999) Personal communication with Levis anti-counterfeit executives, 29 June.

Kagan, D. and Kagan, F.W. (2000) *While America Sleeps: Self-Delusion, Military Weakness and the Threat to Peace Today*. New York, St. Martin's Griffin.

Kates, R.W. (1976) 'Risk Assessment of Environmental Hazard', *SCOPE Report No. 8 International Council of Scientific Unions*, Scientific Committee on Problems of the Environment, Paris.

Kaufman, J. (2011) *The Personal MBA*. London, Penguin.

Kelly, R.J., Maghan, J. and Serio, J.D. (2005) *Illicit Trafficking: A Reference Handbook*. Santa Barbara, CA, ABC Clio.

Kendra, J.M. and Wachtendorf, T. (2003) 'Elements of Resilience after the World Trade Centre Disaster: Reconstituting New York City's Emergency Operations Centre', *Disasters*, Vol. 27, No. 1, 37–53.

Kennan, G. (1947) 'The Sources of Soviet Conduct', *Foreign Affairs*, Vol. 25, No. 4, 566–582.

Kennedy, P.M. (1989) *The Rise and Fall of the Great Powers; Economic Change and Military Conflict From 1500 to 2000*. London, Vintage Press.

KGB (1999) Former Head of KGB revealed in Discovery Channel News Bulletin that KGB has been instrumental in the Nestlé Baby Milk Case, 21 April.

Khan, M. (2012) Personal communication, 27 April. Majid Khan is a Pakistani Elder in the Stoke on Trent Muslim community and Labour Councillor.

Khandani, A.E. and Lo, A.W. (2008) 'What Happened to the Quants in August 2007? Evidence from Factors and Transactions Data', Working Paper 14465, National Bureau of Economic Research. Washington, USA.

Kim, D.H. (1993) 'The Link between Individual and Organisational Learning', *Sloan Management Review*, Vol. 35, No. 1, 37–50. Available at http://sloanreview. mit.edu/the-magazine/articles/1993/fall/3513/the-link-between-individual-and-organisational-learning/ (accessed: 12 April 2010).

King, S. (2012) Chief Economist, HSBC, personal conversation, 19 April.

Kissinger, H.A. (1995) *Diplomacy*. New York, Pocket Books.

Klein, N. (2000) *No Logo*. New York, Flamingo.

Knight, R. and Pretty, D. (2000) 'The Impact of Catastrophes on Shareholder Value'. Available at http://www.readysolutionsinc.com/assets/oxford-rpt-cat-sh-value.pdf (accessed: 14 February 2010).

Koskenalusta, K. (1998) Interview with Maitland P. Hyslop, 23 November.

Kotler, P. and Keller, K.L. (1994) *Marketing Management*, 8th edition. New York, Prentice Hall.

Kotler, P. and Keller, K.L. (2008) *Marketing Management*, 13th edition. New York, Prentice Hall.

KPMG (2000) See comments. Available at www.bloorresearch.com/analysis/4164/kpmg-proves-y2k-impact.html (accessed: 28 August 2012).

KPMG (2010) 'Data Loss Barometer'. Available at www.kpmg.com/uk/en/issuesandinsights/articlespublications/pages/data-loss-barometer.aspx (accessed: 28 August 2012).

Krause, D.G. (1995) *Sun Tsu: The Art of War for Executives*. London, Nicholas Brealey.

Krauthammer, C. (2001) 'This is Not a Crime, This is War'. Available at www.jewishworldreview.com/cols//krauthammer091201.asp (accessed 30 October 2011).

Kroll, Inc. (2000) 'Study on the Links between Organised Crime and Corruption'. Available at http://ec.europa.eu/homeaffairs/doc.centre/crime/docs/study_on_links_between_organised_crime_and_corruption.en.pdf (accessed: 12 December 2011).

Kvashny, K. (2003) *Modern Maritime Piracy in Asia*. University of California, Irvine.

Lace, G. (1983) *Effective Marketing*. London, Scope Books.

Lalvani, J. (2006) Personal communication. Jetu Lalvani heads the corporate interests of the Lalvani family (India), 26 December.

Leake, J. (1998) 'Rural Rising', *The Sunday Times* (UK), 8 February, p15.

Lemagnen, P. (2005) 'Steady Shift to the East', 5 January. Available at www.fdi magazine.com/news/fullstory.php/aid/999/Steady_shift_to_the_east.html (accessed: 12 April 2010).

Leong, A.V.M (2004) 'Definitional Analysis: The War on Terror and Organised Crime', *Journal of Money Laundering Control*, Vol. 8, No. 1, pp19–36.

Levin, J.A. and Fox, J.A. (2010) *Elementary Statistics in Social Research*. Boston, Mass., Allyn and Bacon.

Lewis, T. (2010) 'New Glass-Steagall Will Shake Private Equity', *Financial News*, 22 January.

Linklaters (2010) Senior Partner interview with Maitland P. Hyslop, 20 June.

Lippmann, W. (1955) *Essays in Public Philosophy*. New York, Little Brown.

Lombardi, V. (1965) Available at www.vincelombardi.com/about.html (accessed: 28 August 2012).

London Resilience (2005) Available at www.londonresilience.gov.uk (accessed: 24 October 2012).

London Resilience (2012) Available at www.london.gov.uk/priorities/london-prepared/home (accessed: 24 October 2012).

Lorenz, A. and Alexander, G. (1998) 'Reuters Hits Trouble with Bloomberg', *The Sunday Times* (UK), 8 February, p3.

Lowe, M. (2012) Interview with Maitland P. Hyslop, 15 February.

Luce, R.D. and Raiffa, H. (1959) *Games and Decision: Introduction and Critical Survey*. New York, Wiley.

Luttwak, E.N. (1987) *Strategy: The Logic of War and Peace*. Cambridge, Mass., Belknap.

Lyotard, J. (1984) *The Post Modern Condition: A Report on Knowledge*. Manchester, Manchester University Press.

MacDonnell, E. and Lublin, J. (1998) 'In the Debris of a Failed Merger: Trade Secrets', *The Wall Street Journal*, 10 March.

MacDonnell, E. and Lublin, J.S. (1998) 'In the Debris of a Failed Merger: Trade Secrets', *The Wall Street Journal*, 10 March, pB1.

Machiavelli, N. (1521) *The Art of War*. Various.

Machiavelli, N. (1535) *The Prince*. Various.

Magnusson, D. (1995) 'Holistic Interactionism: A Perspective for Research on Personality Development', Pervin, L.A. and John, O.P. (Eds), *Handbook of Personality: Theory and Research*, New York, Guilford Press, 219–247.

Mainelli, M. and Harris, I. (2011) *The Price of Fish*. London, Nicholas Brealey.

Mann, J. (2012) Interview with Evan Davis on 'Today' Radio 4, 9 August.

Mann, R.D. (1959) 'A Review of the Relationship between Personality and Performance in Small Groups', *Psychological Bulletin*, Vol. 56, 241–270.

Mann, S. (2009) 'Resilience Still Lacking in UK plc', *Professional Manager*, Chartered Management Institute, London, May.

Maqbool, K. (2000) 'Strategy for Combating Corruption in Pakistan'. Available at http://unpan.1.unorg/intradoc/groups/public/documents/APCITY/UN0 10357.pdf (accessed: 12 April 2010).

March, J.G. and Olsen, J.P. (1975) 'The Uncertainty of the Past; Organisational Ambiguous Learning', *European Journal of Political Research*, Vol. 3, 147–171.

March, S.J. (1995) 'Counterfeit Products in the Russian Federation', *Organised Crime in Russia Conference*, RIIA, London, 6 March.

Margenau, H. (1961) *Open Vistas New Heaven*. New Haven, Yale University Press.

Maritime Security Review (2012) Available at www.marsecreview.com (accessed: 28 August 2012).

Marr, A. (2012) 'The History of the World', *BBC One*, 7 October, 2100hrs.

Marsh Inc. (2009) 'Business Continuity Survey'. Available at www.bcifiles.com/ BCM2009_Marsh.pdf (accessed: 28 August 2012).

Marsh Inc. (2010a) *2010 EMEA Business Continuity Benchmark Report*, Marsh Inc.

Marsh Inc. (2010b) Interview with Senior Director with Maitland P. Hyslop, 4 November.

Marwick, A. (1968) *Britain In The Century of Total War*. London, Pelican.

Marx, K. (1897) (reprinted 1 April 1994) *The Eastern Question*. Taylor and Francis Group, London.

Marx, K. and Engels, F. (1888) *The Communist Manifesto*. Various.

Maslow, A.H. (1954) *Motivation and Personality*. New York, Harper and Row.

Maudesley, R. (2009) Interview with Maitland P Hyslop, 15 December.

May, T. (1997) *Social Research*. Maidenhead, Open University Press.

Mayo, E. (2003) *The Human Problems of an Industrial Civilization*. New York, Routledge.

McAfee (2011) 'Fourth Quarter Threat Report 2011'. Available at www. mcafee.com/us/resources/reports/rp-quarterly-threat-q4-2011.pdf (accessed: 28 August 2012).

McCarthy, E.J. (1975) *Basic Marketing*. Toronto, Irwin.

McCrossan, L. (1991) *A Handbook for Interviewers*. London, HMSO.

McDonald, M.B. (1999) *Marketing Plans*. London, Butterworth-Heinemann.

McHugh, D., Groves, D. and Alker, A. (1998) 'Managing Learning: What Do We Learn from a Learning Organisation?', *The Learning Organisation*, Vol. 5, No. 5, 209–220.

McIvor, G. (1998) 'Doing Business in Russia', *Financial Times*, 6 March, p31.

McKee, M. (2007) 'Cochrane on Communism: The Influence of Communism on the Search for Evidence', *International Journal of Epidemiology*, Vol. 36, No. 2, 269–273.

McLaren F1 (2010) Managing Director interview with Maitland P. Hyslop, 20 October.

McSpotlight (1999) Available at www.mcspotlight.org (accessed: 12 April 2010).

Metropolitan Police (2012) Former Chief Constable interview with Maitland P. Hyslop, 9 July.

Metz, S. and Johnson, D.V. (2001) *Asymmetry and US Military Definition, Background and Strategic Concepts*. Carlisle, PA, Strategic Studies Institute.

Metz, S. and Kievit, J. (1995) *Strategy and the Revolution in Military Affairs: From Theory to Policy*. Darby, Diane Publishing.

MI5 (2010) 'Threats to the United Kingdom'. Available at www.mi5.gov.uk/output/the-threats.html (accessed: 19 April 2010).

Miller, K.D. (1992) 'A Framework for Integrated Risk Management in International Business', *Journal of International Business Studies*, Vol. 23, No. 2, 311–331.

Millman, G.J (1995) *The Vandals Crown*. New York, Free Press.

Mises, L. von (1936) *Socialism*. New Haven, Yale University Press.

Mises, L. von (1949) *Human Action*. New York, Foundation for Economic Education.

Mises, L. von (1962) *Liberalism*. New York, Foundation for Economic Education.

Mises, L. von (1956) *The Anti-Capitalistic Mentality*. New York, D. Van Nostrand Company.

Mobily, T. (2004) *Hardening Apache*. Berkeley, CA, Apress.

Moore, G.E. (1965) 'Cramming More Components onto Integrated Circuits', *Electronics Magazine*, Vol. 38, No. 8, 114–117.

Morgan, S. (1998) Personal communication with the Director Europe for the Cleveland, USA, Growth Partnership, 8 February.

Moss Kanter, R. (1995) *World Class*. New York, Simon and Schuster.

Moteff, J. and Parfomak, P. (2004) *Critical Infrastructure and Key Assets: Definition and Identification*. Newbridge, CRS.

Mumford, M.D., Zaccaro, S.J., Harding, F.D., Jacobs, T.O. and Fleishman, E.A. (2000) 'Leadership Skills for a Changing World Solving Complex Social Problems', *The Leadership Quarterly*, Vol. 11, Issue 1, 11–35.

Murden, T. (2008) 'Vision to Bank On', 11 May. Available at http://business.scotsman.com/clydesdalebank/Vision-to-bank-on-Lynne.4071206.jp (accessed: 14 February 2010).

NASA (2000) 'NASA Risk Approach'. Available at www.hq.nasa.gov/office/codeq/risk/docs/rmt.pdf (accessed: 14 February 2010).

National Fire Protection Agency (2009) 'Standard 1600'. Available at www.npfa.org (accessed: 12 April 2010).

National Risk Register (2012) Available at www.cabinetoffice.gov.uk/resource-library/national-risk-register (accessed: 8 August 2012).

National Science Foundation (2002) Available at www.nsf.gov/crssprgm/nano/reports/nbic_roco_04_0422_@aaas_57sl.pdf (accessed: 28 August 2012).

National Security Council (2002) *The National Security Strategy of the United States*. Washington, DC, National Security Council.

Naylor, R.T. (1994) *Hot Money*. Montreal, Black Rose Books.

Nestlé (1991) Senior Executive personal communication with Maitland P. Hyslop, 18 February.

Nestlé (1992) Head of Security personal communication with Maitland P. Hyslop, 15 June.

Network Security Management Limited (1987) *Crisis Management*. London, Hambros.

Neumann, J. Von and Morgenstern, O. (1953) *Theory of Games and Economic Behaviour*. Princeton, Princeton University Press.

New Zealand Government (2006) 'Protecting New Zealand's Critical Infrastructure'. Available at www.e.govt.nz/archive/policy (accessed: 6 January 2007).

Newton, I. (1664) Laws of Motion. Available at http://csep10.phys.ukk.edu/astr161/lect/history/newton3laws.html (accessed 12 April 2010).

NHS (2010) This is an Anonymised NHS PCT Risk Register Summary from a PCT in the South of England.

NHS South East Coast (2010) Chief Executive interview with Maitland P. Hyslop, 4 April.

NHS Surrey (2011) Chief Executive interview with Maitland P. Hyslop, 10 April.

Nimmo, I. (1995) Honeywell IAC, 'Abnormal Situation Management', *9th Symposium on Microprocessor Based Protection Systems*, 7 December.

NISCC (2006) 'The NISCC Good Practice Guide to Telecommunications Resilience', Centre For The Protection Of National Infrastructure, London, UK, 30 March. Available at www.cpni.gov.uk/docs/re-20040501-00393.pdf (accessed: 1 October 2009).

Nonaka, I. and Takeuchi, H. (1995) *The Knowledge Creating Company*. New York, Oxford University Press. Available at http://books.google.com/books?id=B-qxrPaU1-MC (accessed: 27 April 2010).

Noona, W. (2004) *Hardening Network Infrastructure*. Emeryville, CA, Osborne McGraw-Hill.

Norberg, J. (2005) *In Defence of Global Capitalism*. Washington, DC, Cato Institute.

O'Brien, G. and Hope, A. (2010) 'Localism and Energy: Negotiating Approaches to Embedding Resilience in Energy Systems', *Energy Policy*, Vol. 38, No. 12, 7550–7558.

O'Keefe, P., Manyena, B., O'Brien, G. and Rose, J. (2011) 'Disaster Resilience: A Bounce Back or Bounce Forward Ability?', *Local Environment*, Vol. 16, No. 6, 1–8.

O'Keeffe, T. (2002) 'Organisational Learning: A New Perspective', *Journal of European Industrial Training*, Vol. 26, No. 2, 130–141.

O'Neill, J. (2001) *The Growth Map: Economic Opportunity in the BRICKS and Beyond*. London, Penguin.

OECD (2006) 'The Digital Economy'. Available at www.oecd.org/document/6/ 0,3343,en_2649_201185_35930118_1_1_1_1,00.html (accessed: 12 April 2010).

OECD (2011) Various Publications. Available at www.oecds-ilibrary.org and www.oecd.org/topic (accessed: 30 October 2011).

OilServ (2009) Chief Executive interview with Maitland P. Hyslop, 21 June.

Oliver-Smith, A. (1998) 'Disasters, Social Change, and Adaptive Systems', Quarantelli, E.L. (Ed.), *What is a Disaster?* London, Routledge, 231–233.

Oliver-Smith, A. (1998) 'Global Changes and the Definition of Disaster', Chapter 15 in Quarantelli, E.L. (Ed.), *What Is A Disaster?* London and New York, Routledge, 177–194.

Omar, R. (2011) 'The Life of Muhammad', *BBC Two*, 11 July. Available at www. bbc.co.uk/programmes/b012mkg5 (accessed: 28 August 2012).

ONS (2011) Available at www.ons.gov.uk/ons/rel/lms/labour-market-statistics/ december-2011/index.html (accessed: 28 August 2012).

Oppenheim, A.N. (1973) *Questionnaire Design and Attitude Measurement*. London, Heinemann.

Oppenheim, A.N. (1992) *Questionnaire Design, Interviewing and Attitude Measurement*. London, Pinter.

Otway, H.J. (1973) 'Risk Estimation and Evaluation', *Proceedings of the HASA Planning Conference on Energy Systems, HASA-PC3*, Luxembourg, Austria: International Institute for Applied Systems Analysis.

Owens, W.A. (2000) 'Revolutionising Warfare', *Blueprint Magazine*, DLC, January.

Oxfam (1999) 'IMF Product Recall', Advertisement, *Financial Times*, 27 September, p5.

Parker, E. (2012) UBS Manager interview with Maitland P. Hyslop, 19 April.

Partnoy, F. (1997) *F.I.A.S.C.O.* Norton, New York.

Patriot Act (2002) Available at http://thomas.loc.gov/cgi-bin/bdquery/z?d 107:H.R.3162 (accessed: 24 October 2012).

Patterson, D. (2010) 'Creating a Security Conscious Corporate Culture', *Proceedings CPM East 2010*, Jacob K. Javits Conference Centre, New York, USA, 3–4 November.

Patterson, S. (2010) *The Quants*. Crown Business, New York.

Pedler, M., Burgogyne, J. and Boydell, T. (1997) *The Learning Company: A Strategy for Sustainable Development*, 2nd edition, London, McGraw-Hill.

Pelling, M. (Ed.) (2003) *Natural Disasters and Development in a Globalizing World*. London, Routledge.

Perrier (1990) Available at (amongst others) http://brandfailures.blogspot.co.uk/2006/12/brand-pr-failures-perriers-benzene.html (accessed: 28 August 2012) and www.mindspring.com (accessed: 28 August 2012).

Perrow, C. (1984) *Normal Accidents: Living With High Risk Technologies*. New York, Basic Books.

Perry, R.W. and Quarantelli, E.L. (Eds) (2005) *What is a Disaster? New Answers to Old Questions*. Philadelphia, Xlibris Press.

Perry, S. (1995) 'Economic Espionage and Corporate Responsibility', Available at www.acsp.ulc.edu, *CJ International*, March–April.

Pervan, G.P. (1994b) 'A Case for More Case Study Research in Group Support Systems', *TC8 AUS IFIP Conference*, Bond University, Gold Coast, Qld, 8–11 May, 485–496.

Pervez, M. (2012) Personal communication, 27 April. Mohammed Pervez is the Muslim Labour Leader of Stoke-on-Trent City Council.

Peston, R. (2007) at the BBC. Available at www.bbc.co.uk/blogs/thereporters/robertpeston (accessed: 1 October 2009).

Peterson, M. (2002) 'The Limits of Catastrophe Aversion', *Risk Analysis*, Vol. 22, No. 3, 527–538.

Phillips, W. (1989) *Confessions of a Marketer*. London, Mercury.

Piper, F. (2009) Fred Piper is Professor of Mathematics at London University. Personal discussion regarding how organisations are going to manage themselves, and particularly Information Assurance, in the future, 20 June.

Plato (2007) *The Republic*. London, Penguin Classics.

Plutarch (2001) *Lives*. New York, Modern Library.

Politech Institute (2007) Available at www.politech-institute.org (accessed: 24 October 2012).

Popper, K. (1935) *Logik der Forschung (The Logic of Research)*. Vienna, Austria, Julius Springer Verlag.

Popper, K. (1972) *Objective Knowledge: An Evolutionary Approach*. Oxford, UK, Clarendon Press.

Porter, M.E. (1980) *Competitive Strategy*. Free Press, New York.

Porter, M.E. (1990) *The Competitive Advantage Of Nations*. New York, Free Press.

Porter, M.E. (1995) 'The Competitive Advantage of the Inner City'. Available at http://www.uc.edu/cdc/urban_database/food_resources/competitive-advantage-of-inner-city.pdf (accessed: 31 August 2013).

Pretty, D. (2000) *Catastrophes, Reputation and Shareholder Value*. Templeton College, Oxford, UK, 21 September.

Pretty, D. (2008) 'Impact of Crisis Leadership on Shareholder Values', *The BCI Symposium*, Brighton, UK, 9/10 October.

PwC (2010) 'Information Security Breaches Report'. Available at www.pwc.co.uk/audit-assurance/publications/isbs-survey-2010.jhtml (accessed: 28 August 2012).

Rand, A. (1943) *The Fountainhead*. New York, Signet.

Rand, A. (1957) *Atlas Shrugged*. New York, Random House.

Rand, A. (1966) *Capitalism: The Unknown Ideal*. Indianapolis, Bobbs Merrill.

Randall, J. (2007 onwards) of *The Daily Telegraph*. Available at, for example, www.telegraph.co.uk/finance/comment/jeffrandall/4528718/Were-in-denial-afraid-to-face-up-to-the-real-causes-of-recession.html# (accessed: 1 October 2009).

Rathmell, A. et al. (Anonymous Contributors) (1997) 'The IW Threat from Sub-State Groups: an Interdisciplinary Approach', *3rd International Symposium on Command and Control Research and Technology*, Institute for National Strategic Studies, National Defense University, June 17–20. Available at www.kcl.ac.uk/ (accessed: 1 October 2009).

Ray, J.J (1973) 'Conservatism, Authoritarianism, and Related Variables: A Review and Empirical Study', Wilson, G.D. (Ed.), *The Psychology of Conservatism*, New York, Academic Press, Chapter 2, 17–35.

RBS (2009) Chief of Technology interview with Maitland P. Hyslop, 10 January.

Reform Institute (2008) 'Hardening the Global Supply Chain'. Available at www.reforminstitute.org/uploads/publications/supply-chain-2-19-08_inn_template03-06-08.pdf (accessed: 1 October 2009).

Rewick, C.J. (1999) 'Wall Street Sure Doesn't Like Sara Lee', *Crain's Chicago Business*, May, p1.

Richardson, A. and Cooley, W. (2011) *Regulating Wall Street*. New York, Wiley.

Rider, B.A.K. (Ed.) (1991) 'Economic Crime – Due Diligence', *Proceedings 9th Symposium on Economic Crime*, Jesus College, Cambridge.

Rivers Capital (2012) Chief Executive interview with Maitland P. Hyslop, 13 March.

Roberts, M. (2005) 'Resilience for a Top FTSE 100 Company – an Insight from a BT Perspective', *3rd Annual European Telecommunications Resilience and Recovery Association Conference*, Sophia Antipolis, France, 29–30 June.

Robinson, J. (1995) *The Laundrymen*. New York, Pocket Books, p16.

Rochlin, G.I., La Porte, T.R. and Roberts, K.H. (1987) 'The Self-Designing High Reliability Organisation: Aircraft Carrier Flight Operations at Sea', *Naval War College Review*, Autumn, 76–90.

Rommel, E. (2011) 'Infantry Attacks'. Available at www.bnpublishing.com (an online reprint of the 1937 original) (accessed: 24 October 2012).

Rose, B. (1999) 'Iridium Mess: Fallout for Motorola', *Crain's Chicago Business*, 10 May, Vol. 22, Issue 19, p1.

Rosen, D. (1998) *Behind the Open Door*. Washington, DC, International Institute for Economics.

Rosenberg, M. (1957) *Occupations and Values*. Glencoe, IL, Free Press.

Ross, S.J. (2003) 'Business Continuity Management: An American Perspective', *1st European Telecommunications Resilience and Recovery Association Conference*, Newcastle, UK, 11–13 June.

Rother, M. (2009) *Toyota Kata*, New York, McGraw-Hill. Available at http://books.google.com/books?id=_1lhPgAACAAJ&dq=toyota+kata (accessed: 12 April 2010).

Rough Guide (2009) *The Internet*, 14th edition, London, Penguin.

Rout, L. (1999) 'Ten Years Later: The State of Capitalism a Decade after the Fall of the Wall', *The Wall Street Journal*, World Business Report, 27 September, R1–R32.

Rowe, W.D. (1977) *An Anatomy of Risk*. New York, John Wiley and Sons.

Royds, J. (2005) 'Business Continuity', *North East Business Continuity Conference*, Sage Centre, Gateshead, UK, 18 February.

Royds, J. (2008) Personal communication with Maitland P. Hyslop, 1 October.

Rudd, D. (1995) 'Five Have a Gender-ful Time: Blyton, Sexism and the Infamous Five', *Children's Literature in Education*, Vol. 26, No. 3, 185–196.

Saunders, J. (1988) *Nightmare*. London, Arrow Books.

Scruton, R. (2003) *The West and the Rest: Globalization and the Terrorist Threat*. Wilmington, Intercollegiate Studies Institute.

Seligman, M.E.P. (2004) 'Can Happiness be Taught?', *Daedalus*, Spring, 133 (2), 80–87.

Senge, P.M. (1990) *The Fifth Discipline*. New York, Doubleday/Currency.

Serenko, A., Bontis, N. and Hardie, T. (2007) 'Organisational Size and Knowledge Flow: A Proposed Theoretical Link', *Journal of Intellectual Capital*, Vol. 8, No. 4, 610–627.

Serrano, A. (2009) 'Explaining the Link between Organisational Resilience and Crisis Management'. Available at www.continuitycentral.com/feature0636.html (accessed: 1 October 2009). This online article contains a paragraph on 'Hardening' and was first published in Continuity Forum News. Available at www.continuity.net.au (accessed: 1 October 2009).

Severson, C. (2010) 'The Science of Happiness'. Available at www.retirement lifematters.com/new-aging/the-science-of-happiness (accessed: 12 February 2011).

Sharp, J. (2003) 'BC Developments', *1st European Telecommunications Resilience and Recovery Association Conference*, Newcastle, UK, 11–13 June.

Sharpe, W.F. (1964) 'Capital Asset Prices: A Theory of Market Equilibrium under Conditions of Risk', *Journal of Finance*, Vol. 19, No. 3, 425–442.

Shaw, K. (2012) 'The Rise of the Resilient Local Authority', *Local Government Studies*, Vol. 38, No. 3, 281–300.

Shell (2012) Finance Director interview with Maitland P. Hyslop, 26 April.

Shelley, L.I. (2005) *Methods and Motives: Exploring Links Between Transnational Organized Crime and International Terrorism*. Available at www.ncjrs.gov/ pdffiles1/nij/grants/211207.pdf (accessed: 15 April 2010).

Shipp, S. (1987) 'Modified Vendetta Sanctions', *Journal of Business Ethics*, Vol. 6, No. 8, 603–612.

Sirkin, H.L., Hemerling, J. and Bhattacharya, A. (2008) *Globality*. London, Headline.

Sjuve, S. (2010) Head of Risk, National Australia Bank Group, Personal communication, 9 February.

Smith, A. (2008) 'Security of Europe's Critical Infrastructures to be Strengthened by Major International Project'. Available at www3.imperial.ac.uk/news andeventspggrp/imperialcollege/newssummary/news_15-7-2008-13-35-25? newsid=40474 (accessed: 12 April 2010).

Smith, C.S. (1997) 'Chinese Discover Product Liability Suits', *The Wall Street Journal*, 13 November, p1.

Smith, D. and Fischbacher, M. (2009) 'The Changing Nature of Risk and Risk Management: The Challenge of Borders, Uncertainty and Resilience', *Risk Management*, Vol. 11, Issue 1, 1–12.

Smith, J.A. and Foti, R.J. (1998) 'A Pattern Approach to the Study of Leader Emergence', *Leadership Quarterly*, Vol. 9, No. 2, 147–160.

Smith, R. (2012) quoted in Steelhenge (2012) and Personal communication with Maitland P. Hyslop, 15 August.

Snopes (1997) Available at http://snopes.simplenet.com (accessed: 28 August 2012).

Snyder, C. (1940) *Capitalism the Creator*. London, Macmillan.

Soros, G. (2009) *The Crash of 2008 and What it Means: The New Paradigm for Financial Markets*. New York, Public Affairs.

Spaander, H. (2008) 'Global Hardening', ABN-AMRO. Available at http://redhat .sns.ro/files/done/Hans_Spaander_Redhat_ABNAmro.pdf (accessed: 1 October 2009).

Spinks, D. (2005) 'Telecommunications Resilience', *3rd Annual European Telecommunications Resilience and Recovery Association Conference*, Sophia Antipolis, France, 29–30 June.

Staffordshire Fire Service (2012) Chief Executive interview with Maitland P. Hyslop, 9 January.

Staffordshire Police (2012) Chief Constable interview with Maitland P. Hyslop, 9 January.

Stamatis, D.H. (2004) *Six Sigma Fundamentals: A Complete Guide to the System, Methods, and Tools*. New York, Productivity Press.

Standard Chartered Bank (2012) Available at www.bbc.co.uk/news/business-19253666 (accessed: 28 August 2012).

Starkman, D. (1997) 'Secrets and Lies: The Dual Career of a Corporate Spy', *The Wall Street Journal*, 23 October, p1.

Staten, C.L. (1997) 'Reflections on the 1997 Commission on Critical Infrastructure Protection (PCCIP) Report'. Available at www.emergency.com/pcciprpt.htm (accessed: 1 October 2009).

Staten, C.L. (1999) 'Asymmetric Warfare, the Evolution and Devolution of Terrorism: The Coming Challenge for Emergency and National Security Forces', *Journal of Counterterrorism and Security International*, Winter. Available at www.emergency.com/asymetrc.htm (accessed: 1 October 2009).

Steelhenge (2012) *Crisis Management Key Themes for Success: The Cornerstones of Crisis Management*. Steelhenge, London, August. (This is the first paper in a major new series entitled, Crisis Management: Key Themes for Success, written by Dominic Cockram and Dr Claudia van den Heuvel.) Available at http://www.steelhenge.co.uk/index.php/kz-thought-lead (accessed: 28 August 2012).

Steelite (2012) Chief Executive interview with Maitland P. Hyslop, 18 May.

Stennet, T. (2009) Personal communication, conversation with the Head of Technology at Royal Bank of Scotland, 12 October.

Stiglitz, J. (2003) *Globalisation and its Discontents*. New York, Penguin.

Stiglitz, J. (2007) *Making Globalisation Work*. New York, Penguin.

Stockwell, S. and Muir, A. (2004) 'FCJ-04 The Military-Entertainment Complex: A New Facet of Information Warfare'. Available at http://one.fibreculturejournal.org/fcj-004-the-military-entertainment-complex-a-new-facet-of-information-warfare (accessed: 13 August 2012).

Stogdill, R.M. (1948) 'Personal Factors Associated with Leadership: A Survey of the Literature', *Journal of Psychology*, Vol. 25, 35–71.

Strachan, C. (2003) 'Security and Accessibility', *1st European Telecommunications Resilience and Recovery Association Conference*, Newcastle, UK, 11–13 June.

Strauss, A.L. and Corbin, J. (1990) *Basics of Qualitative Research: Grounded Theory Procedures and Techniques*. London, Sage.

Sullivan, G.R. (1996) *Hope Is Not A Method*. New York, *Times Business* (and personal communication).

Sunday Times (1999) 'Macro-Virus'. Available at http://articles.cnn.com/key word/macro-virus (accessed: 24 October 2012).

Sunday Times (2011) 'Stuxnet'. Available at www.thetimes.co.uk/tto/news/ world/middleeast/article3433284.ece (accessed: 24 October 2012).

Taepke, L. (1998) Vice President Bank One personal communication with Maitland P. Hyslop, 26 April.

Tafani, C. (2007) French intelligence agent personal communication with Maitland P. Hyslop, Nice, France, 21 June.

Taleb, N.N. (2007) *Black Swan*. London, Allen Lane.

Tata (2012) Senior Executive interview with Maitland P. Hyslop, 24 July.

Taylor Johnson Garrett (1999) 'Drug Pricing In Europe', *Biotech, '99*, Boston, MA, 19 May.

Taylor Nelson Sofres Intersearch (1999) quoted in and available at http://www. religioustolerance.org/rel_rate.htm (accessed: 28 August 2012).

Taylor, F.W. (1911) *Principles of Scientific Management*. London, Harper.

Tead, O. (1933) *Human Nature and Management: The Applications of Psychology to Executive Leadership*. New York, McGraw-Hill.

Terpstra, J.H. (2004) *Hardening Linux*. Emeryville, CA, Osborne McGraw-Hill.

Tetra Pak (2009) Managing Director interview with Maitland P. Hyslop, 4 February.

Thomson, D. (2009) '"Unravelling Lehman" Business Turnaround', *The Economist*, London, UK, 14 May.

Times, The (2011a) 'Global Risk', 13 January, p40.

Times, The (2011b) 'Sovereign Dominoes' Leader, 16 November.

Tolchin, M. and Tolchin, S.J. (1992) *Selling Our Security*. New York, Knopf.

Tong, R. (1989) *Feminist Thought*. Boulder, Westview Press.

Torrey, R.A. (Ed.) (1909) *The Fundamentals: A Testimony to the Truth*. Ada, Baker Books.

Trim, P.R.J. and Lee, Y. (2007) 'A Strategic Marketing Intelligence and Multi-Organisational Resilience Framework', *European Journal of Marketing*, Vol. 42, No. 7/8, 731–745.

Trim, P.R.J. (2004) 'The Strategic Corporate Intelligence and Transformational Marketing Model', *Marketing Intelligence and Planning*, Vol. 22, No. 2, 240–246.

Trim, P.R.J. (2005) 'The GISES Model for Counteracting Organised Crime and International Terrorism', *International Journal of Intelligence and Counter-Intelligence*, Vol. 18, 451–472.

Trim, P.R.J. (2010) 'Summary', *2nd CIIP Workshop*, Birkbeck College, University of London, UK, 29 March.

Trim, P.R.J. and Caravelli, J. (Eds) (2009) *Strategizing Resilience and Reducing Vulnerability*. Hauppage, NY, Nova Science.

Trim, P.R.J. and Lee, Y. (2006) 'The Role of Marketing Intelligence Officers in Strategy Formulation and Implementation', *Handbook of Business Strategy*, Vol. 7, Issue 1, 125–130.

Trim, P.R.J., Jones, N.A. and Brear, K. (2009) 'Building Organisational Resilience through a Designed in Security Management Approach', *Journal of Business Continuity and Emergency Planning*, Vol. 3, No. 4, August, 345–355.

TseTung, M. (1964) *Quotations from Chairman Mao Tsetung*. China, Government of the People's Republic of China.

Tucker, E. (1997) 'Branson to Tell EU of Illegal BA Practices', *Financial Times*, 22 October, p10.

Turnbull, J. (2004) *Hardening Linux*. Berkeley, CA, Apress.

Turner, A. (2009) 'The Turner Review'. Available at http://www.fsa.gov.uk/ Pages/Library/Corporate/turner/index.shtml (accessed: 14 February 2010).

UBS (2012) Senior executive interview with Maitland P. Hyslop, 22 March.

UK Mail (2012) Director interview with Maitland P. Hyslop, 21 November.

US Army (2009) Chief of Staff interview with Maitland P. Hyslop, 15 November.

US Army (2010) 'Comprehensive Soldier Fitness'. Available at http://csf.army. mil/ (accessed: 24 October 2012).

US Banking Act (1933) Available at www.spartacus.schoolnet.co.uk/USAR banking.htm (accessed: 24 October 2012).

US Constitution (1787) Available at www.usconstitution.net/const.html (accessed: 24 October 2012).

US Declaration of Independence (1776) Available at www.loc.gov/rr/program/ bib/ourdocs/DeclarInd.html (accessed: 24 October 2012).

USJFCOM (2008) 'Commander's Guidance for Effects-based Operations', Autumn. Available at www.carlisle.army.mil/USAWC/parameters/Articles /08autumn/mattis.pdf (accessed: 24 October 2012).

Van Assen, M., van den Berg, G. and Pietersma, P. (2009) *Key Management Models: The 60+ Models Every Manager Needs to Know*. London, FT Prentice Hall.

Van Duijn, P. (1965) 'The Interaction of Theories and Experiments in Science', Dockx, S. and Bernays, P. (Eds), *Information and Prediction in Science*, New York, Academic Press.

Vanguard (2012) Personal communication with Maitland P Hyslop, 1 March.

Viano, E.C., Magallenes, J. and Bridel, L. (2003) *Transnational Organized Crime: Myth, Power, and Profit*. Durham, NC, Carolina Academic Press.

Vickers Report (2011) Available at http://bankingcommission.independent. gov.uk/ (accessed: 28 August 2012)

Vistica, G. (1999) 'We're In The Middle of a Cyberwar', *Newsweek*, 20 September, p52.

Von Neumann, J. and Morgenstern, O. (2007) (1944) *Theory of Games and Economic Behaviour*, Commemorative edition, Princeton, Princeton University Press.

Vreede, G.J. de (1995) 'TRW Scientist Pleads Guilty To Giving China Nuclear Information', *Facilitating Organisational Change: The Participative Wall Street Journal* (1997), 9 December, p1.

The Wall Street Journal (1999) 'Microsoft and Netscape'. Available at http://online. wsj.com/article/SB101183050852731680.html (accessed: 24 October 2012).

Walter, P. (2010) Personal communication with this risk management consultant to the banking and legal sectors, 15 October.

Wang, C.L. and Ahmed, P.K. (2003) 'Organisational Learning: A Critical Review', *The Learning Organisation*, Vol. 10, No. 1, 8–17.

Ward, K. (2011) *The World in 2050*. London, HSBC Global Research.

Watson, M. (2011) 'Crisis Management Planning', Working Paper, 24 August. (Unfortunately Marilyn died in a tragic diving accident whilst this paper was being developed.)

Wayper, C.L. (1973) *Political Thought*. London, EUP.

Weber, M. (1997) *The Theory of Social and Economic Organisation*. New York, Free Press.

Weber, R. (2004) 'Editor's Comments: The Rhetoric of Positivism versus Interpretivism: A Personal View', *Journal MIS Quarterly*, Vol. 28, No. 1, March, iii–xii.

Weller, S.C. (1998) 'Structured Interviewing and Questionnaire Construction', Bernard, H.R. (Ed.), *Handbook of Methods in Cultural Anthropology*, London, Sage, 365–409.

Wellington College (2011) 'Happiness'. Available at www.wellingtoncollege. org.uk/news-archive/archive/wellbeing (accessed: 27 April 2012).

Whessoe (1992) Chief Executive personal communication with Maitland P. Hyslop, 15 June.

White, G.F. (1974) 'Natural Hazards Research: Concepts, Methods, and Policy Implications', White, G.F. (Ed.), *Natural Hazards: Local, National and Global*, New York, Oxford University Press, 3–16.

Wiger, D.E. and Huntley, D.K. (2002) *Essentials of Interviewing*. New York, Wiley.

Williams, P. (2002) 'Organized Crime and Cybercrime – Implications for Business'. Available at www.cert.org/archive/pdf/cybercrime-business.pdf (accessed: 12 April 2010).

Wilson, J. (1999) Personal communication with this senior Baker and Mckenzie lawyer, 6 April (cf. Winne, B.W.).

Winne, B.W. (1999) Personal communication with this senior Andersen Consulting executive, 6 April (cf. Wilson, J.).

Wisner, B. (2003) 'Disaster Preparedness and Response; Why is the 'Phone Off the Hook', *1st European Telecommunications Resilience and Recovery Association Conference*, Newcastle, UK, 13 June.

Wisner, B., Blaikie, P., Cannon, T. and Davis, I. (2002) *At Risk: Natural Hazards, People's Vulnerability and Disasters*. New York, Routledge.

Wolf, M. (2005) *Why Globalisation Works*. New Haven, Yale University Press.

Wood, J.C. and Wood, M.C. (2002) *Fayol: Evaluations in Business Management*. London, Routledge.

Wood, R. (2000) *Managing Complexity*. London, Economist Books.

Woodman, P. (2008) *Business Continuity Management 2008*. London, Chartered Management Institute.

Woodman, P. and Hutchings, P. (2010) *Disruption and Resilience, The 2010 Business Continuity Management Survey*. London, Chartered Management Institute and the Cabinet Office.

Woodman, P. and Kumar, V. (2009) 'A Decade of Living Dangerously', Chartered Management Institute and the Cabinet Office. Available at www.Managers.org.uk/bcm2009 (accessed: 1 October 2009).

World Population Balance (2012) Available at www.worldpopulationbalance.org (accessed: 28 August 2012).

Yale (2013) The Avalon Project. Available at www.avalon.yale.edu (accessed: 1 October 2009).

Yates, S. (2003) 'Failure To Prepare Is Preparing To Fail', *1st European Telecommunications Resilience and Recovery Association Conference*, Newcastle, UK, 11–13 June.

Yip, C. and Palivos, T. (1997) 'Gains from Trade for a Monetary Economy Once Again', *Canadian Journal of Economics*, Canadian Economics Association, Vol. 30, Issue 1, 208–223, February.

Young, B. (2011a) 'The Need for Integration: The Failure of Risk Management Part 1', *Business Continuity*, January/February.

Young, B. (2011b) 'The Need for Integration: The Failure of Risk Management Part 2', *Business Continuity*, March/April.

Zaccaro, S.J. (2007) 'Trait-based Perspectives of Leadership', *American Psychologist*, Vol. 62, No. 1, 6–16.

Zaccaro, S.J., Gulick, L.M.V. and Khare, V.P. (2008) 'Personality and Leadership', Hoyt, C.J., Goethals, G.R. and Forsyth, D.R. (Eds), *Leadership at the Crossroads*, Vol. 1, Westport, CT, Praeger, 13–29.

Index